Access My eLab Leap 3

leap 3
NEW EDITION
READING AND WRITING
JULIA WILLIAMS
Pearson · GSE

TO REGISTER

❶ Go to **mybookshelf.pearsonerpi.com**

❷ Follow the instructions. When asked for your access code, please type the code provided underneath the blue sticker.

❸ To access **My eLab** at any time, go to http://mybookshelf.pearsonerpi.com.
Bookmark this page for quicker access.

Access to My eLab is valid for 12 months from the date of registration.

STUDENT ACCESS CODE

LEAPST-STONK-CINCH-SPECS-ALLOT-THRAW

WARNING! This book CANNOT BE RETURNED if the access code has been uncovered.

Note: Once you have registered, you will need to join your online class. Ask your teacher to provide you with the class ID.

TEACHER Access Code

To obtain an access code for My eLab, please contact your Pearson ELT consultant.

 1 800 263-3678, ext. 2
pearsonerpi.com/help

W138568 (A39001)

leap 3

NEW EDITION

READING AND WRITING

JULIA WILLIAMS

Pearson

Product Owner
Stephan Leduc

Managing Editor
Sharnee Chait

Project Editor
Emily Harrison

Copy Editor
Mairi MacKinnon

Proofreader
Paula Sarson

Rights and Permissions Coordinator
Aude Maggiori

Text Rights and Permissions
Rachel Irwin

Art Director
Hélène Cousineau

Graphic Design Manager
Estelle Cuillerier

Book and Cover Design
Frédérique Bouvier

Book Layout
Marquis Interscript

Cover Photos
Getty Images © Hero Images
Shutterstock © TAVEESUK

Dedication

As always, I send more than my thanks to Wayne, Sam, Scott, Carolyn, Ron, Garth, Nicole, Ross, and Mary.

The publisher wishes to thank the following people for their helpful comments and suggestions:

Janelle Caballero, English Language Institute, University of British Columbia

Susan A. Curtis, English Language Institute, University of British Columbia

Michelle Duhaney, Seneca College

Izabella Kojic-Sabo, University of Windsor

Laura Parker, University of Oklahoma

Hélène Prévost, Cégep de l'Outaouais

Jamie Tanzman, Texas A&M International University

1611 Crémazie Boulevard East, 10th Floor
Montréal, Québec H2M 2P2
Canada
Telephone: 1 800 263-3678
Fax: 1 514 334-4720
information@pearsonerpi.com
pearsonerpi.com

Registration of copyright—Bibliothèque et Archives nationales du Québec, 2018
Registration of copyright—Library and Archives Canada, 2018

Printed in Canada   123456789   II   21 20 19 18
ISBN 978-2-7613-8568-8   138568 ABCD   OF10

INTRODUCTION

Welcome to the new edition of *LEAP 3: Reading and Writing*. In this new edition, you'll recognize many of the characteristics of the earlier editions:

- engaging chapter topics about technology, science, and education;
- readings in a variety of genres that reflect interesting and often divergent perspectives;
- Warm-Up Assignments positioned mid-chapter that help you develop the skills you need to succeed in the final assignments;
- explicit attention to vocabulary, in particular AWL words, with multiple exercises that allow for lots of practice;
- reading and writing instruction that support the development of essential academic skills like citing, paraphrasing, and summarizing.

You'll also discover new features that will help you achieve your academic objectives:

- Focus on Critical Thinking sections to encourage you to develop your own opinions about the readings;
- Focus on Accuracy sections to draw your attention to language details.

Several chapter topics are completely new while other topics have been significantly revised based on reviewer feedback.

I hope this new edition will help you reach your academic goals.

ACKNOWLEDGEMENTS

I would like to begin by warmly thanking my former colleagues at Carleton University, who set the stage for the development of the first edition of *Learning English for Academic Purposes*. My colleagues at Renison University College at the University of Waterloo have also supported me with their comments, ideas, and encouragement. My great appreciation goes to my teaching colleagues: Judi Jewinski, Tanya Missere-Mihas, Stefan Rehm, Pat Skinner, Agnieszka Wolczuk, Nancy Oczkowski, Christa Schuller, Maggie Heeney, Maria Pop, Elizabeth Matthews, Keely Cook, Dara Lane, Stephen Hill, Christine Morgan, Raveet Jacob, Nela Maluckov, Kim Burrell, Margaret Wardell, Dianne Tyers, Audrey Olson, Bruce Russell, Winona Phachanla, Andrea Brandt, and Louann Nhan.

A special word of thanks is also due to Dr. Ken Beatty, who enthusiastically took on the writing of *LEAP: Listening and Speaking*, and has been instrumental in building the initial books into a full series. Special thanks to Sharnee Chait and the editing team at Pearson ERPI, who have been supportive and patient as we have worked through multiple drafts.

Julia Williams, Renison University College,
University of Waterloo, Canada

HIGHLIGHTS

Gearing Up uses images and infographics to spark reflection and discussion about the chapter topic.

Vocabulary Build strengthens comprehension and builds awareness of key vocabulary on the Academic Word List.

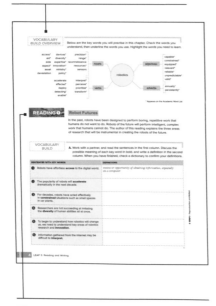

The **overview** outlines the chapter's objectives.

Three **readings** in each chapter come from a variety of sources including academic textbooks and journal articles. The readings offer different perspectives on the chapter theme, providing content for writing tasks.

Before, **while**, and **after** reading activities focus on comprehension and critical thinking.

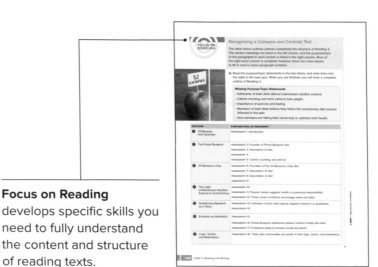

Focus on Writing develops specific skills you need to write effective academic English.

Focus on Reading develops specific skills you need to fully understand the content and structure of reading texts.

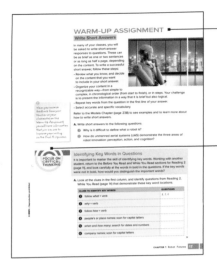

The **Warm-Up Assignment** explores a writing task and prepares you for the final assignment.

Focus on Critical Thinking introduces you to strategies for thinking critically about what you read and how to apply these strategies to writing tasks.

My eLab provides practice and additional content.

Focus on Accuracy draws attention to important language details that you can apply when reading and writing academic English.

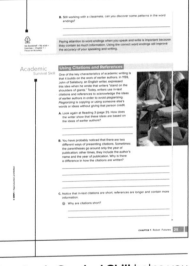

Academic Survival Skill helps you understand and practise effective classroom and study skills.

Critical Connections allows you to reinvest what you learned in the chapter while applying critical thinking.

The **Final Assignment** synthesizes the chapter content and theme through a writing task.

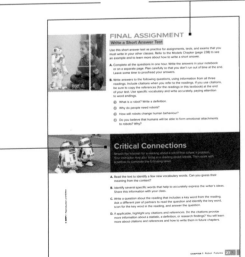

The **Models Chapter** provides instructions and models for the writing tasks in the coursebook.

SCOPE AND SEQUENCE

CHAPTER	READING	CRITICAL THINKING	WRITING
CHAPTER 1 **ROBOT FUTURES** SUBJECT AREAS: engineering, robotics, technology	• Learn strategies to understand new words in context	• Identify key words in questions - Scan for answers while reading	Improve your writing with specific vocabulary
CHAPTER 2 **INTERNATIONALIZATION OF EDUCATION** SUBJECT AREAS: education, psychology	• Skim a text to gather information	• Consider characteristics of a text for efficient reading	• Vary sentence structures to create interest
CHAPTER 3 **BUYING AND SELLING INNOVATIVE PRODUCTS** SUBJECT AREAS: marketing, business	• Understand writer and reader responsibility - Learn tips to make your writing easy to understand	• Apply knowledge to new contexts - Generate unique thoughts	• Write definitions - Recognize typical sentence patterns for definitions
CHAPTER 4 **THE SOCIAL IMPACT OF MARKETING** SUBJECT AREAS: marketing, social psychology	• Understand how authors introduce examples into an academic text	• Predict an author's opinion - Consider the author, the audience, and the type of text	• Present your views by conceding and refuting
CHAPTER 5 **THE SCIENCE OF NUTRITION** SUBJECT AREAS: biology, health, nutrition	• Recognize a compare and contrast text - Identify purpose/topic statements	• Evaluate information based on prior knowledge	• Consider the academic perspective - Adopt an objective perspective
CHAPTER 6 **DIGITAL CURRENCIES** SUBJECT AREAS: business, economics, mathematics	• Learn how to annotate texts to remember information	• Contextualize information - Place new information in a larger context to understand it better	• Write in the third person - Explore problems and solutions
CHAPTER 7 **THE INTERNET OF THINGS** SUBJECT AREAS: business, computer science, technology	• Recognize the differences between academic and popular texts	• Weigh advantages and disadvantages to develop a unique opinion	• Summarize and reference to avoid plagiarism
CHAPTER 8 **THE SLOW FOOD MOVEMENT** SUBJECT AREAS: agriculture, political science	• Read multi-clause, multi-phrase sentences - Identify the start and end points of clauses and phrases	• Find an academic source - Learn how to research your topic	• Choose effective vocabulary to express opinions

ACCURACY	ACADEMIC SURVIVAL SKILL	ASSIGNMENTS	My eLab
• Use word forms accurately	• Identify and understand academic citations and references	• Write short answers • Write a short answer test	
• Introduce statistics in your writing	• Ask questions using correct word order 　- Survey other students and collect data	• Write a short report • Design a survey and write an extended report	
• Use parallelism when writing 　- Help readers understand content quickly	• Learn to read smart 　- Read quickly, understand the main points, and think critically about what you read	• Write a short process essay • Write a longer process essay	• Online practice for each chapter: 　- More comprehension exercises for the readings 　- Vocabulary review 　- Accuracy practice 　- Writing focus review 　- Chapter test
• Represent cause and effect accurately	• Learn strategies to become an independent learner 　- Improve your English language learning	• Write a short cause and effect essay • Write a longer cause and effect essay	
• Use conjunctions to compare and contrast	• Quote and reference to avoid plagiarism 　- Write in-text citations and references accurately	• Write a short compare and contrast essay • Write a longer compare and contrast essay	• Additional online reading texts: 　- Extra reading with comprehension and critical thinking questions • Study resources in Documents including: 　- Referencing 　- Irregular Verbs List
• Write conditional sentences 　- Understand the first, second, and third conditionals	• Paraphrase to avoid plagiarism 　- Learn paraphrasing techniques	• Paraphrase a paragraph • Write a cause and effect essay that includes paraphrases of two paragraphs	
• Use the passive voice 　- Learn how and when to use the passive voice	• Edit your own writing 　- Identify your top three challenges needing improvement	• Write a short summary • Integrate a summary into a persuasive essay	
• Clarify the subject of a sentence	• Express opposing ideas 　- Learn sentence frames to help you express opposing thoughts	• Write a short persuasive essay • Write an extended persuasive essay	

TABLE OF CONTENTS

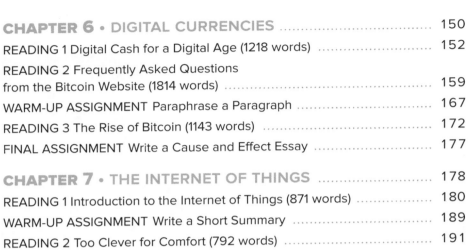

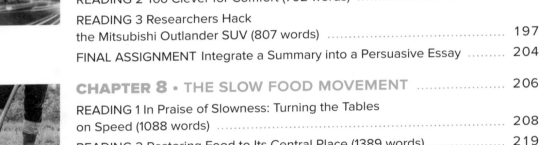

CHAPTER 1
Robot Futures

When you think about robots, do you think of the robots in the famous *Star Wars* movies (R2-D2, C-3PO, and BB-8), robotic machines building cars, or humans with superpowers? How about advanced drones that can help people recover from natural disasters, or even personal nurses that can provide care for older people? Robots serve many different purposes and come in many different forms, but one thing is certain—robots are changing our world, and in the process, they will change how we think and behave. How will we share our world with these rapidly evolving machines?

In this chapter, you will

- use vocabulary related to robotics;

- learn strategies to understand new words in context;

- identify key words in questions to scan for answers when reading;

- improve your writing with specific vocabulary;

- write word forms accurately;

- identify and understand academic citations and references;

- write short answers and a short answer test.

GEARING UP

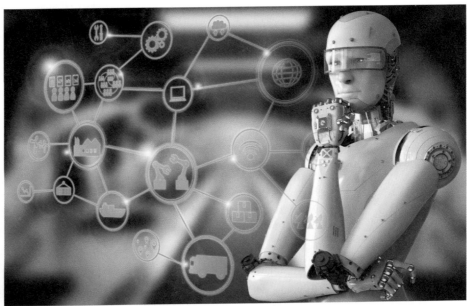

Robots are designed to help humans with their most significant problems.

A. The table below lists two human problems and robot solutions discussed in Readings 2 and 3. Working with a small group of students, brainstorm other problems and possible solutions, and write them in the blank rows of the table. When you have finished, share your suggestions with the class.

HUMAN PROBLEMS	ROBOT SOLUTIONS
1 Natural disasters, like landslides and hurricanes, create dangerous conditions for rescue workers trying to help people.	Flying robots (unmanned aerial systems) can take pictures of unsafe land and send them back to people on safe ground.
2 There are not enough young people to take care of older people.	Robots can help care for older patients by moving them, spending time talking to them, etc.
3	
4	

Below are the key words you will practise in this chapter. Check the words you understand, then underline the words you use. Highlight the words you need to learn.

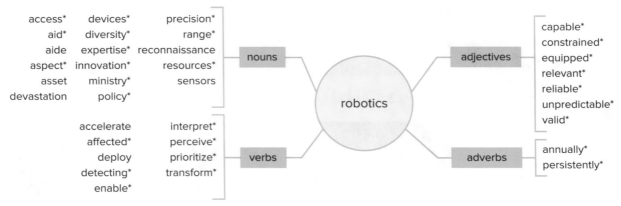

nouns		
access*	devices*	precision*
aid*	diversity*	range*
aide	expertise*	reconnaissance
aspect*	innovation*	resources*
asset	ministry*	sensors
devastation	policy*	

verbs	
accelerate	interpret*
affected*	perceive*
deploy	prioritize*
detecting*	transform*
enable*	

adjectives
capable*
constrained*
equipped*
relevant*
reliable*
unpredictable*
valid*

adverbs
annually*
persistently*

robotics

* Appears on the Academic Word List

Robot Futures

In the past, robots have been designed to perform boring, repetitive work that humans do not want to do. Robots of the future will perform intelligent, complex work that humans cannot do. The author of this reading explains the three areas of research that will be instrumental in creating the robots of the future.

A. Work with a partner, and read the sentences in the first column. Discuss the possible meaning of each key word in bold, and write a definition in the second column. When you have finished, check a dictionary to confirm your definitions.

SENTENCES WITH KEY WORDS	DEFINITIONS
❶ Robots have effortless **access** to the digital world.	*means or opportunity of obtaining information, especially on a computer*
❷ The popularity of robots will **accelerate** dramatically in the next decade.	more powerful, increasing speed quickly
❸ For decades, robots have acted effectively in **constrained** situations such as small spaces in car plants.	restriction, or limitation limited space of time
❹ Researchers are not succeeding at imitating the **diversity** of human abilities all at once.	The inclusion of people from different races
❺ To begin to understand how robotics will change us, we need to understand key areas of robotics research and **innovation**.	Introduction of Something New
❻ Information gathered from the Internet may be difficult to **interpret**.	To Explain or Tell The meaning

SENTENCES WITH KEY WORDS	DEFINITIONS
7 Modern robotics is about how anything can **perceive** the world, make sense of its surroundings, then act on the world and make change.	To attain Awareness (notice)
8 An automotive assembly plant robot moves with great speed and **precision**, repeating the same complex motion thousands of times a day.	Accuracy
9 But there is one special quality of modern robotics that is very **relevant** to how our world is changing: robots are a new form of living glue between our physical world and the digital universe we have created.	Evidence Tending To prove or disprove The matter at issue or under discussion (related directly)
10 Robots have physical **sensors** and motors—they can operate in the real world just as well as any software program operates on the Internet.	a particular motion devices heat light move
11 Robots will have capabilities that will **transform** human lives.	To change character or Condition (completely change)
12 Acting in our social, human world means moving from the constraints of the factory floor to the dynamic, **unpredictable** world in which we raise our families.	declare in Advance hard to know what will happen next

B. Suffixes (letters added to the end of a word) and prefixes (letters added to the beginning of a word) can change a word form or meaning. Compare the words in the table below to the key words in the table above. Put a check mark in the column that explains how each of the new words was formed. When you are finished, confirm your answers with a partner.

NEW FORM OF KEY WORD	ADDED PREFIX	ADDED SUFFIX	REMOVED PREFIX OR SUFFIX	WORDS WITH SIMILAR PREFIX/ SUFFIX PATTERNS
1 accessible		✓		*visible – vision*
2 acceleration	/			deceleration
3 unconstrained	/		X	constrained (uncertain)
4 diverse		X	/	diversity / Active- Activity
5 innovate		X	/	innovation- accumulation
6 misinterpret	/		X	interpret mispell
7 perception	/			reception
8 precise	X		/	diverse- diversion precisely precision
9 irrelevant	—		X	relevant regular
10 sense	X		/	survive—survival Presence
11 transformative	/		X	complete Competitive Transformative
12 predictable	X		/	Unpredictable

word Start R   in
Pre   Un

C. In the last column of the table above (page 5), write the word pairs from the word box below that follow the same prefix/suffix pattern as the new words. The first one has been done for you.

accumulate – accumula**tion**	**ir**regular – regular
active – activ**ity**	**mis**understand – understand
available – **un**available	recep**tion** – receive
competit**ive** – compete	survive – surviv**or**
diverse – diver**sion**	**un**happy – happy
invita**tion** – invite	~~visible – vision~~

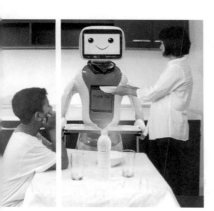

Before You Read

A. With a partner, look at the picture of a robot working. Discuss the following questions.

1. What is the robot doing?

2. What problem does the robot solve?

3. To function well,
   • what does the robot need to "see" in its environment?
   • what action does the robot need to perform?
   • what decisions does the robot need to make?

Thinking about this information will help you understand Reading 1.

While You Read

B. This reading can be divided into several sections. As you read, write the number of each paragraph next to the section in which it belongs.

SECTIONS OF THE READING	PARAGRAPH NUMBERS IN THAT SECTION
Introduction	1 3
Areas of research in robotics	4
Explanation of the areas of research	5, 6, 7
Conclusion	8

Robot Futures

1. Robot technologies seem magical because they are transformative. A product we simply use becomes something that sees us, hears us, and responds to our needs. Robotics makes the products around us more aware and more alive, a trend that will **accelerate** dramatically in the next decade. This is because the **ambition** of robotics is no longer limited only to copying us—making walking, talking androids that are indistinguishable from humans. Robotics has grown up.

2. Modern robotics is about how anything can **perceive** the world, make sense of its surroundings, then act on the world and make change. But never ask a **roboticist** what a robot is. The answer changes too quickly. By the time researchers finish their most recent debate on what is and what isn't a robot, the frontier moves on as whole new interaction technologies are born.

ambition (n.): strong desire to achieve something

5

roboticist (n.): someone who designs and builds robots

10

3. But there is one special quality of modern robotics that is very **relevant** to how our world is changing: robots are a new form of living glue between our physical world and the digital universe we have created. Robots have physical **sensors** and
15   motors—they can operate in the real world just as well as any software program operates on the Internet. They will be embedded in our physical spaces—our sidewalks, bedrooms, and parks—and they will have minds of their own thanks to artificial intelligence (AI). Yet robots are also fully connected to the digital world— they are far better at navigating, sharing information, and participating in the
20   online world than humans can ever be. We have invented a new species, part material and part digital, that will eventually have superhuman qualities in both worlds at once, and the question that remains is, how will we share our world with these new creatures, and how will this new ecology change who we are and how we act?

25   ...

4. To begin to understand how robotics will change us, we need to understand key areas of robotics research and **innovation**. We take inspiration from humans, and so the first question roboticists ask is, what makes humans intelligent? We think of human intelligence as a quality that is living and interactive, [part of] the world
30   in which we function. Therefore, intelligence depends on two things: being meaningfully connected to our environment, and having internal decision-making skills to consider our circumstances and then take action. The environmental connection is two-way, and we term the inputs as *perception* and the outputs back to the world as *action*. The internal decision-making that **transforms** our senses
35   about the world into deliberate action is *cognition*.

5. *Perception* is the ability to collect and **interpret** information about the world using sensors—digital cameras, sonar rangefinders, radar, light sensors, artificial skin, and many others. Perception is easy on the Internet because everything has a digital form—online sensors are easy to build, and the signals are easy to interpret. An
40   online artificial intelligence can play video games [just as well as] humans because it can see as well as humans can online. But robot perception in the real world means recreating the [complex] physical and visual processing systems we have— feeling a firm handshake, recognizing faces, animals, textures, and fleeting smiles.

6. *Action* is the power to effect change in the world. For decades, robots have acted
45   effectively in **constrained** situations such as automotive **assembly** lines. Robots are historically hard, heavy machines with powerful motors and little flexibility. An automotive assembly plant welding robot moves with great speed and **precision**, repeating the same complex motion thousands of times a day, all in a steel cage that is off-limits to humans, because the robot could thoughtlessly kill with a single
50   blow. But acting in our social, human world means moving from the constraints of the factory floor to the dynamic, **unpredictable** world in which we raise our families. Instead of speed and power, social robots need elasticity, pliability, and gentleness of touch. This has motivated researchers to invent new types of motors with built-in springs, and new control systems to push a shopping cart or unscrew
55   a jar of honey.

7. *Cognition* is the ability to reason, to make decisions about what to do next. Cognition is close to the traditional AI dream of thinking like a human: if a robot can sense the world through perceptions and change the world through action, then cognition

assembly* (adj.): putting parts together

60 is about making decisions about what to do next. It is the glue that connects perception to action, just as our brains absorb information using the five senses, then make decisions about how to behave next, connecting our senses to our muscles using reflexes and thought. Cognition is also the area in which robots [differ] from how natural animals operate, with local brains that must make decisions independently. Robots have effortless **access** to the digital world [which

65 includes] both massive data and superhuman processing power. Every robotic decision can be informed by everything its shared network of robot "brothers and sisters" have encountered, and even the decision-making process itself is subject to outsourcing—a robot can use powerful online computing services so that its own circuitry can stay lightweight and power-efficient.

70 ...

8. The three core strands of robotics research inquiry—perception, action, and cognition—do not proceed at the same rate, nor are researchers succeeding in [imitating] the **diversity** of human abilities all at once. Rather, our research is [an uneven] frontier that, in some cases, already exceeds human capabilities in peculiar

75 ways and, in other cases, seems to be refusing every effort at advancement. We are not really on a straight path to the artificial human, but rather on the road to a strange [collection] of mechanical creatures that have both subhuman and superhuman qualities all jumbled together, and this near future is for us, not just for our descendants.

(963 words)

Nourbakhsh, I. R. (2013). *Robot futures* (pp. xiv–xviii). Cambridge, MA: MIT Press.

After You Read

C. Compare your answers from the table in While You Read with those of a classmate. If your answers are different, explain your reasoning to each other. Confirm your answers with the class.

D. Answer the questions to check your comprehension.

1 At the end of the first paragraph, why does the author write, "Robotics has grown up"?

_____

_____

2 Why should you never ask what a robot is?

_____

3 What two worlds do robots "glue" together?

physical & Digital

_____

4 How will the new species of robots change humans?

How we Act

_____

⑤ What are the three key areas of robotic research and innovation?

action,

⑥ What is *perception*?

using sensors to see and understand

⑦ What is *action*?

the ability to do something

⑧ What is *cognition*?

the ability

⑨ Why do you think these three areas of robotics research are not developing at the same rate?

⑩ The author suggests that in the future, robot perception will be able to sense very small differences in humans, robot action will be gentle, and robot cognition will be intelligent. What do you think these perceptive, gentle, and intelligent robots will be able to do? Discuss your ideas with a partner.

My Bookshelf > My eLab > Exercises > Chapter 1 > Robot Futures

FOCUS ON READING

Strategies for Understanding Words in Context

Learning as many new English words as you can will help you understand what you read. However, you may still see words that you are not familiar with. What do you do then?

A. Discuss with the class what you do when you see a word you don't know. Decide together which methods will help you learn and remember new words most effectively.

Here are some strategies that might help you with unfamiliar vocabulary.

Strategy 1: Guess the meaning from the context.

One of the strategies successful students use when they see new vocabulary is to try to guess the meaning of the word from the context (or the words around the unfamiliar word).

Example: Robot researchers constantly develop new technology to expand the **frontier** of knowledge.

You may not be familiar with the word *frontier*, but you do know that

• the reading is about robots of the future;

• *frontier* is the object of the verb *expand* (What must be expanded to develop new technology?);

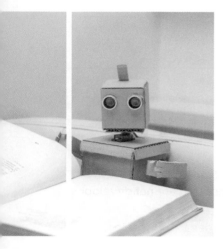

- the word *frontier* is followed by a prepositional phrase: *of knowledge*. You know that developing new ideas usually means expanding knowledge;
- *frontier* is preceded by *the*; therefore, you know that it is a noun.

You may still not understand the exact meaning of *frontier*, but you have a good idea what the sentence means. Now read the sentence that comes after.

> Example: Robot researchers constantly develop new technology to expand the **frontier** of knowledge. As the **frontier** is pushed back, scientists discover more ways in which robots can help solve human problems.

The second sentence gives you more information about the meaning of the word *frontier*. You now know that

- the *frontier* is something that is pushed back;
- as the *frontier* is pushed back, scientists discover more ways to solve human problems.

You can probably guess that frontier refers to the limits of knowledge that scientists *expand* or *push back* to make new discoveries. Now you know the meaning of the word, and you didn't have to look it up in the dictionary.

Strategy 2: Guess the meaning from root words, prefixes, and suffixes.

You can also use what you know about root words, prefixes, and suffixes to help you guess the meanings of words.

> Example: Never ask a **roboticist** what a robot is.

You may not know what *roboticist* means. However, you can figure out that the word

- contains the root *robot*, which you know means a machine that does the work of a human;
- is a noun, because the article *a* precedes it, and articles introduce nouns;
- refers to a person because of the verb *ask*; you ask *people* questions;
- ends with the suffix *–ist*, which looks similar to the suffix on the word scient*ist*, which you may be familiar with.

As a result, you can probably guess that *roboticist* means "person who develops robots"—without needing to consult a dictionary.

It may be helpful to know that prefixes change the meaning of words. For example:

- *pre*requisite, *pre*condition, *pre*determined (*pre–* means "before")
- *re*place, *re*think, *re*store (*re–* means "again")
- *in*considerate, *in*consistent, *in*convenient (*in–* means "not")

Suffixes change the form of the word (or part of speech), but the meaning remains similar to the meaning of the root word. For example:

- activ*ity* (n.), act (v.), activ*e* (adj.), activ*ely* (adv.)
- impres*sion* (n.), impress (v.), impress*ive* (adj.), impress*ively* (adv.)
- rebell*ion* (n.), rebel (v.), rebell*ious* (adj.), rebell*iously* (adv.)

Strategy 3: Continue reading without knowing the meaning of every word.

Successful students know they may have to continue reading—even if they don't know the meaning of every word—in order to finish the reading quickly. Sometimes it isn't necessary to understand every word to grasp the meaning of the reading.

> Example: Perception is the ability to collect and interpret information about the world using sensors—digital cameras, **sonar rangefinders**, radar, light sensors, artificial skin, and many others.

You may not know what *sonar rangefinders* are. However, you can continue reading without worrying about the exact meaning because you observe other things:

- *Sonar rangefinders* are included in a list of items that collect information about the world;
- This is the only time the words *sonar rangefinders* are used in the reading.

As a result, you can probably guess that the words *sonar rangefinders* refer to equipment that gathers information. As the term is mentioned only once, you probably don't need to understand its exact meaning in order to continue reading. You must decide if the new term is important, or if you can still understand the main points of the reading without knowing its exact meaning.

B. Discuss with the class how to decide if it is essential or not to understand the exact meaning of a word. Here are some clues.

NOT ESSENTIAL TO THE MEANING OF THE READING	**ESSENTIAL** TO THE MEANING OF THE READING
• The word isn't repeated often.	• The word is repeated frequently.
• The word is included in a list of examples.	• The word is included in the title or subheading(s).
• The word is an adjective that you can guess is positive or negative.	• The word is highlighted in some way (in bold or italics).

C. As you read the next text, use these strategies to help you with unfamiliar vocabulary.
- Guess the meaning of the word from its context.
- Guess the meaning of the word from its root word, or by removing its prefix or suffix.
- Decide if you can continue reading without knowing the exact meaning of the word.

 **Press Release from Aeryon Labs**

Aeryon Labs makes small flying robots (unmanned aerial systems or UAS) that are used to help people after a natural disaster like a hurricane or a landslide. After these disasters, the ground may not be safe for humans, so UAS robots can help humans "see" what help is needed.

A. Read each sentence, and circle the letter of the answer that best matches the meaning of the word in bold. When you have finished, check your answers with a partner and confirm these with the class.

1 "GlobalMedic immediately offered support to the communities **affected** by Irma," said Rahul Singh, Executive Director, Global Medic.

a) changed by   b) created by   c) deployed by

2 In areas where the majority of the buildings have been destroyed, these maps will also provide valuable information that will **aid** in the rebuilding efforts.

a) enable   b) detect   c) assist with

3 Aeryon's unmanned aerial systems (UAS) are built for extreme conditions like high winds and heavy rain, making them the perfect aerial **asset** for disaster response efforts.

a) influential thing   b) valuable thing   c) interesting thing

4 The Aeryon SkyRangers used in the Caribbean are equipped with thermal cameras to help locate survivors by **detecting** body heat.

a) prioritizing   b) deploying   c) finding

5 Aeryon **deployed** UAS and pilots to assist after the Nepal earthquake in 2015, the Ecuador earthquake in 2016, and the Columbian landslides earlier this year.

a) hid   b) used   c) found

6 Last week, Hurricane Irma, a Category 5 storm with winds of over 185 mph (298 kph), tore through the Caribbean leaving **devastation** in its path.

a) deletion   b) detection   c) destruction

7 UAS **enable** ground-based rescue teams to collect critical aerial intelligence quickly in difficult situations.

a) destroy   b) allow   c) rely

8 GlobalMedic will use the SkyRangers to create detailed maps of the area, so first responders can **prioritize** supplies and coordinate the most effective response.

a) list in order of importance   b) determine to be   c) fix in order

9 Using UAS for aerial intelligence and **reconnaissance** enables rescuers to rapidly determine how and where to help the people who need it the most.

a) investigation   b) explanation   c) destruction

10 Aeryon's UAS are built for **reliable** operations in extreme conditions.

a) unthinkable   b) believable   c) dependable

11 "UAS enable ground-based rescue teams to collect critical aerial intelligence and deploy rescue **resources** quickly where they are needed most," said Bill McHale of Aeryon Labs.

a) books   b) supplies   c) revisions

B. In this reading, you will find some words that fit together to form expressions. These expressions are called *collocations*, meaning words that "locate together." Learning these expressions will improve your reading and writing fluency.

Use the line numbers from Reading 2 in the first column to find collocations that match the definitions in the third column. Write the collocations in the second column. When you have finished, compare your answers with a partner's.

LINE NUMBER	COLLOCATIONS	DEFINITIONS
LINES 3, 12	*disaster recovery efforts*	attempts to help people after a natural disaster has occurred
LINE 4		group that helps people and countries that have experienced natural disasters
LINE 5		people who arrive first in a country to provide aid
LINE 11		dangerous and life-threatening circumstances
LINE 11		high-speed winds
LINE 12		heavy rain

Before You Read

When you have a text followed by a set of questions, reading the questions first can help you find the answers faster. Identify key words (or their synonyms) in the questions, and scan for these to help you locate the answers in the reading.

A. Read the questions below, and scan the first paragraph of the reading for words (or synonyms) that match the words in bold. This will help you find the answers to the questions quickly.

B. Write your answers in one or two sentences, repeating the key words in your answers. Compare your answers with a classmate's.

① What does **Aeryon Labs manufacture?**

Aeryon Labs manufactures unmanned aerial systems (UAS) called SkyRangers.

② How is this equipment **used** (synonym for deployed)?

_____

_____

③ What **organization** does Aeryon Labs **work with** (synonym for partner with)?

_____

_____

④ Whey they work together, what services do they **provide**?

_____

_____

While You Read

C. Read the following questions and note the key words in bold. Scan Reading 2 for the key words (or their synonyms) and answer the questions. In your answers, write one or two sentences. If possible, repeat the key words from the questions.

1 **When** was this reading posted to the Internet?

_____

_____

2 What happened in **Saint Martin last week** (i.e., the week before the article was posted)?

_____

_____

3 According to **Rahul Singh**, why are UAS **perfect aerial assets**?

_____

_____

_____

4 How do **Aeryon SkyRangers find survivors**?

_____

_____

_____

5 According to **Bill McHale**, what will Aeryon Labs **continue doing** in the future?

_____

_____

_____

6 Aside from search and rescue work, what else does **GlobalMedic use the SkyRangers for**?

_____

_____

7 How **many times** have Aeryon Labs and GlobalMedic **worked together**, and **why**?

_____

_____

_____

_____

Aeryon Deploys SkyRangers to Support Hurricane Irma Response

SAINT MARTIN – 2017, September 12 – Aeryon Labs Inc., the premier manufacturer of small unmanned aerial systems (UAS), has **deployed** SkyRanger UAS and an expert pilot to help support the disaster recovery efforts after Hurricane Irma. Starting in Saint Martin, Aeryon has partnered with the relief organization GlobalMedic to provide aerial
5 intelligence to first responders and international disaster relief teams on the ground.

Last week, Hurricane Irma, a Category 5 storm with sustained winds of over 185 mph [295 kph], tore through the Caribbean leaving **devastation** in its path. "GlobalMedic immediately offered support to the communities **affected** by Irma," said Rahul Singh, Executive Director, Global Medic. "Using UAS for aerial intelligence and **reconnaissance**
10 **enables** us to rapidly determine how and where to help the people who need it the most. Aeryon's UAS are built for reliable operations in extreme conditions like high winds and torrential rain, making them the perfect aerial **asset** for our disaster recovery efforts."

The Aeryon SkyRangers deployed to the Caribbean are **equipped** with Aeryon SR-EO/
15 IR Mk II thermal cameras to help locate survivors by **detecting** body heat. In addition, Aeryon's HDZoom30 cameras deliver powerful zoom capabilities and can provide detailed facial recognition from over 1000 feet away.

"UAS enable ground-based rescue teams to collect critical aerial intelligence and deploy rescue **resources** quickly and where they are needed most," said Bill McHale,
20 CEO at Aeryon Labs. "We are proud to be able to support the Irma relief efforts and to continue developing advanced UAS technology that helps save lives."

In addition to search and rescue work, GlobalMedic will use SkyRangers to create detailed **2-D and 3-D** maps of the affected areas, so that first responders can **prioritize** resources and coordinate the most effective response. In areas where the majority
25 of the buildings have been destroyed, these maps will also provide valuable information that will **aid** in the rebuilding efforts.

The Hurricane Irma response is the fourth time Aeryon has partnered with GlobalMedic and their RescUAV program, which uses innovative UAS technology to aid in disasters. Aeryon deployed UAS and pilots to assist after the Nepal earthquake in 2015, the
30 Ecuador earthquake in 2016, and the Columbian landslides earlier this year.

(360 words)

CEO (n.): Chief Executive Officer (head of an organization)

2-D and 3-D (adj.): referring to images in two dimensions and in three dimensions

Aeryon Labs. (2017, September 12). *Aeryon deploys SkyRangers to support Hurricane Irma response* [Press Release]. Retrieved from https://www.aeryon.com/press-releases/aeryon-deploys-skyrangers-support-hurricane-irma-response

After You Read

D. Compare your answers with a classmate's. Are any of your answers different? If so, confirm your understanding with your class.

E. With your class, discuss other ways the UAS systems could be used in the areas of pipeline inspection, public safety, ground mapping, traffic reconnaissance, border security, and wildlife monitoring. What problems do these robot applications solve?

My Bookshelf > My eLab >
Exercises > Chapter 1 >
Press Release from Aeryon Labs

FOCUS ON WRITING

Improving Your Writing with Specific Vocabulary

You can quickly improve your written and spoken English by selecting specific and descriptive vocabulary. This will allow your readers and listeners to "see" your exact meaning. However, better vocabulary is not only useful for academic writing—it is *essential*. Academic writing is used to express complex ideas. If you choose words that are not specific, your reader may not understand your exact meaning.

You do not need to spend a lot of time looking in a dictionary or thesaurus to find better vocabulary. Think of words that you already recognize but have yet to use. The words don't have to be long or complicated. Spend time searching your mind for better words; consult a dictionary or thesaurus only as a last resort.

Look at these sentences that roboticists might say about their robots. The underlined words indicate non-specific and inaccurate verbs, adjectives, and nouns. The words in bold indicate better vocabulary.

> Example #1: If the robot <u>does</u> this work, it will <u>get</u> success.

Better vocabulary:

> If the robot **performs** this work, it will <u>achieve</u> success.

> If the robot <u>accomplishes</u> this work, it will be **successful**.

> Example #2: First responders <u>can help people</u> better if they use unmanned aerial systems to see <u>where they can't go</u>.

Better vocabulary:

> First responders can **support survivors** better if they **employ** unmanned aerial systems for **reconnaissance**.

> or

> First responders can **assist victims** better if they **deploy** unmanned aerial systems for **investigations**.

A. Now look at these sentences that news reporters might say to describe disaster relief efforts. Work with another student to identify the non-specific words, and then select better verbs, adjectives, and nouns.

1 There was a bad storm that caused <u>some</u> damage.

* there was

> There was a neggative weather condition that caused destruction

2 After the storm, people and some robots went to Saint Martin to help.

> supportive Survivors Assist Some victims

3 The work was difficult, and the robots did a lot of work.

My Bookshelf > My eLab >
Exercises > Chapter 1 >
Focus on Writing

WARM-UP ASSIGNMENT

Write Short Answers

In many of your classes, you will be asked to write short-answer responses to questions. These can be as brief as one or two sentences or as long as half a page, depending on the content. To write a successful short answer, follow these steps:

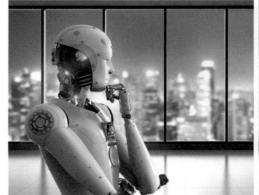

- Review what you know, and decide on the content that you want to include in your short answer.
- Organize your content in a recognizable way—from simple to complex, in chronological order (from start to finish), or in steps. Your challenge is to present the information in a way that it is brief but also logical.
- Repeat key words from the question in the first line of your answer.
- Select accurate and specific vocabulary.

Refer to the Models Chapter (page 238) to see examples and to learn more about how to write short answers.

A. Write short answers to the following questions.

When you receive feedback from your teacher or your classmates on this Warm-Up Assignment, you will have information that you can use to improve your writing on the Final Assignment.

  1 Why is it difficult to define what a robot is?

  2 How do unmanned aerial systems (UAS) demonstrate the three areas of robot innovation: perception, action, and cognition?

FOCUS ON CRITICAL THINKING

Identifying Key Words in Questions

It is important to master the skill of identifying key words. Working with another student, return to the Before You Read and While You Read sections for Reading 2 (page 11), and look carefully at the words in bold in the questions. If the key words were not in bold, how would you distinguish the important words?

A. Look at the clues in the first column, and identify questions from Reading 2, While You Read (page 14) that demonstrate these key word locations.

CLUES TO IDENTIFY KEY WORDS	QUESTIONS
1 follow *what* + verb	*2, 5, 6*
2 *why* + verb	
3 follow *how* + verb	
4 people's or place names; scan for capital letters	
5 *when* and *how many*; search for dates and numbers	
6 company names; scan for capital letters	

B. Highlight the key words in the questions below. Then scan the first paragraph of Reading 3 (page 21) to find the answers.

① According to this reading, what can Japan's citizens look forward to?

_____

② What is the current life expectancy for men and women in Japan?

_____

_____

③ Between 2010 and 2025, what is the expected increase in the number of Japanese people older than age sixty-five?

_____

_____

④ By 2050, what percentage of people in Japan will be over age sixty-five?

_____

 **READING ③**　**Here Come the Robots**

Reading 2 described how robots (UAS) help first responders provide relief after a natural disaster has made the surrounding environment unsafe. Reading 3 describes another problem that robots help solve: the world's population is aging, and older people sometimes need help. In many countries, there aren't enough young people to take care of all the older people. Robots are being built to help older people live independently.

VOCABULARY BUILD	

A. Guess the meaning of the words in bold in the sentences in the first column of the table. Match each word to the correct definition in the second column. Confirm your answers with the class.

SENTENCES WITH WORDS		DEFINITIONS
① Toyota built a nursing **aide** named Robina as part of their Partner Robot Family, a line of robots to take care of the world's aging population.	_h_	a) way of doing something that has been officially agreed on
② Japan allows only 50,000 work visas **annually**, and unless something changes, there will not be enough nurses to care for the older people.	_____	b) important or useful
③ Most companies that build robots didn't enter the caretaking field with a good idea of how to forge an emotional connection with people, which is an important **aspect** of eldercare.	_____	c) built; supplied
④ It remains difficult to design robots **capable** of intimate activities like bathing patients or brushing their teeth.	_____	d) every year

SENTENCES WITH WORDS		DEFINITIONS
❺ Honda is also focusing much of its research and commercialization on robotic arms and legs and assistance **devices** that are robotic but not free-standing robots.	_____	e) number of people or things that are different but of the same type
❻ **Equipped** with cameras that function as eyes, ASIMO can follow voice commands, shake hands, and answer questions with a nod or by voice.	_____	f) continuously; with perseverance
❼ Japanese companies Toyota and Honda are using their **expertise** in mechanical engineering to invent the next generation of robots.	_____	g) government department responsible for an area like education or health
❽ Japan's **Ministry** of Health, Labour, and Welfare predicts a need for four million eldercare nurses by 2025.	_____	h) person whose job is to help others
❾ With Japan's **persistently** strict immigration policies limiting the number of workers in the country, there will not be enough humans around to do the job at all.	_____	i) able to do something
❿ Although its one-child **policy** is over, Chinese women have on average 1.4 children, well below the replacement rate of 2.1, resulting in too few young people to provide for the elderly.	_____	j) one part of a situation that has many parts
⓫ For an elderly patient, ASIMO can fulfill a **range** of tasks from helping the patient get out of bed to holding a conversation.	_____	k) special skills learned through training and experience
⓬ These questions about technical and emotional robot abilities are **valid**.	_____	l) machines or tools that do a special job

My Bookshelf > My eLab > Exercises > Chapter 1 > Vocabulary Review

Before You Read

A. While You Read below lists questions for Reading 3. Highlight the key words in these questions. Compare your key words with a classmate's. Discuss any differences you might have.

While You Read

B. Working on your own, scan the text for the highlighted key words to find the answers to the questions.

❶ Why does the author think that taking care of one's grandparents will no longer be possible in Japan?

_____

❷ How many eldercare nurses will be required in 2025? How many are there now?

_____

_____

❸ Why will the labour shortage be worse in the field of eldercare?

_____

_____

❹ Which Japanese companies are developing eldercare robots?

_____

5 What robots has Toyota developed and what can they do?

_____

_____

_____

_____

6 What robot has Honda developed and what can it do?

_____

_____

_____

7 What is a technical challenge for companies that design robots?

_____

_____

_____

8 a) What does Sherry Turkle question?

_____

_____

b) What does Turkle warn us about?

_____

_____

c) What does Turkle argue?

_____

_____

_____

9 If robots are accepted as caregivers in Japan, what will that do to Japan's economy?

_____

10 What other countries are also experiencing aging populations?

_____

_____

_____

11 What will be a rare phenomenon related to robot technology?

_____

_____

Welcome your new job takers and caregivers. The [future] will see societies transform as humans learn to live alongside robots.

Japan is home to the longest-living citizens on earth and the biggest elderly population of any country—and it's not getting any younger. Japan's current life expectancy is
5 80 years for men and 87 years for women and is expected to rise to 84 and 91, respectively, over the next 45 years (National Institute of Population and Social Security Research in Japan, 2012). Between 2010 and 2025, the number of Japanese citizens 65 years or older is expected to increase by seven million (American Society for Quality, 2013). Today, 25 percent of Japan's population is age 65 or older (World Bank,
10 n.d.) ... By 2020, this is projected to increase to 29 percent, and reach 39 percent by 2050 (Japan **Ministry** of International Affairs and Communications, 2014).

All of those long-living elderly will need caretakers. Yet Japan's low birth rates mean that what once was [typical] of Japanese family life—taking care of one's grandparents and great-grandparents—will no longer be [possible] at the scale the nation needs.
15 There will not be enough grandchildren.

With Japan's **persistently** strict immigration policies [limiting] the number of workers in the country, there will not be enough humans around to do the job at all. Japan's Ministry of Health, Labour, and Welfare predicts a need for four million eldercare nurses by 2025. Right now there are only 1.49 million in the country (Difference
20 engine: The caring robot, 2013). Japan allows only 50,000 work visas **annually**, and unless something changes, the math does not work.

This labour shortage will hit service-industry jobs like eldercare and will be worsened because caretakers have a high job turnover rate due to low pay and high rates of work-related injury from lifting patients.

25 Enter the robots.

Our future caretakers are being developed in a Japanese factory right now. Just as Japanese companies reinvented cars in the 1970s and consumer electronics in the 1980s, they are now reinventing the family. **Rival** Japanese companies Toyota and Honda are using their **expertise** in mechanical engineering to invent the next
30 generation of robots. Toyota built a nursing **aide** named Robina ... as part of their Partner Robot Family, a line of robots to take care of the world's growing **geriatric** population. Robina is a "female" robot, 60 kilograms in weight and 1.2 metres tall, that can communicate using words and **gestures**. She has wide-set eyes, a [stylish haircut], and even a flowing white metallic skirt.

35 Robina's brother, Humanoid, serves as a multi-purpose home assistant. He can do the dishes, take care of your parents when they're sick, and even provide entertainment; one model plays the trumpet, another the violin. Both versions [look like] the famous *Star Wars* robot C-3PO although in white instead of gold (Toyota, n.d.).

In response, Honda has created ASIMO (the Advanced Step in Innovative Mobility
40 robot), a fully functional humanoid that looks like a 4-foot-tall astronaut stuck on Earth. ASIMO is sophisticated enough to interpret human emotions, movements, and conversation. Equipped with cameras that function as eyes, ASIMO can follow voice commands, shake hands, and answer questions with a nod or by voice. He even bows

rival (adj.): competing

geriatric (adj.): relating to medical care of older people

gestures (n.): movements of part of your body to express a feeling or meaning

to greet others, demonstrating good Japanese manners (Obringer & Strickland, 2007).
45 For an elderly patient, ASIMO can fulfil a **range** of tasks from helping the patient get out of bed to holding a conversation (Seven robots that can help, 2013).

Honda is also focusing much of its research and commercialization on robotic limbs and assistance **devices** that are robotic but not free-standing robots. Its Walking Assist device wraps around the legs and back of people with weakened leg muscles, giving
50 them extra power to move on their own (Honda, n.d.). In the future, expect to see Honda making robotic hands and arms. Its goal is nothing less than helping **paraplegics** walk and the very frail rediscover the speed and power of their youth.

…

Nevertheless, challenges remain. On the technical side, it remains difficult to design
55 robots **capable** of intimate activities like bathing patients or brushing their teeth (Difference engine: The caring robot, 2013). And most Japanese companies that are developing these robots specialize in industrial motors and electronic automation. They didn't enter the caretaking field with a keen grasp of how to forge an emotional connection, [which is an important] **aspect** of eldercare. Even as they improve, some
60 observers—like Sherry Turkle, a professor of the social studies of science and technology at MIT—question whether patients will ever be able to form a true emotional connection with robot caretakers. As Turkle warns, "For the idea of artificial companionship to be our new normal, we have to change ourselves, and in the process we are remaking human values and human connection." If robot nurses catch on, she explains, they
65 may even create a [damaging gap] between younger and older generations. "It's not just that older people are supposed to be talking," Turkle argues, referring to the goal of creating robots that can hold conversation, "younger people are supposed to be listening. We are showing very little interest in what our elders have to say. We are building the machines that will let their stories fall on deaf ears" (Moskowitz, 2013).

70 These technical questions (Can a robot brush a person's teeth?) and almost-spiritual doubts (Can, and should, emotional connections be made between humans and robots?) are both **valid.** [As] robot technology and applicability continue to advance in Japan, answers to these questions will [be increasingly important]. With too few caretakers, robots [are likely to] become a regular part of the Japanese family system.

75 If the aging nation can pull it off, robot caretakers will be a **boon** for Japan's economy and will soon make the jump to the global economy, with potentially far-reaching consequences.

Much of the rest of the industrialized world is on the verge of a period of advanced aging that will mirror Japan's own. In Europe, all 28 member states of the European
80 Union have populations that are growing older, and in the decades ahead, the percentage of Europe's population aged 65 and older will grow from 17 percent to 30 percent (European Commission, 2012; Eurostat, 2017). China is already entering a period of advanced aging even as it continues to develop. Although its one-child **policy** is already being phased out … Chinese women have on average 1.4 children,
85 well below the replacement rate of 2.1, resulting in too few young people to provide for the elderly. The notable exception is in [North America], where immigration policies partially diminish the effects of an aging population.

paraplegic (n.): person who can't move the lower part of the body, including the legs

boon (n.): great benefit

As the populations of developed nations continue to age, they create a big market for Japanese robots. And
90 caretaking robots, alongside robotic limb technology, may simply be the first in a new wave of complex robots entering our everyday lives. Robots will be the rare technology that reaches **mainstream** society through elderly users first, spreading down [through
95 the generations] as grandma shows off her next cutting-edge robot to the kids and grandchildren.

mainstream (adj.): accepted by most people in society

(1163 words)

References

American Society for Quality. (2013, June 12). Japan moving toward nursing robots for elderly. *Japan Economic Newswire*. Retrieved from http://asq.org/qualitynews/qnt/execute/displaySetup?newsID=16207

Difference engine: The caring robot. (2013, May 24). *Economist: Babbage*. Podcast retrieved from http://www.economist.com/blogs/babbage/2013/05/automation-elderly

European Commission. (2012, May 15). 2012 Ageing report: Europe needs to prepare. Retrieved from https://ec.europa.eu/eip/ageing/news/2012-ageing-report-europe-needs-prepare_en

Eurostat. (2017). Population structure and ageing. Retrieved from http://epp.eurostat.ec.europa.eu/statistics_explained/index.php/Population_structure_and_ageing

Honda. (n.d.). Walking assist: Supporting people with weakened leg muscles to walk. Retrieved from http://world.honda.com/Walking-Assist/

Japan Ministry of International Affairs and Communications, Statistics Bureau. (2014). *Statistical handbook of Japan – 2014*. Retrieved from http://www.stat.go.jp/english/data/handbook/index.htm

Moskowitz, C. (2013, February 18). Human-robot relations: Why we should worry. *Live Science*. Retrieved from https://www.livescience.com/27204-human-robot-relationships-turkle.html

National Institute of Population and Social Security Research in Japan. (2012). Population projections for Japan (January 2012): 2011–2060. Retrieved from http://www.ipss.go.jp/site-ad/index_english/esuikei/ppfj2012.pdf

Obringer, L. A. & Strickland, J. (2007, April 11). How ASIMO works. Retrieved from http://science.howstuffworks.com/asimo.htm

Seven robots that can help aging Americans. (2013, May 2). *Fiscal Times*. Retrieved from http://www.thefiscaltimes.com/Media/Slideshow/2013/05/02/7-Robots-That-Help-Aging-Americans.aspx?index=2#zFQXE8DZODxK7z2p.99

Toyota. (n.d.). Partner robot family. Retrieved from http://www.toyota-global.com/innovation/partner_robot/family_2.html

World Bank. (n.d.). Population ages 65 and above (% of total). Retrieved from http://data.worldbank.org/indicator/SP.POP.65UP.TO.ZS

_____

Ross, A. (2016). Here come the robots. In *The Industries of the Future* (pp. 15–19). New York, NY: Simon & Schuster.

After You Read

C. Working with two other students, compare and confirm your answers from While You Read. How did the key words from the questions help you find the answers?

D. Still with your small group, search the Internet for the percentage of people over the age of sixty-five in the country where you live. Then compare that number to the percentages of people over age sixty-five in neighbouring countries, and/or in other countries that interest you. Do you believe that looking after older people will be a problem in your country or other countries? Do you think older people will be content to be cared for by robots? Share your answers with your class.

My Bookshelf > My eLab > Exercises > Chapter 1 > Here Come the Robots

FOCUS ON ACCURACY

Writing Word Forms Accurately

In English, word endings provide a lot of information. When you work in your second or additional language(s), it can be difficult to pay attention to a word's ending because you are more focused on the meaning, indicated by the root word. Once you understand the meaning, you might easily miss the ending, which can give you more detailed information about the word.

You already know that in English, word endings contain information about
• number (add –*s* or –*es* to nouns to show plural);
• agreement with the subject (add –*s* or –*es* to regular present tense verbs in the third-person singular);
• tense (add –*ed* to regular past tense verbs);
• continuous action (add –*ing* to continuous or progressive verb forms).

A. In addition, word endings can indicate part of speech: noun, verb, adjective, or adverb. The sentences below contain some words from Readings 1, 2, and 3 that appear in different forms. Read each sentence, determine the form (part of speech) of each word in bold, and write the word in the appropriate column in the table. When you have finished, compare your answers with a classmate's.

① Lack of money is a **constraint** on the robot development process.

② Robots work well in **constrained** spaces.

③ When the **environment** is unsafe, UAS can see where people can't.

④ To be intelligent, robots must have an **environmental** connection.

⑤ According to Nourbakhsh, there are three key areas of robot **innovation**.

⑥ Roboticists must be very imaginative to **innovate**.

⑦ Aeryon Labs uses **innovative** technology to respond to natural disasters.

⑧ In the future, robots and humans will have regular **interactions**.

⑨ Scientists design **interactive** technology to develop robots.

⑩ **Perception** is the ability to connect the environmental conditions to action.

⑪ Future robots can **perceive** their environment and take action.

⑫ Robot **technology** is becoming increasingly complex.

⑬ Building robots is becoming increasingly **technical**.

NOUN	VERB	ADJECTIVE	ADVERB
	constrain	constrained	*no adverb form*
	no verb form	environmental	*environmentally*
	innovating	innovative	*innovatively*
	interact	interactive	*interactively*
	no verb	*perceptive*	*perceptively*
	no verb form	technical	*technically*

B. Still working with a classmate, can you discover some patterns in the word endings?

_____

_____

My Bookshelf > My eLab > Exercises > Chapter 1 > Focus on Accuracy

Paying attention to word endings when you speak and write is important because they contain so much information. Using the correct word endings will improve the accuracy of your speaking and writing.

Academic
Survival Skill

Using Citations and References

One of the key characteristics of academic writing is that it builds on the work of earlier authors. In 1159, John of Salisbury, an English writer, expressed this idea when he wrote that writers "stand on the shoulders of giants." Today, writers use in-text citations and references to acknowledge the ideas of earlier authors in order to avoid plagiarizing. _Plagiarizing_ is copying or using someone else's words or ideas without giving that person credit.

A. Look again at Reading 3 (page 21). How does the writer show that these ideas are based on the ideas of earlier authors?

_____

_____

B. You have probably noticed that there are two different ways of presenting citations. Sometimes the parentheses go around only the year of publication; other times, they include the author's name and the year of publication. Why is there a difference in how the citations are written?

Citation is shorter quoting what author is written

_____

_____

C. Notice that in-text citations are short; references are longer and contain more information.

① Why are citations short?

To utilize keyword from the Title

_____

② Why are the references at the end of the reading?

To avoid plagiarism

Evaluate when to use primary sources

③ Each reference contains a lot of information that would distract the reader if it was included in the text. Why do readers need so much information?

It helps recall information as stabelize your emotions

④ What kind of information is included in a reference?

_____

_____

_____

_____

D. Most often, writers use citations when they want to acknowledge an earlier author for a statistic, a quote, or statement of fact that shows or proves something. Three of the citations from Reading 3 are listed below. For each citation, write the reason for the citation (statistic, quote, or statement of fact) in the column beside it. Check your answers with the class.

CITATION	REASON FOR USING THE CITATION
(Obringer & Strickland, 2007)	quote : to confirm what ASIMO can do
(Moskowitz, 2013)	statement of fact : to state a negative outcome of using robots to care for elderly people
(National Institute of Population and Social Security Research in Japan, 2012)	statistic : to prove the Japanese population is aging

E. Authors use academic citations and references to accomplish several goals. Look at the list of these goals. With a partner, check two or three of the goals that you consider the most important. Discuss your choices with the class.

☑ To recognize the work of earlier authors

☑ To give credit to earlier authors

☐ To give the writing an academic look

☑ To avoid plagiarism

☐ To demonstrate that the authors are familiar with research and their field of study

FINAL ASSIGNMENT
Write a Short Answer Test

Use this short answer test as practice for assignments, tests, and exams that you must write in your other classes. Refer to the Models Chapter (page 238) to see an example and to learn more about how to write a short answer.

A. Complete all the questions in one hour. Write the answers in your notebook or on a separate page. Plan carefully so that you don't run out of time at the end. Leave some time to proofread your answers.

B. Write answers to the following questions, using information from all three readings. Include citations when you refer to the readings. If you use citations, be sure to copy the references (for the readings in this textbook) at the end of your test. Use specific vocabulary and write accurately, paying attention to word endings.

1. What is a robot? Write a definition.

2. Why do people need robots?

3. How will robots change human behaviour?

4. Do you believe that humans will be able to form emotional attachments to robots? Why?

Critical Connections

Search the Internet for a reading about a robot that solves a problem. Your instructor may also bring in a reading about robots. Then work with a partner to complete the following tasks.

A. Read the text to identify a few new vocabulary words. Can you guess their meaning from the context?

B. Identify several specific words that help to accurately express the writer's ideas. Share this information with your class.

C. Write a question about the reading that includes a key word from the reading. Ask a different pair of partners to read the question and identify the key word, scan for the key word in the reading, and answer the question.

D. If applicable, highlight any citations and references. Do the citations provide more information about a statistic, a definition, or research findings? You will learn more about citations and references and how to write them in future chapters.

CHAPTER 2

Internationalization of Education

Around the world, colleges and universities are internationalizing. You may be part of this internationalization process. Are you an international student, studying abroad (outside your home country)? Are you an exchange student, studying outside your home country for a limited time? Or are you a domestic student, studying in your own country but with the opportunity to meet students from abroad? These questions relate to internationalization from a student perspective. However, the term doesn't just apply to students; it applies to instructors and your area of study as well. Where is your instructor from? Do you learn about global issues at school? These questions suggest that you don't always have to travel to benefit from international education. How does the internationalization of education affect you?

In this chapter, you will

- learn vocabulary related to the internationalization of education;

- recognize sentence patterns and use varied sentence structure in your writing;

- consider characteristics of various types of text to read more efficiently;

- ask questions using correct word order to survey other students and collect data;

- learn how to skim a text for general comprehension;

- introduce statistics in your writing;

- design a survey and write an extended report based on the data you collect.

GEARING UP

How much evidence of internationalization do you see at your educational institution?

A. Working with a small group, brainstorm all the things you see and experience that contribute to internationalization at your school. You can use the following questions to guide your discussion.

- Are there international and exchange students in your classes?
- What services are available to support these students?
- Are there international instructors and staff to teach and assist you?
- Do you have the opportunity to learn about international issues in class?

B. Write down all your ideas. When you are finished, share them with the class.

Below are the key words you will practise in this chapter. Check the words you understand, then underline the words you use. Highlight the words you need to learn.

colleagues*
curriculum vitae (CV)
distribution*
drivers
motive*
partnerships*

rationales
respondents*
strategies*
target*
trends*

nouns

affiliated (with)
analyze*
challenging*
conducted*
demonstrate*
engage

enhance*
facilitate*
fostering
implement*
rely (on)*

verbs

internationalization of education

adjectives

aggregate*
core*
fundamental*
pervasive
prestige
potential*

other words

step out of your comfort zone (exp.)
outgoing student mobility (exp.)

* Appears on the Academic Word List

READING ❶ Profile of an International Student

In this reading, you will learn about a student's experience of studying at the University of Sheffield in the United Kingdom (UK). The student offers some advice to other international students and to students who may be thinking of studying abroad.

Key words and phrases from Reading 1 are listed in the box. In the table below, complete the sentences in the first column with the appropriate words or phrases from the box. Then follow the instruction in the second column to use each key word orally in a sentence. The first one is done for you as an example.

affiliated with	curriculum vitae (CV)	potential
analyze	enhance	rely on
challenging	facilitate	step out of their comfort zone

SENTENCES WITH KEY WORDS	USE THE KEY WORDS
❶ When two schools are connected (for example, a high school is connected with a university or college), they are _____ *affiliated with* _____ each other.	Name two things that are connected in this way. *The badminton club is affiliated with the Student Sports Association.*
❷ During orientation week, student leaders _____ orientation activities. They help students meet each other and participate in fun activities.	Explain how computers can help you learn.

SENTENCES WITH KEY WORDS	USE THE KEY WORDS
❸ When a student decides to examine some data closely in order to learn more about it, the student decides to _curria_ the data.	Name one more thing that students examine closely to learn more about it.
❹ When applying for a job, a student will prepare a _curriculum vitae_ that lists her or his education and previous work experience.	Explain who will read this document. the applicants must submit curriculum vitae before the interview
❺ When a student finds schoolwork difficult, that school work is _challenging_.	Name two more things that students might find difficult. students in Vancouver but challe
❻ Experienced international students may advise younger students to try something new and _sep out of their comfort zone_	Describe something that would encourage students to try something new.
❼ Studying in a new country can be challenging, so universities develop services that students can _____ to support them.	Describe other people or things that help international students.
❽ When students have valuable work experiences, those experiences can _____ their CVs.	Describe other kinds of experiences that can make your CV look good.
❾ When a student is interested in a specific major, that field may present a _____ career for them in the future.	Describe the future benefit of a college diploma or a university degree.

Before You Read

A. Working with a partner, on a separate page, list the benefits and challenges of being an international student. Whether you are an international student, know international students in your classes, or simply have an idea of what it would be like to study abroad, use what you know or imagine to further develop a table like the one below.

BENEFITS OF BEING AN INTERNATIONAL STUDENT	CHALLENGES OF BEING AN INTERNATIONAL STUDENT
• *Experience a different culture*	• *You must buy a new cellphone plan*

B. When you have finished, share your answers with the class. Discuss strategies (a series of planned actions) international students might use to overcome the challenges.

While You Read

C. As you read, on a separate page, summarize the student's experiences of studying abroad in a table like the one below. The headings and first points are provided here to help you begin. When you have finished, compare your table with a partner's.

BENEFITS OF INTERNATIONAL STUDY EXPERIENCE	CHALLENGES OF AN INTERNATIONAL STUDENT
• *Professors are amazing*	• *Was not able to attend the university's open days*

Profile of an International Student

BA Economics

1. My high school was **affiliated with** Beijing International Studies University where I studied for one year. Wanting to try something different and improve my English skills, I decided to study abroad at the University of Sheffield after my first year.

5 2. I was not able to attend the university open days in advance, so I did not know what to expect at Sheffield. However, I could **rely on** information from the university rankings and online student blogs. I wanted to study economics, and Sheffield is ranked in the top ten universities in economics, and the online student comments were very positive. I was confident that Sheffield would be a good place for me
10 to study.

3. I really enjoy studying economics at Sheffield. The professors are amazing! The profs plan their lectures clearly, and the tutors are super helpful. As long as you attend classes regularly, you are well prepared for your assignments and exams; I really enjoy studying my program here.

15 4. As there are students from all over the world at Sheffield, it is possible to discuss and **analyze** many various economic systems. It's so interesting to consider how other societies and markets are structured and organized. As I love learning about markets, this program is perfect for me.

5. Also, the courses here are organized in a way that makes learning easy. Most
20 courses are two hours per week; one hour is a lecture with the professors, and one hour is a seminar with the tutors. The tutorials allow students to apply what they have learned in the lectures, and I enjoy the real-world application of theory.

6. Of course, it is important to find time to practice. To encourage this, in our second year, there are mandatory study hours every two weeks. During these periods, you
25 can study the way you like best as long as what you study is relevant to your subject. Lecturers are always available to **facilitate** student learning by answering questions. And because students are all together, it's an efficient way to study. Professors post all the course materials, like slides and handouts, on the online course platform; as a result, we can study and review at any time.

30 7. I was happy to be successful in my first year. This year, I'm enjoying my courses more, and I intend to place all of my effort into my experiences here. My goal is to achieve a first-class standing in my degree.

8. Students here study and participate in a variety of activities. There is always something interesting to do. After all, you can't study all the time. When you participate in
35 activities outside the classroom, you can make new friends, and gain confidence through practising your English language.

9. If you decide to come to Sheffield, check out the Students' Union. It has everything a student will need. There are student societies (I joined the Business Student Society), clubs (I joined the photography club), and many events like visiting
40 speakers to keep you interested. I've made lots of awesome friends, and I'm not surprised that students vote Sheffield as number one for student experience.

10. I have also found some opportunities to gain work experience. Job vacancies are advertised online, and I can develop new job skills that will help me in the future. Before I finish my program, I want to try a lot of different things to **enhance** my
45 **curriculum vitae (CV)**.

11. My first job experience was as an orientation leader. This experience taught me teamwork and how to communicate well with others. In my second year at Sheffield, I worked as a teaching assistant to support the Conversation Partner program. I'm also a program leader, so I represent my classmates' views at
50 meetings with our program administration. This way, I'm building my visibility, and the extra work forces me to be really organized. All of these skills will be valuable to me in my future career. Next year I hope to find an **internship** in economics so I can learn more about the **potential** jobs in my field and prepare for my first job post graduation.

internship (n.): job lasting for a short time that students do to gain experience

55 12. Some international students feel stressed, but you should be brave. When you come, you should try to **step out of your comfort zone** and meet students from all over the world. Although you will likely be most comfortable with people who come from your country or speak your language, it is a precious experience to meet friends from all over the world; if you don't, you might be wasting your
60 time. At first, I was lonely, but now I enjoy **challenging** myself to try new things. It was not always easy to do at the beginning, but it's really important to try. Once you meet many people from all over the world, you will have many awesome friends and learn more about the world. You will also learn more about yourself, and slowly you will mature. This is the real benefit of studying internationally.
65 Your experience of studying abroad could be one of the most exciting experiences of your life.

(867 words)

This reading is a compilation of international student profiles drawn from examples on Sheffield University's International Student website: https://www.sheffield.ac.uk/international/countries/asia/east-asia/china/studentprofiles/undergraduate/

After You Read

D. Answer the following questions about this student's experience studying abroad.

1 How do you know that the student's experience was mostly positive?

_____

_____

_____

2 What do you think the student's recommendations for other students might be?

_____

_____

_____

_____

My Bookshelf > My eLab > Exercises > Chapter 2 > Profile of an International Student

Using Varied Sentence Structure

Understanding basic sentence structure makes it easier to move on to more complex language tasks such as paraphrasing and summarizing. Simple sentences are the building blocks of writing. After you learn to write simple sentences, you can combine them in various ways to make your writing more interesting.

Pattern 1: Use a single *independent clause* (IC).

A simple sentence expresses a full thought. It consists of an independent clause (IC) that includes a subject and a verb.

An IC can be very short or it can have two or more subjects and verbs.

Examples are: Students study. (Full thought; subject + verb)
Marina and Olga study and travel each term. (Full thought; two subjects + two verbs)

Here are some patterns that you can use to combine independent clauses to make your writing more interesting.

Pattern 2: Combine a *phrase* with an IC.

A phrase is a group of words that are joined together to create meaning, but that do not contain a subject + verb combination.

Examples are:

• in 2020

• at the end of the term

• with her decision

phrase + comma + IC	**In 2020,** he decided to study abroad.
	At the end of the term, Hiromi decided to travel.
	Hoping to improve his English, he decided to study at an English university.
IC + phrase (no comma)	She was an undergraduate student **at her home university**.
	Her parents were happy **with her decision**.
	Ruizhe wanted to study abroad **to broaden her experience**.

Pattern 3: Combine a *dependent clause* (DC) with an IC.

A dependent clause (DC) expresses an incomplete thought. It begins with a subordinate conjunction and includes a subject and a verb.

Examples are:

- when she started
- since exercise is important
- before the instructor assigned the homework

DC + comma + IC	**When she started,** she was excited.
	After Xi arrived at her new university, she joined a conversation partner program.
	Since exercise is important, Yizhi played badminton to keep healthy.
IC + DC (no comma)	She was excited **when she started**.
	Mohammed registered early for classes **although he didn't know anyone else in the school**.
	He did a lot of research **before he made his decision to study abroad**.

The following are some of the more common subordinate conjunctions and their functions.

SUBORDINATE CONJUNCTION	FUNCTION	SUBORDINATE CONJUNCTION	FUNCTION
after/before	to establish a sequence	if/unless	to set a condition
although / even if / even though	to present opposing ideas	since/when	to refer to a point in time
as / just as	to make a comparison	where/wherever	to introduce a place
because	to give a reason	while	to show simultaneous actions

A. Return to Reading 1, and underline the topic sentence (the first sentence) of each paragraph. Then write the paragraph numbers corresponding to the correct topic sentences to answer the following questions.

   1 Which topic sentences are independent clauses (pattern 1)? ___*3,*___

   2 Which topic sentences combine a phrase with an independent clause (pattern two)? ___*5,*___

   3 Which topic sentences combine a dependent clause with an independent clause (pattern 3)? ___*1,*___

B. Practise sentence patterns 1, 2, and 3. On a separate page, write five sentences: one consisting of an independent clause (pattern 1); two including phrases at the beginning or end of an independent clause (pattern 2); and two with dependent clauses joined to independent clauses (pattern 3).

C. When you have finished, exchange your sentences with another student. Can you recognize your partner's sentence patterns? Help each other correct any errors.

Pattern 4: Combine an IC with an IC using a *coordinate conjunction*.

When combining independent clauses, insert a comma before the coordinate conjunction.

IC + comma + coordinate conjunction + IC	She wanted to travel, **and** she hoped for adventure.
	She wanted to travel, **but** she was nervous about leaving home.
	She wanted to travel, **so** she checked the World University Rankings to learn about the best universities.

Here is a list of coordinate conjunctions and their functions.

COORDINATE CONJUNCTION	FUNCTION	COORDINATE CONJUNCTION	FUNCTION
and	to add to	or	to show an alternative
but	to contrast	so	to show a result
for	to introduce a reason	yet	to introduce two opposing ideas
nor	to add an idea after a negative statement		

Pattern 5: Combine an IC with an IC using a *semicolon (;)*.

Use a semicolon between two independent clauses when the meanings of the clauses are very close.

| IC + semicolon + IC | He considered many universities; he decided to study in Spain. |
| | There is a lot of information to consider; the rankings help students make decisions about where to study. |

Pattern 6: Combine two ICs using a *semicolon* and an *adverbial conjunction*.

Place a comma after the adverbial conjunction.

| IC + semicolon + adverbial conjunction + comma + IC | He wanted to travel; **however,** he found studying abroad hard. |
| | He wanted to travel; **consequently,** he decided to study abroad. |

These are some of the most common adverbial conjunctions and their functions.

ADVERBIAL CONJUNCTION	FUNCTION	ADVERBIAL CONJUNCTION	FUNCTION
accordingly/ as a result/ consequently	to show a result	likewise/similarly	to show similarity
also/furthermore/ moreover	to add to	meanwhile/at the same time	to show simultaneous actions
however/ nevertheless	to contrast	otherwise	to show an alternative consequence

Composed w/ even

D. Observe the sentence patterns in Reading 1 and answer these questions.

1 Which topic sentences combine two independent clauses with a coordinate conjunction (pattern 4)? _____2,_____

2 In paragraph 5, find a sentence that combines two independent clauses with a semicolon (pattern 5). Highlight the sentence in your reading.

3 In paragraph 6, find a sentence that combines two independent clauses with a semicolon and an adverbial conjunction (pattern 6)? Highlight the sentence in your reading.

E. You now know six different sentence patterns. Read the following paragraphs. All the sentences consist only of independent clauses. Writing in this way is grammatically correct but boring to read. Working with another student, on a separate page, use what you know about combining independent clauses to make these paragraphs more interesting.

Qi and Peter were finishing high school; They were good students, and had high marks, They could go to almost any university, Their parents suggested studying abroad. Qi was excited about the possibility; Peter was less excited. Both Qi and Peter spoke with their friends; Some of their friends also wanted to study abroad. Most of their friends were going to study at home, Qi and Peter did some research together, They looked at the World University Rankings; They looked at the universities' internationalization scores. The scores helped them decide.

as a result

Qi wanted to study in an English university. The university she liked was big. It had many international students. Her university was ranked in the top ten universities of the world. Qi looked forward to meeting students from all over the world. Peter decided to go to a small university. His uncle and aunt lived abroad. Peter could live with them. The university he liked had many support services for international students. It had many clubs he could join. It had a conversation partner program. He wanted to be a conversation partner to meet new people. Both Qi and Peter made good decisions. They enjoyed their time studying abroad.

My Bookshelf > My eLab > Exercises > Chapter 2 > Focus on Writing

FOCUS ON CRITICAL THINKING

Considering the Characteristics of a Text

When you read, it is helpful to know what type of text you are reading: textbook, report, course notes, magazine article, newspaper story, essay, email, website, or novel. Each type has different characteristics including purpose, organization, language, and key features, and these characteristics may change how you approach the reading.

A. Read the information in the following table. Some of the boxes have been left blank. As a class, discuss what information should be added to the blank boxes.

TYPE OF TEXT	CHARACTERISTICS OF TEXT	HOW TO READ EFFICIENTLY
TEXTBOOK	• provides information • content is organized under chapter titles, headings, and subheadings • usually contains a table of contents and an index • sometimes key words or concepts are defined in text boxes in the margins • may contain in-text citations and references • language is formal	• in each chapter, skim to learn the topic and main points. • scan to look for specific details. • highlight important information.
COURSE NOTES PROVIDED BY INSTRUCTOR	• provide information • content is organized by topic or date • usually include key information • may leave some information out, so students are required to complete the notes as they listen to the lecture • language is most likely formal	
MAGAZINE ARTICLE	• written to attract interest • topic may be of current interest in the media • may start with the story of an individual • language may be informal and/or idiomatic • writer may use quotations	• read quickly for interest • understand the main point or concept
NEWSPAPER STORY		• read quickly for information • may read only the first few paragraphs, then skim the rest of the story
REPORT	• provides information about a specific, limited topic • usually divided into sections: introduction, methods, results, and discussion or recommendations • often has statistics, charts, graphs, and tables • may contain citations and references • language is formal and professional	

audience genre to publish on article
genre
purpose: argue
inform
entertain

peer-reviewed - write critics
criticise others -

TYPE OF TEXT	CHARACTERISTICS OF TEXT	HOW TO READ EFFICIENTLY
EXECUTIVE SUMMARY OF A REPORT	• summarizes a report; only the most important points are included • points are short; not much development; may be presented in point form • usually divided into sections with headings and subheadings • often has statistics, charts, graphs, and tables • language is formal and professional	
ESSAY		• read to find the thesis statement • read topic sentences to confirm main points • may read paragraphs for details • conclusion should confirm main points from thesis
EMAIL OR TEXT	• written for a wide variety of purposes • is often short • language may be formal or informal, depending on topic, writer, or recipient	
BLOG	• written in the first-person perspective; often tells a story or a narrative • language may be informal	
WEBSITE		• skim to identify the topic/subject • scan for details you want to know about

B. Find the text types in this chapter.

1. Review Reading 1 (page 32). What type of text is it? How do you know?

    ____

    ____

2. Look ahead to Reading 2 (page 45). What type of text is it? How do you know?

    ____

    ____

    ____

    ____

3 Look ahead to Reading 3 (page 52). What type of text is it? How do you know?

_____

_____

_____

_____

_____

Academic
Survival Skill

Asking Questions Using Correct Word Order

Writing and asking questions are essential skills that will help you find important information. During your years of study, you will need to ask questions of other students, teaching assistants, instructors, and professors. It is important to use correct question format; this will increase your confidence as well as your chances of being understood and of obtaining the information you need.

Although you may find it difficult at first, don't be afraid to ask other students or teachers for help. Remember that it is often easy for other students to help you, and it is the job of teachers to provide you with the information you need. A good way to ask for information is to say, "Excuse me" and then ask your question. Don't forget to smile. Students and teachers will be glad to help you.

Yes/No Questions

Generally, for questions with simple *yes* or *no* answers, an auxiliary verb (*be, have, do*) or a modal auxiliary (*can, could, may, might, must, shall, should, will, would*) precedes the subject of the sentence. The main verb follows the subject.

AUXILIARY (*BE/HAVE/DO*)	SUBJECT	MAIN VERB	REST OF SENTENCE
Is	he	enjoying	studying abroad?
Have	you	benefited	from travelling?
Does	the university	encourage	student exchanges?

MODAL AUXILIARY	SUBJECT	MAIN VERB (BASE FORM)	REST OF SENTENCE
Can	you	recommend	the best university?
Should	parents	decide	for their children?
Would	your parents	approve	of that university?

An exception is when *be* is the main verb. Then your questions look like this:

VERB *BE*	SUBJECT	REST OF SENTENCE
Is	he	interested in his program?
Was	she	happy at university?
Were	they	well informed about their university choices?

When you ask a question that has a yes/no answer, raise the pitch of your voice at the end of the question.

Information Questions

Generally, to request information, a question word (*who, what, where, when, why, how*) is followed by either

• an auxiliary verb (*be/have/do*); or

• a modal auxiliary (*can, could, may, might, must, shall, should, will, would*).

These are followed by the subject and main verb of the sentence.

QUESTION WORD	AUXILIARY / MODAL AUXILIARY	SUBJECT	MAIN VERB	REST OF SENTENCE
What	did	you	study	at university?
What benefits*	did	you	experience	when you studied abroad?
Why	are	so many students	studying	abroad?
How	should	universities	support	student exchanges?

*The question word *what* is often accompanied by a noun.

An exception is when *be* is the main verb. Then your questions look like this:

QUESTION WORD	*BE* (MAIN VERB)	SUBJECT	REST OF SENTENCE
When	is	our next English class?	
Why	are	you	so determined to study abroad?

Another exception is *who* questions that require an answer that becomes the subject of the next sentence.

QUESTION WORD AS SUBJECT	MAIN VERB	REST OF SENTENCE
Who	studied	abroad last semester? (Saroj and Raoul studied abroad.)

When you ask an information question, do not raise the pitch of your voice at the end of the sentence.

A. Working with two other students and using some of the ideas from Gearing Up (page 29) and Reading 1, think of at least six questions you would like to ask about the benefits and challenges of being an international student. These questions are your survey. You may be in a class of international or exchange students. In that case, you can ask your classmates your questions. If you know international or exchange students in other classes, you can ask them your questions.

B. Use the forms you have learned to write accurate questions on a separate page. Your teacher will review your questions to make sure they are correct.

C. Once your teacher has checked your questions, write them in the left-hand column of the table. Then, write the names of the two other students at the top of the other columns to the right. Take turns asking and answering the questions. Practise raising your pitch for yes/no questions, or keeping your pitch level at the end of information questions. As you listen to the students' responses, write brief, point-form notes in the columns under their names.

D. When you have finished, you will have some data about the benefits and challenges of studying abroad that you will use to complete the Warm-Up Assignment.

QUESTION	NAME: _____	NAME: _____
❶ What challenges do international students face when they study abroad?		

E. After completing the table, select the most interesting piece of information and discuss it with the class.

WARM-UP ASSIGNMENT

Write a Short Report

A. Use the information you collected in your survey about the benefits and challenges of studying abroad to write a short two-page report.

B. Review the characteristics of a report in Focus on Critical Thinking (page 38). Your report should include an introduction, description of methods, presentation of results, and discussion. If possible, present the data you collected in Academic Survival Skill in a table, chart, or graph. In your results and discussion sections, write about the benefits and challenges of studying abroad from the point of view of the people you surveyed.

C. Write sentences that follow the patterns you learned in Focus on Writing (page 34). Refer to the Models Chapter (page 240) to see an example and to learn more about how to write a report.

When you receive feedback from your teacher on this Warm-Up Assignment, you will have information that you can use to improve your writing.

FOCUS ON READING

Skimming a Text to Gather Information

When you skim a text, you look over the text quickly to determine

- how long it is (to estimate how much time it will take to read);
- what type of text it is (to understand the author's method of organization);
- who wrote it (to determine if the author has a unique perspective on the topic);
- when it was written (to know how recent it is);
- the main topic (to recognize what you are reading about);
- the main points (to have an idea what the author is going to say before you begin to read more closely).

You can discover most of this information by simply looking at the text (or in this textbook, at the citation at the end of each reading). However, it may be more difficult to discover the main points of a text. To skim for the main points, quickly read

- the title;
- subheadings;
- captions for pictures or charts;
- the introduction;
- the first sentence of each paragraph;
- the conclusion.

You will practise your skimming skills in the Before You Read sections for Readings 2 and 3.

The Contemporary Landscape of University Internationalization

You may wonder how your own school, college, or university is internationalizing. The next reading is from a national report on internationalization in colleges and universities in Canada.

VOCABULARY BUILD

A. Use the line numbers in column 1 to find key words in the reading that match the definitions in column 2. Write the key words in column 3. The first one has been done for you.

LINE NUMBERS	DEFINITIONS	KEY WORDS
81	people you work with, usually at your job	(n.) *colleagues*
78, 114	most important (or central) part of something	(adj.)
9	things that cause other things to happen	(n.)
3, 111, 119	do, or become involved in an activity	(v.)
27, 81	helping something to develop over time	(v.)
25, 27, 34	reason that makes someone do something, or underlying cause	(n.)
14, 32, 36, 51, 52, 60, 79	relationships between two people, countries, or organizations	(n.)
2	existing everywhere	(adj.)
12, 37, 39	respect and admiration people or organizations get because of their success	(n.)
24	reasons for a decision, belief, etc.	(n.)
11	quality of directly relating to something	(n.)
54	planned series of actions to achieve something	(n.)

B. Some of these key words are commonly used with other words to form collocations. Learning these words together can help you learn more words quickly, and improve your reading, listening, speaking, and writing fluency.

Using the line numbers, find these words in Reading 2 again, and fill in the blanks with the words near them. These word combinations are collocations.

① Line 78: core _____*element*_____

Line 114: core academic _____

② Line 3: engage (to some degree) _____

Line 111: engage _____

Line 119: engage _____

③ Line 34: motive _____

4 Line 32 and 60: partnerships _____

Line 51: _____ partnerships

Line 36: _____ partnerships

Line 60: _____ partnerships

5 Line 11: _____ relevance _____

Before You Read

A. Answer the following questions.

1 Review your answer to task B, question 2 in Focus on Critical Thinking (page 39). What type of text is Reading 2 and how do you know?

_____

_____

_____

2 Skim Reading 2 to identify its length, author, date of publication, and main topic.

_____

_____

3 After skimming the title and the first sentence of each paragraph in the first section, list some of the main points:

- _____

- _____

- _____

- _____

B. After you have finished answering these questions, check your answers with a classmate.

While You Read

C. This reading is divided into three sections. The section headings are listed here, out of order. As you read, write the heading that best fits each section on the line at the top of the section. Confirm your answers with a classmate.

- Challenges of Internationalization
- Why Canada Pursues Internationalization
- Statistics on Internationalization in Canadian Colleges and Universities

The Contemporary Landscape of University Internationalization

Section 1: _____

In recent decades, globalization has become a pervasive force shaping higher education. Today almost all institutions … around the world engage to some degree in activities aimed at **forging** global connections and building global competencies

forging (v.): forming or developing something strong and enduring, especially relationships between people or groups

backdrop (n.): conditions or situation in which something happens

umbrella term (exp.): word or phrase whose meaning includes many different elements or concepts

lament (v.): feel or express sadness or disappointment about

5 among their students, faculty, and administrative units. Developing such activities at many levels within universities is now a central part of institutional planning, structures, and programming—a phenomenon known as the internationalization of higher education.

These activities are taking place against the **backdrop** of multiple drivers shaping the
10 national and international higher education landscape. Universities are increasingly called upon to demonstrate their economic relevance to society, including through their internationalization activities; there is greater competition for prestige, funding, and student recruitment among universities at both national and international levels; and research increasingly involves international co-authorships and partnerships.

15 Though these and other processes have been variously conceptualized under the **umbrella term** of "internationalization," in AUCC's [Association of Universities and Colleges of Canada] definition the term refers to "institutional efforts to integrate an international, global and/or intercultural dimension into the teaching, research, and service functions of universities." Importantly, internationalization is not a unitary
20 set of goals and processes unfolding in the same way everywhere. It occurs with different emphases, at different paces, and in different ways in various institutions, regions, and countries. This survey reviews the state of internationalization efforts across Canada's university campuses.

A wide range of rationales inform Canadian universities' efforts at internationalization.
25 Among the most prominently discussed are two traditionally academic motives: creating globally aware graduates with skills suited to the jobs of today and tomorrow, and fostering globally connected research and scholarship. Other motives are more directly connected to national well-being and prosperity. University internationalization helps develop a globally competitive national labour force, and attracts international
30 students who may become needed new citizens and workers. Some universities also highlight their internationalization efforts as advancing international development or supporting scientific diplomacy through partnerships with overseas universities and researchers.

Another motive for university internationalization is competition for international
35 students, whose tuition fees bring in revenue and (in some cases) offset declining domestic enrolments. As well, international partnerships have become a component of institutional prestige in an era of ever more fiercely competitive national and global rankings of universities. Some observers of trends in global higher education **lament** the growing influence of financial, competitive, and prestige-oriented considerations
40 in internationalization.

...

Section 2: _____

• The most prominent finding of AUCC's 2014 survey is that Canadian universities are deeply committed to internationalization. Fully 95 percent identify it as part
45 of their strategic planning and 82 percent view it as one of their top five priorities. This commitment is deeply embedded at senior administrative levels of most institutions and is being translated into action with increasing urgency: 89 percent of respondents say that the pace of internationalization on their campuses has accelerated (either greatly or somewhat) during the past three years.

50 • Universities' commitment to internationalization is also growing more sophisticated. For example, the pursuit of high-quality partnerships (as opposed to simply total numbers of partnerships) is a priority at 79 percent of institutions. Evaluation is also growing: today, 59 percent of Canadian universities track the implementation of their internationalization strategies within their quality assessment and assurance

55 procedures, and just over three-fifths assess their success in supporting international students.

• Institutions' most common top priority for internationalization is undergraduate student recruitment, identified by 45 percent as their highest priority and by 70 percent as among their top five goals. The next top-rated priorities are pursuing

60 strategic partnerships with overseas higher education institutions and expanding international academic research collaboration.

• In the sphere of Canadian education abroad, more than 80 percent of responding universities offer a degree or certificate program abroad with international partners and 97 percent offer opportunities for Canadian students to do academic coursework

65 abroad.

• However, outward student mobility is still low: just 3.1 percent of full-time undergraduates (about 25,000) had an international experience in 2012–2013, and only 2.6 percent had a for-credit experience abroad (up very slightly from 2.2 percent in 2006). Cost and inflexible curricular or credit transfer policies are

70 perceived as major barriers to greater student participation.

• China is overwhelmingly the top focus of almost all facets of Canadian universities' internationalization activities. Although the geographic focus of universities' internationalization efforts leans heavily toward developing powers, students' preferred destinations for overseas experience remain the traditional ones of

75 English-speaking and major western European nations.

…

Section 3: _____

As the results of AUCC's 2014 survey show, internationalization has become a core element of Canadian universities' activities. Partnerships and programs abroad are

80 growing, more international students are studying in Canada, and Canadian researchers' collaboration with colleagues abroad is flourishing. Fostering, coordinating and assessing these activities are high on the agenda of most of Canada's university administrators. At the same time, many points for further investigation and follow-up emerge from these findings.

85 One issue that suggests the need for better coordination among all stakeholders is the limited extent to which outward student mobility has been increasing, despite the shared ambitions of Canada's universities, businesses, and governments, including through the federal International Education Strategy. Moreover, students do not seem to favour the parts of the world where universities, business, and government are

90 eager to encourage greater ties (i.e., China and other emerging powers in Asia and Latin America). To better understand why this geographic **misalignment** exists, further reflection is needed on Canadian students' perceptions of barriers to their outward mobility, their reasons for continuing to prefer traditional foreign destinations, as well as what institutional or policy supports might help expand students' choices. Both

95 increased financial support and curricular adjustments may be part of the solution.

misalignment (n.): incorrect alignment or position of something in relation to something else

The shared interest among universities and governments in recruiting more international students offers great promise for expanded enrolment numbers. The chance of success for these students is far greater if a full range of support services is in place for them. Appropriate and adequate support services offered by universities
100 will ensure that Canada maintains its strong reputation as a quality international education destination.

In turn, issues of equity and access also raise questions about whether all Canadian students are benefiting equally from opportunities for international experience. More research is needed to understand which students currently benefit from such
105 opportunities and what can be done to broaden the profile of students who go abroad.

On a related note, given that the vast majority of students will continue to have their university education inside Canada, there is also opportunity for continued reflection on "internationalization at home," so that some of the benefits of internationalization extend fully to all university graduates.

110 As the internationalization efforts of Canadian universities grow and mature, institutional leaders are ready to engage on issues of values, benefits, and risks that are becoming more prevalent in global discussions of higher education. While strengthening international linkages will continue to serve a range of interests among various stakeholders, all parties will want to ensure that core academic values, quality
115 and equity, remain paramount considerations.

As the national association that represents Canada's universities, AUCC will continue to monitor and support our member institutions' internationalization efforts. As the global higher education landscape and discussion evolves, we will continue to advance the dialogue on internationalization and to engage with a broad range of stakeholders
120 both in Canada and internationally, on issues affecting our member institutions' internationalization activities.

(1219 words)

Association of Universities and Colleges of Canada. (2014). *Canada's universities in the world: AUCC internationalization survey*. Retrieved from https://www.univcan.ca/wp-content/uploads/2015/07/internationalization-survey-2014.pdf

After You Read

Section 1 Questions

D. Write T (for true) or F (for false) next to the statements below, based on your understanding of information in the first section of the reading. When you have finished, compare your answers with a classmate's.

1. The internationalization of higher education is a global phenomenon. _____

2. Higher education institutions want to attract international research funding, university students, and research colleagues. _____

3. Higher education institutions are all internationalizing in the same ways and at the same pace. _____

4. Universities and colleges want to internationalize for the following reasons:
   a) To ensure their students are aware of global issues _____
   b) To increase the commercialization of education _____

c) To encourage global research _____

d) To attract educated international students to stay and work in the country _____

e) To increase international development and scientific diplomacy _____

f) To increase the competitive nature of education _____

g) To increase revenues through international tuition fees _____

h) To increase the prestige that comes from building international partnerships _____

Section 2 Questions

E. To summarize the information in the second section, scan for the statistics that match the following statements adapted from Reading 2.

STATEMENTS	STATISTICS FROM RESPONDING INSTITUTIONS (%)
❶ Internationalization is part of the institutional plan.	*95%*
❷ Internationalization is a top priority.	
❸ Internationalization is increasing.	
❹ Institutions are making high-quality partnerships a priority.	
❺ Institutions are tracking and evaluating the progress of their internationalization strategies.	
❻ Institutions are making the recruitment of international students a top five priority.	
❼ Institutions collaborate with international partners to offer a degree or a certificate program	
❽ Institutions offer domestic students a chance to study abroad.	
❾ Domestic students are studying abroad.	

Section 3 Questions

F. There are seven paragraphs in the third section of the reading. The main points are listed below (out of order). Number each point (from 1 to 7) to show the order in which the points are presented in the reading. When you are finished, compare your order with a classmate's.

Main Points

_____ Many Canadian students do not study abroad. Efforts are needed to understand how these students can benefit from internationalization while staying at home.

_____ Outward student mobility remains low.

_____ Not all Canadian students have equal opportunities to study abroad.

_____ The AUCC will continue to survey Canadian universities and colleges.

_____ Universities must develop a range of support services to help international students succeed.

___1___ There are internationalization issues in Canada that require further thought.

_____ Higher education institutions in Canada must work for greater internationalization while maintaining core values of quality and equity.

G. What problem does the AUCC report note about outward student mobility? Why is this a problem? Discuss these questions with a partner.

My Bookshelf > My eLab > Exercises > Chapter 2 > The Contemporary Landscape of University Internationalization

READING ③

READING 3

The Internationalization of Higher Education

You have read about the internationalization of higher education at a national level. You may also be interested to know that the International Association of Universities tracks internationalization statistics at a global level. Read the following text to find information about the internationalization of higher education around the world.

VOCABULARY BUILD

A. Working with a partner, read the sentences in the first column of the table, and write a definition for the words in bold in the second column. Use a dictionary if needed. After, compare your definitions with those of another pair of students. Then answer the questions in task B below.

VOCABULARY WORDS	DEFINITIONS
❶ The survey results are presented at the **aggregate** level.	_total amount after all figures have been added together_
❷ The survey was **conducted** in May 2013.	something done
❸ The results **demonstrate** that internationalization of higher education is growing.	
❹ The geographic **distribution** of responding universities is shown in the table.	shared different parts
❺ The **fundamental** values of the universities are reflected in their answers to survey questions. _essential_	Important part of something basic part of something.
❻ The majority of universities have already begun to **implement** internationalization policies.	Something that has been officially decided Start to happen
❼ Unfortunately, **outgoing student mobility** remains lower than anticipated.	going away from particular place
❽ The majority of **respondents** were from Europe.	

VOCABULARY WORDS	DEFINITIONS
9 Approximately 50 percent of respondents indicated they had a **target** for international student recruitment.	*approximately*
10 The survey reports on **trends** in higher education related to internationalization.	*general direction of changing*

B. Using the table above, answer the following questions.

1 Which words would be used often in a survey?

aggregate, _____

2 Which words have the opposite meaning to "incoming international student mobility"?

_____

3 Which verb collocates with the noun *policy*? _____

4 Which verb is a synonym for *show*? _____

5 Which word can mean "basic," "central," or "essential"? _____

My Bookshelf > My eLab > Exercises > Chapter 2 > Vocabulary Review

Before You Read

A. Answer the following questions, then check your answers with a partner.

1 Review your answer to task B, question 3 in Focus on Critical Thinking (page 40). What type of text is Reading 3 and how do you know?

_____

_____

_____

2 Skim Reading 3 to identify its length, author, date of publication, and main topic.

_____

_____

3 After skimming the title, headings, and table, list some of the main points:

- _____

_____

- _____

_____

While You Read

B. There are eleven numbered sections in this reading; they all are indicated by headings, in the same font style and positioned next to the left margin (so they all look the same). There is no indication that some are main section headings and some are subheadings. However, there are only four **main sections** in this reading. As you read, write down the numbers of the main headings, and the numbers that are subheadings.

C. When you are finished, you will see the structure of the full report. Confirm your answers with your class.

MAIN SECTION NUMBERS	SUBHEADING SECTION NUMBERS
1,	

The Internationalization of Higher Education

1. Introduction

The purpose of the International Association of Universities (IAU) Global Surveys is to provide data and analysis of developments in internationalization of higher education. Alongside its data collection on the importance, the activities, and priorities
5 of this process, this fourth edition of the IAU Global Survey adds an important focus on values and principles, as well as the potential benefits and risks of current trends in internationalization of higher education for both institutions and society.

2. Methodology and Respondents

The IAU Fourth Global Survey took place approximately four years after the previous
10 one. The report is based on responses from 1336 institutions of higher education located in 131 countries in every world region. The number of responses was nearly double that of the previous survey. The dominant institutional profile of responding higher educational institutions (HEIs) is public, focused on both teaching and research, offering programs at all degree levels, and relatively small in size in terms of student
15 enrolment (under 5000 students). The table below presents the geographic **distribution** of **respondents**:

Table 1: Geographic Distribution of Respondents

REGION	PERCENTAGE OF RESPONDENTS	NUMBER OF HEIS
AFRICA	9 percent	114
ASIA AND PACIFIC	12 percent	164
EUROPE	45 percent	604
LATIN AMERICA AND THE CARIBBEAN, INCLUDING MEXICO	11 percent	141
MIDDLE EAST	4 percent	60
NORTH AMERICA	19 percent	253

In total, 6879 institutions worldwide were contacted. They were instructed to provide data for the start of the 2012 academic year, and the survey was **conducted** between May and September, 2013. The questionnaires and a glossary of terms and definitions
20 were made available in English, French, and Spanish. In all results, the n = 1336 unless otherwise indicated. Results are presented at the aggregate/global level.

3. Highlights of Findings

The results of the Fourth Global Survey bring some good news starting with an almost 20 percent rate of response, itself a measure of success. The findings **demonstrate**
25 that internationalization remains, or indeed grows in importance for higher education institutions. It is being **driven**, in large measure, by the most senior levels of leadership

driven (v.): strongly influenced to do something

infrastructure (n.): basic systems and structures a country needs to work properly, for example, roads, railroads, banks, etc.

of the institutions. The majority of the institutions already have or are developing policies to **implement** the process and have the key elements of supportive **infrastructure** in place to move forward and monitor progress.

30 Results show that internationalization has fairly clear [benefits related to] student learning and student mobility. Student knowledge and appreciation of international issues is also a significant expected benefit, though institutions also perceive risks, at both institutional and societal levels.

Responses to specific questions … demonstrate that higher education institutions …
35 express concern about equal access to international opportunities for all students and about the commodification and commercialization of education. They are also [concerned] that more competition among higher education institutions will arise as a result of internationalization.

Finally, … when both societal and institutional risks in the Fourth Global Survey are
40 compared with the perceived risks in the previous two surveys, practically the same issues are identified: commodification/commercialization, brain drain, difficulty in assessing quality of foreign programs. At the same time, there are some new issues being reported such as the risk of growing gaps in quality and/or prestige among institutions in a given country.

45 ## 4. Internationalization Policy/Strategy and Infrastructural Supports

- 53 percent of the respondents have an institutional policy/strategy and 22 percent report that one is in preparation; 16 percent indicate that internationalization forms part of the overall institutional strategy.

- 61 percent of the institutions report having a dedicated budget for internationalization,
50 compared to 73 percent reporting one in the previous survey.

- The most frequently assessed areas of internationalization are international student enrolment, outbound student mobility and partnerships.

5. Importance of Internationalization and Expected Benefits

- 69 percent of the respondents report that internationalization is of high importance
55 for the leadership of their institution.

- In terms of change in the past three years, 27 percent report that over this period, internationalization has remained very important; 30 percent report that it has substantially increased in importance, and for another 31 percent it has increased in importance.

60 - For 32 percent of the respondents, the top-ranked expected benefit is students' increased international awareness and engagement with global issues. This is followed by improved quality of teaching and learning. Revenue generation is the lowest-ranked benefit overall.

6. Risks of Internationalization to Institutions and to Society

65 - Respondents perceive, as the most significant risk of internationalization for institutions, that international opportunities will be available only to students with financial resources; 31 percent of the respondents cited this as the most significant risk. This top-ranked risk is followed by the difficulty of local regulation of the quality of foreign programs (13 percent of respondents selected this as their top choice),
70 and by excessive competition among HEIs.

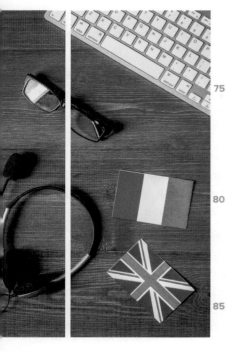

- The most significant potential risk of internationalization for society is commodification of education, ranked first by 19 percent of the respondents. The unequal sharing of benefits of internationalization among partners was ranked at the top by 18 percent. When all three top-ranked responses are brought together, in third place is growing gaps between HEIs within the country.

7. International Student Enrolment

- Just over 50 percent of the respondents report that international degree-seeking undergraduate students represent less than 5 percent of their total enrolment.
- Just over a quarter of the respondents report that international degree-seeking students represent between 6 percent and 15 percent of their total enrolment at the undergraduate level.
- 64 percent of the respondents report that shorter-term, credit-earning international students represent up to 5 percent of their overall student enrolment at the undergraduate level.

8. Outgoing Student Mobility

- 15 percent of the respondents report that their institutions do not offer undergraduate students short/medium (three to twelve months) outgoing mobility opportunities.
- 63 percent of the respondents report that up to 5 percent of their students at the undergraduate level participate in short/medium-term mobility opportunities.
- Short-term (less than three months) outgoing mobility opportunities are not available at 26 percent of institutions for any students at the undergraduate level.
- 59 percent of the respondents report that up to 5 percent of their enrolled undergraduates can take advantage of such short-term international mobility opportunities.

9. Recruitment of International Students

- Respondents are almost equally distributed between those that have specific **targets** for international student recruitment and those that do not.
- Among those that have such a target, nearly a quarter set it at 5 percent of their total enrolment; another quarter set this target at between 6 percent and 15 percent of their enrolment.
- Asia and Pacific is the geographic region most often prioritized for international student recruitment, followed by Europe.

10. Internationalization at Home

- Requiring a foreign language was most frequently ranked first among internationalization activities that respondents reported undertaking as part of the formal curriculum; 26 percent cited it as their top-ranked activity.
- Integrating the contributions of international students into the learning experience is ranked second last in importance.
- The top ranked extracurricular activity is events that provide an intercultural or international experience, followed by mentor or partner **schemes** linking international and home students.

schemes (n.): official plans intended to help people in some way

~~11.~~ Conclusion

The IAU Fourth Global Survey report, *Internationalization of Higher Education: Growing Expectations,* **Fundamental** *Values,* offers a **vast** amount of data and information.
115 Some of it provides support for anecdotal evidence and observable trends. In some cases, the report offers new information and expands the knowledge base about [internationalization] …

As was the case for previous IAU surveys, the results should stimulate new thinking about internationalization and point to many new areas for further research … The
120 report does, however, add to overall knowledge about internationalization processes in higher education institutions across the globe, raises critical questions about similarities and differences in trends, and can serve as a useful resource to policy makers, higher education leaders, and other stakeholders as they develop new strategies.

(1262 words)

Egron-Polak, E. & Hudson, R. (2014, April). *IAU 4th global survey. Executive summary – Internationalization of higher education: Growing expectations, fundamental values.* Paris, France: International Association of Universities.

After You Read

D. Write short answers to the following questions. Use the critical thinking skills you learned in Chapter 1 to identify key words in the questions, and then scan for the answers. When you have finished, compare your answers with a partner.

1 What is the purpose of the IAU Global Survey on the Internationalization of Higher Education?

_____

2 What information does this Fourth Global Survey add to previous surveys?

_____

_____

3 How many institutions were contacted, and how many responded? What languages did the survey use? How many universities from your region of the world responded to the survey?

~~6879~~ , 20% response, French, Spanish, English
1336 5 / 131 countries

_____

4 What was the response rate for the survey? Do the authors think this is a good rate of response?

_____

_____

5 Who drives (or encourages) the internationalization of higher education?

_____

E. In the table below, list in point form the benefits and risks of the internationalization of higher education as they are described in lines 30-75.

BENEFITS OF INTERNATIONALIZATION	RISKS OF (CONCERNS ABOUT) INTERNATIONALIZATION
• Student learning	• Not all students have equal access

F. According to the conclusion, what does this survey offer?

_____

_____

_____

_____

My Bookshelf > My eLab >
Exercises > Chapter 2 >
The Internationalization
of Higher Education

FOCUS ON ACCURACY

Introducing Statistics in a Text

When you write a report based on a survey, the report will include statistics. You can use several patterns to introduce statistics.

The table below presents four different patterns. The examples in the second column come from section 2 of Reading 2 (page 46); the examples in the third column come from Reading 3 (page 52). There are more examples of each pattern in Readings 2 and 3.

A. To find two or three other examples in the readings, scan for percentages, and then place each example in the row corresponding to that pattern. When you complete the table, you will have multiple examples of each pattern.

WAYS TO INTRODUCE STATISTICS IN A TEXT	READING 2 (SECTION 2) EXAMPLES	READING 3 EXAMPLES
Pattern 1 Start the sentence (or independent clause) with a percentage.	*82 percent view …* 80% Hry education institution 20	*53 percent of respondents have …*
Pattern 2 Use the verb *was* + past participle + *by* + percent. (Put percentage information near the end of a sentence.)	*was identified by 45 percent …*	• *was ranked at the top by 18 percent* (no more examples of this pattern in Reading 3)

WAYS TO INTRODUCE STATISTICS IN A TEXT	READING 2 (SECTION 2) EXAMPLES	READING 3 EXAMPLES
Pattern 3 Use a short word + percentage (to introduce an independent clause).	*at 79 percent of institutions, …* (no more examples of this pattern in Reading 2)	*for another 31 percent, it has …*
Pattern 4 Use an adverb + percentage	*Fully 95 percent identify …*	*Just over 50 percent of respondents …*

B. On a separate page, and based on the statistics (in percentages) in the table below, write two sentences using each pattern. When you have finished, write your sentences on the board, and ask for feedback from your classmates and instructor.

STATEMENTS		REPORTED STATISTICS
❶	Higher education institutions have support services for students studying abroad.	75 percent
❷	Higher education institutions have an early orientation week for international students.	23 percent
❸	Higher education institutions have visa consultants for students studying abroad.	50 percent
❹	Higher education institutions have conversation partner programs that help students studying abroad meet domestic students.	47 percent
❺	Higher education institutions offer domestic students opportunities to study abroad.	98 percent

My Bookshelf > My eLab >
Exercises > Chapter 2 >
Focus on Accuracy

FINAL ASSIGNMENT
Design a Survey and Write an Extended Report

Use what you know about question format, and design a survey to discover how your school assists international students to deal with the challenges of studying abroad. What services or support can international students access to help them succeed at school? You will want to direct questions to your school's counsellors, homestay coordinators, teachers, writing (or communications) centre tutors, librarians, or anyone else who helps international students.

By asking your survey questions, you will generate statistics that you can use to write a report.

A. The people you survey are called *participants or respondents*. Compose at least five questions to discover what the participants do to help international students. You can ask *closed* questions, *Likert scale* questions, and *multiple-choice* questions.

- Closed questions have *yes* or *no* answers.

  Example: (Ask an instructor or an administrative assistant)
  Is a counsellor available to help international students on campus?   Yes   No

- Likert scale questions ask people to rate their opinions on a scale of 1 to 5.

  Example: (Ask an instructor)
  How important is it to teach international issues in university or college classes?
  1   very important
  2   somewhat important
  3   neither important nor unimportant
  4   unimportant
  5   completely irrelevant

- Multiple-choice questions offer several possible answers.

  Example: (Ask a writing centre administrator)
  At the writing centre, what percentage of students seeking help are international students?
  a)   approximately 5 percent
  b)   approximately 10 percent
  c)   approximately 15 percent
  d)   approximately 20 percent
  e)   approximately 25 percent

B. Once you have a set of questions, ask a classmate or your teacher to review them. Make sure you are using correct question format. Write the questions on a separate page. Leave space to record the answers.

C. Conduct your survey. Ask at least four respondents.

D. Show your results in a table, chart, or graph.

E. Write a report based on the information you gathered. Your report should include the four sections that are characteristic of reports: introduction, methods, results, and discussion. Use your knowledge of sentence structure to add interest to your writing. Refer to the Models Chapter (page 239) to see examples and to learn more about how to design and write a survey and a report.

Critical Connections

To practise recognizing characteristics of texts and other skills you have learned in this chapter, consider other universities. Working with a partner, select a university or college anywhere in the world that you

• attend now;

• would like to attend in the future;

• would like to know more about.

A. To practise your skimming skills, research the university or college in various places. Try to find at least three different types of texts that give information about the institution. For example, you might find a website, a brochure, and a magazine article.

B. To practise your question formation skills, develop three questions about the institution you selected. At least one question should require a quantitative (or statistical) answer. Try to find the answers to your questions in the texts you identified.

C. To practise recognizing characteristics of texts, read the texts carefully to determine if they demonstrate the characteristics common to those types of texts.

D. To practise using varied sentence structure and introducing statistics, write a short paragraph about your selected institution. Explain why you are interested in the school, and describe the types of texts you found to learn more about it. Present the questions that you developed about the institution, and the answers. Be sure to include at least one statistic in your paragraph and write using varied sentence structure.

CHAPTER 3
Buying and Selling Innovative Products

It seems that there are always new and improved products in the stores. Why do companies constantly develop and market new products? The answer to this question is related to product life cycles, product design characteristics, and consumer buying behaviour. Once a company knows its consumers, it can market products effectively to the group of consumers it wants to target. How would you market a new product to ensure that it gets adopted successfully?

In this chapter, you will

- use new vocabulary related to buying and selling innovative products;

- understand writer-reader responsibility;

- learn how to "read smart" and apply those skills to read more efficiently;

- use parallelism to write easy-to-understand sentences;

- write definition sentences;

- apply knowledge to new contexts;

- write process essays.

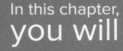

GEARING UP

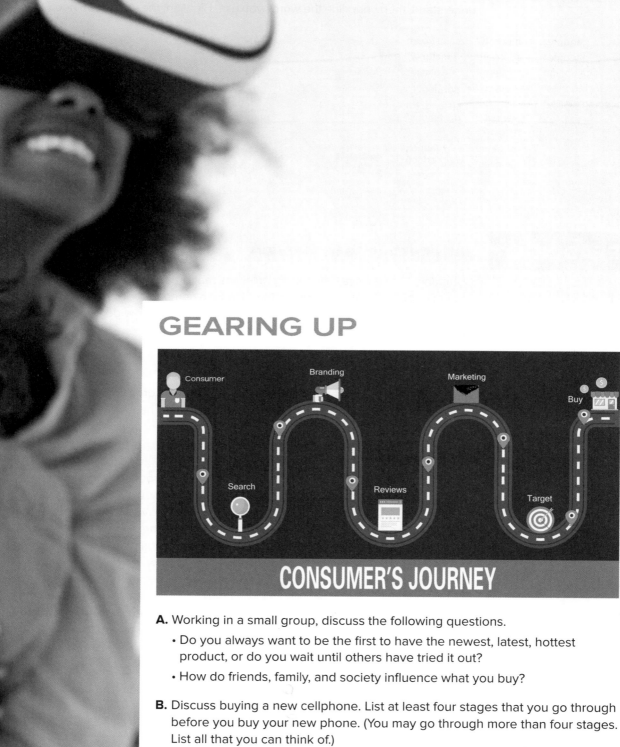

CONSUMER'S JOURNEY

A. Working in a small group, discuss the following questions.

- Do you always want to be the first to have the newest, latest, hottest product, or do you wait until others have tried it out?

- How do friends, family, and society influence what you buy?

B. Discuss buying a new cellphone. List at least four stages that you go through before you buy your new phone. (You may go through more than four stages. List all that you can think of.)

_____

_____

_____

_____

Below are the key words you will practise in this chapter. Check the words you understand, then underline the words you use. Highlight the words you need to learn.

adopter · complexity* · mainstream
attribute* · constant* · maturity*
campaign · consumer* · phase*
categories* · cycle* · sequence*
compatibility* · evaluation* · (standard)
hierarchy* · deviations*

assume* · launch
implies* · (a product)
seek*

nouns

buying and selling

verbs

adjectives

incentive*
lagging
logical*
obsolete

adverbs

eventually*
obviously*
radically*

expressions — (go into) decline*

* Appears on the Academic Word List

READING ❶ Introduction to Innovation

Companies are always developing products that are *new*, *improved*, and *better than ever before*. Why do they do this? How do companies know when to stop selling an old product, and start selling a new one? And how do people make decisions about when to buy a new product?

A. Read the following paragraph, which includes key words (in bold) from Reading 1. Use the context cues in the paragraph to help you match each key word to its definition.

Consumers and Products

We are all **consumers**. We constantly like to buy products and services, and this is good for the economy. We really like innovations such as new computers and smartphones. When we buy an innovative smartphone (for example), we usually throw away our **obsolete** technology, and this **cycle** is repeated over and over. Marketers, who **seek** profit, **launch** new products on the market to match our **constant** desire for new things. The life cycle of these new products goes through **phases**; products are often successful at the beginning when people first buy them, they reach **maturity** when many people have bought them, and they **eventually go into decline** as people stop buying them and look to buy the next innovative technology.

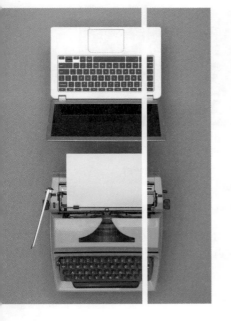

KEY WORDS		DEFINITIONS
❶ constant (adj.)	c	a) decrease in importance, number, or quality
❷ consumer (n.)	e	b) when someone or something is full grown
❸ cycle (n.)	f	c) happening all the time
❹ go into decline (v.)	a	d) stage or step in a process
❺ eventually (adv.)	i	e) someone who buys products and services

KEY WORDS		DEFINITIONS
6 launch (v.)		f) number of related events that happen again and again
7 maturity (n.)		g) start something big
8 obsolete (v.)		h) look for or hope to achieve
9 phase (n.)		i) after a long time, or after a lot of things have happened
10 seek (v.)		j) no longer useful

B. In this chapter, you will often see the word *product. Product* combines repeatedly with other words to form expressions, also called *collocations.* Collocations are groups of words that commonly "locate" together. Learning collocations helps you to increase your listening and reading fluency, and to say and write words more quickly.

The first box below contains collocations that include the word *product.* In the table, write each of the collocations under the heading that best describes the collocation's structure. When you have finished, check your answers with a partner.

COLLOCATIONS		
~~bring a product to market~~	product characteristics	introduce a new product
failed product	new product	product sales
profit from a product	product features	existing product
innovative product	launch a product	product success
product life cycle	put a product on the market	product area
well-established product		develop a new product

VERB + PRODUCT	PRODUCT (USED AS AN ADJECTIVE) + NOUN	ADJECTIVE + PRODUCT
bring a product to market		

Before You Read

A. This graph shows the product life cycle for companies introducing a new product to the market. Look at the graph, and answer the following questions. When you are finished, compare your answers with a partner's.

Figure 3.1 The product life cycle

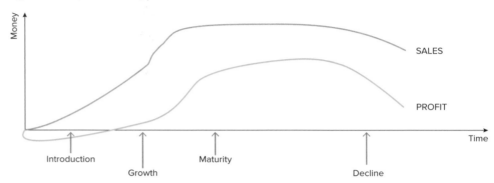

1. How many stages are there in a product's life cycle? Name the stages.

   _____

   _____

   _____

2. Why are sales low in the introduction stage?

   _____

   _____

   _____

3. What happens to company profits in the introduction and growth stages of the product's life cycle? Why?

   _____

   _____

   _____

4. Does this life cycle graph represent all the products on the market? Can you think of products that might not follow this cycle?

   _____

   _____

   _____

5. Can you think of ways this graph fails to represent the life cycle of a product? Are there any limitations to this representation?

   _____

   _____

   _____

While You Read

B. While you read, highlight the five limitations of the product life cycle graph. When you have finished, list them as the answer to the question 3 in After You Read.

Introduction to Innovation

moribund (adj.): no longer active; coming to an end

supersede (v.): replace

Innovation is said to be the lifeblood of successful companies. Firms that fail to innovate are thought to become **moribund** very quickly, and eventually to disappear altogether because competitors introduce new products that **supersede** the old ones. However, this **constant** stream of innovation does create problems from a **consumer**
5 behaviour viewpoint. Decision-making and information-gathering are at their most complex when consumers are considering an innovative product. Thousands of new products are **launched** onto the market every year, with varying success rates; the vast majority never recover their development costs. (Estimates of new-product success rates vary, largely due to the difficulty of defining what constitutes success.)

10 **The Product Life Cycle**

Products are constantly being superseded by newer, more effective products. For this reason, firms **seek** to develop new products; those firms that fail to innovate will, eventually, only be producing products that are **obsolete**. The product life **cycle** illustrates the process of introduction, growth, **maturity** and obsolescence in products.
15 Products tend to lose money when they are first introduced, because the amount of marketing support they need is not justified by the initial sales as the product tries to become established in the market. As the product moves into a growth **phase**, profits begin to come in, and when the product becomes well established (i.e., mature) the profits are also at a peak. Eventually, the product will **go into decline** as competing
20 products enter the market, or fashions change, or the market becomes saturated.

In fact, the situation is often much more complex than this, so the basic product life cycle (as shown in Figure 3.1) does not always describe what actually happens in practice. The product life cycle is a useful concept for explaining what happens to products, but it suffers from a number of weaknesses. First, the model is not useful
25 for making predictions, because there is no good way of knowing what the length of the maturity phase will be: for a fashion item, the maturity phase might only last a few months, whereas for a product such as pita bread the maturity phase has already lasted several thousand years and shows no sign of changing. Second, the model ignores the effects of marketing activities. If a product's sales are declining, marketers
30 might decide to reposition the product in another market, or might run a major promotional campaign, or might decide to drop the product altogether and concentrate resources on another product in the portfolio. These alternatives are shown in Figures 3.2 and 3.3.

in the doldrums (exp.): not developing, not doing well

Third, the model does not account for those products that come back into fashion
35 after a few years **in the doldrums**. Recent examples include the Mini Cooper, the Volkswagen Beetle and the yo-yo (which seems to experience revivals every ten to fifteen years).

Fourth, the model does not take account of the fact that the vast majority of new products fail. This would give a life cycle such as that shown in Figure 3.4, where the
40 product never moves into profit.

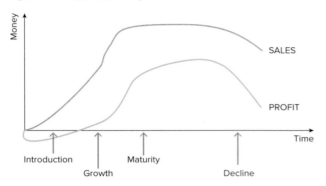
Figure 3.1 The product life cycle

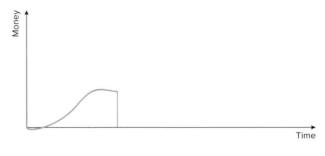
Figure 3.2 Product dropped shortly after introduction

Figure 3.3 Effects of marketing activities on the product life cycle

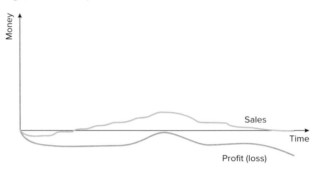
Figure 3.4 Failed product

Finally, the product life cycle looks at only one product, whereas most marketing managers have to balance the demands of many different products and decide which of them is likely to yield the best return on investment (or perhaps which one will take the company nearest to achieving its strategic objectives).

45 The product life cycle can be explained in terms of consumer behaviour. In the introduction and growth stages, innovative consumers are adopting the product. In the maturity phase, more cautious consumers buy the product, until finally another product comes along that has more benefits or that does a better job, and people switch to the new product. The basic problem for marketers lies in knowing how long 50 the maturity phase will last; the product life cycle does tell us, though, that all products **eventually** fade and die, and marketers should therefore develop new products to replace the old ones as these products fall out of favour with consumers.

Although we can be reasonably sure that all old products will eventually fail, we cannot by any means be sure that a new product will succeed. The lack of a good predictive 55 system for forecasting product success wastes resources since producers will spend time and effort making things that consumers do not want to buy. The ideal outcome for a producer is to develop products that become **culturally anchored**—that become part of modern life. Recent examples are the mobile telephone, cable television and the personal computer—none of which would have been part of the average household 60 thirty years ago, but which now would be difficult to manage without. In practice, such breakthroughs are hard to achieve. Understandably, with so much at stake for firms, there has been a great deal of research interest in innovation, with many researchers trying to determine what are the critical factors in new product success.

(829 words)

culturally anchored (adj.): a product that has become part of everyday life

Blythe, J. (2013). *Consumer behaviour* (2nd ed., pp. 305, 307–309). London: Sage.

After You Read

C. Answer the following questions to check your comprehension.

1 Why do companies constantly develop new products?

_____

_____

2 How do new products challenge consumers?

_____

_____

3 What are the limitations of the product life cycle graph?

_____

_____

_____

_____

_____

4 What does it mean when a product becomes culturally anchored? List the examples of culturally anchored products mentioned in this text. Can you

think of others? _____

_____

_____

My Bookshelf > My eLab >
Exercises > Chapter 3 >
Introduction to Innovation

FOCUS ON
READING

Writer and Reader Responsibility

When we write, we always anticipate who our readers will be. As a result, writing involves at least two people: the writer and the reader (sometimes called "the audience"). Both writers and readers share responsibility for successful communication; the writer must present information well, and the reader must try to understand the writing.

You can see an example of how the writer worked hard to help readers understand in Reading 1. Return to lines 21–44 of Reading 1 (page 65).

A. Reread this text carefully and highlight the ways in which you believe the writer (Blythe) made the text easy to understand. Discuss your ideas with your class. When you have finished, read the questions in the first column of the table, and match them with the best answers in the second column.

QUESTIONS		BEST ANSWERS
1 How does the writer first indicate that this section of the text will be about negative aspects of the standard life cycle graph?	_c_	a) The writer uses the word *finally* to introduce the last weakness in the list.
2 How does the writer indicate that this section of the text will list weaknesses?	_d_	b) The writer uses listing and ordering words like *first*, *second*, etc., to highlight the weaknesses of the graph.
3 How does the writer make it easy for the reader to identify the weaknesses of the life cycle graph?	_b_	c) The topic sentence states that the graph does not always describe what happens in real life. This indicates that the writer is moving on to write about the limits or weaknesses of the life cycle graph.
4 How does the writer indicate that the list is coming to an end?	_a_	d) The second sentence of the paragraph uses two independent clauses: the first states that the life cycle graph is useful; the second (introduced by *but*) indicates that there are a number of weaknesses. The reader can anticipate that a list of the weaknesses will follow.

When you write your assignments, you may (or may not) anticipate an audience with specific reader expectations. Keep these tips in mind to make your writing easy to understand:

- Clearly state your topic in your topic sentence.
- Use sentence structure strategically. You can use multi-clause sentences to direct your reader's attention from one section of your text to another. In the first clause, you can summarize previous point(s), and in the second clause, you can redirect the reader's attention to your next point(s).
- Use obvious language to list and order items with words like *first*, *second*, *third ... finally*. If you have a long list of items or steps in a process, using numbers may begin to sound repetitive. In that case, use alternatives like *furthermore*, *moreover*, *in addition*, and *last* or *in conclusion*. Listing and ordering language is common in many essay types, especially process essays.

Using these strategies to facilitate your reader's understanding may help you communicate more clearly.

Learning to Read Smart

Generally, for most of your academic reading, you will want to read fast and remember what you read. In order to accomplish this, you should "read smart." Here are some tips to help you read quickly, understand the main points, and think critically about what you read so that you will remember the content.

Figure out exactly what you are reading.

This is important because different kinds of writing are organized in different ways. If you know how the writing is organized, you can find the main points quickly. This type of reading is called *skimming*.

- Textbooks are usually very structured. They have headings and subheadings, and the topic sentence of each paragraph clearly expresses the main point. Concluding sentences often restate the main points of the paragraph. Of course, you should also look at pictures and read captions.
- Magazine and newspaper articles, including Internet articles, are organized to attract attention. Generally, the main points appear in the first few paragraphs, and the details are discussed in the rest of the article.
- Scholarly essays can be found in academic books, journals, magazines and newspapers, and on the Internet. They are organized according to essay structure, with an introduction and thesis, body, and conclusion.

Consider what you already know about the topic.

If you are reading a textbook, looking at the table of contents can help you see how the information in one chapter relates to information that comes before

and after. For other types of writing, try to remember what you already know about the topic and how it relates to the new information.

Before you begin to read, predict what information you will learn.

What do you expect the text to tell you? If you try to predict what you will read, you will read with greater attention.

Take short, point-form notes on each section of the reading.

The section might consist of one or several paragraphs. Keep your notes short so that they are easy to review. Write in the margins. Highlight key points. Remember, however, that if you highlight too much information, it will be difficult to review quickly later on.

When you have finished reading, use your critical thinking skills.

Write short notes on what you think about the content, not about the content itself. For example, how important is this information? Does the information complement your prior knowledge of the topic? Is the information surprising in any way? Do you agree or disagree with the information? Is the writing biased? All of these observations can help you not only remember the information, but also decide how important it is to your academic success.

You will apply these read smart skills in Reading 2.

The Buyer Decision Process for New Products

As consumers decide to purchase (or not to purchase) a new product, they are influenced by both their own and the product's characteristics. In this text, you will read about personality characteristics and product features that determine what sells, to whom, and when.

VOCABULARY BUILD

In the following exercise, explore key words from Reading 2.

A. Choose the best words to fill in the blanks in the sentences below.

> adopter ~~campaign~~ categories compatibility complexity
> ~~incentive~~ lagging ~~mainstream~~ standard deviations

1. One way to refer to "the majority of consumers" is to compare purchasers to water, specifically to the part of the water flow where the water is deepest. When the majority of consumers have purchased a product, we say that

   the product has been adopted by _____*mainstream*_____ consumers.

2. Companies should research the characteristics of innovators and early

   adopters in their product _**Compatibility**_ and direct initial marketing efforts toward them.

3. A person who buys a product when it is first on the market is called an "innovator"; the person who buys a product just after the innovator is called

   an early _adopter_.

4. Chevrolet developed a promotional _campaign_ to encourage consumers to buy their cars.

5. How early a consumer purchases a product can be measured by

   categories from the mean.

6. Sometimes marketers encourage consumers to buy a product by offering a "two for one" deal, or by including a related product for free when the consumer buys something. This kind of selling plan is a(n)

   incentive campaign.

7. The Blackberry phone is not made anymore; however, it was famous for

   its security. That meant it was _complexity_ with the values of many government workers who wanted complete electronic privacy.

8. The last consumers to purchase a product are called

   lagging adopters.

9. Cellphone plans are all different; some of them have high calling costs; others have high data costs. Selecting the best plan can be difficult.

   Therefore, cellphone plans have a high degree of _standard deviations_, which makes them hard to sell.

Before You Read

A. Reading 2 provides you with the perfect opportunity to practise and apply read smart skills. Work with a partner to answer the following questions.

1 What type of text are you reading? _____

How do you know? _____

_____

2 Skim Reading 2, looking for information contained in the title, headings, and subheadings. Consider what you already know about the topic. Reading 1 (page 65) provided you with information about product life cycles. Predict the information that Reading 2 will add to this knowledge.

_____

_____

3 The headings and subheadings divide the reading into how many sections?

_____

4 What is the purpose of the first section?

_____

_____

5 What is the purpose of the second section?

_____

_____

6 What is the purpose of the third section?

_____

_____

While You Read

B. To continue applying your read smart skills, write short, point-form notes on each section. Notice the definitions in the margins. You will also want to write notes on the main points in the margins.

The Buyer Decision Process for New Products

We are now going to look at how buyers approach the purchase of new products. A **new product** is a good, service, or idea that some potential customers perceive as new. It may have been around for a while, but our interest is in how consumers learn about products for the first time and make decisions on whether to adopt them. The
5 **adoption process** is the mental process that an individual follows from first learning about an innovation to final adoption. Adoption is the decision by an individual to become a regular user of the product (Rogers, 2003). Adoption is the individual's decision to buy a product on a regular basis.

new product (n.): good, service, or idea that some potential customers perceive as new

adoption process (n.): mental process that an individual follows from first hearing about an innovation to final adoption

Stages in the Adoption Process

10 Consumers go through five stages in the process of adopting a new product:

- **Awareness**: The consumer becomes aware of the new product but lacks information about it.

- **Interest**: The consumer seeks information about the new product.

- **Evaluation**: The consumer considers whether trying the new product makes sense.

15 - **Trial**: The consumer tries the new product on a small scale to improve his or her estimate of its value.

- **Adoption**: The consumer decides to make full and regular use of the new product.

This model suggests that **marketers** should think about how to help consumers move through these stages. For example, to help customers past the car-purchase decision 20 hurdle in a still-tight economy, in 2012, Chevrolet launched a "Love It or Return It" guarantee at US dealerships. The program promised uncertain buyers of 2013 models up to sixty days to return cars that had been driven fewer than 4 thousand miles and had no damage. Car maker Hyundai had offered a similar but even greater **incentive** program to help reduce purchasing **barriers** following the economic 25 meltdown in 2008. Its Hyundai Assurance Plan promised to let buyers who financed or leased their new Hyundais to return them at no cost and with no harm to their credit rating if they lost their jobs or incomes within a year. Sales of the Hyundai Sonata [increased] 85 percent in the month following the start of the **campaign** (Bunkley, 2009; O'Leary, 2012).

30 ## Individual Differences in Innovativeness

People differ greatly in their readiness to try new products. In each product area, there are "consumption **pioneers**" and early **adopters**. Other individuals adopt new products much later. People can be classified according to the adopter **categories** shown in Figure 3.5 (Rogers, 2003, p. 281). As shown by the curve, after a slow start, 35 an increasing number of people adopt the new product. As successive groups of consumers adopt the innovation, it eventually reaches its cumulative **saturation** [point]. Innovators are the first 2.5 percent of buyers who adopt a new idea (those beyond two **standard deviations** from mean adoption time); the early adopters are the next 13.5 percent (between one and two standard deviations); and then come 40 early **mainstream**, late mainstream, and **lagging** adopters.

The five adopter groups have differing values. *Innovators* are venturesome—they try new ideas at some risk. *Early adopters* are guided by respect—they are opinion leaders in their communities and adopt new ideas early but carefully. *Early mainstream* adopters are deliberate—although they are rarely leaders, they adopt new ideas before 45 the average person. *Late mainstream* adopters are skeptical—they adopt an innovation only after a majority of people have tried it. Finally, *lagging adopters* are tradition bound—they are suspicious of changes and adopt the innovation only when it has become something of tradition itself.

This adopter classification suggests that an innovating firm should research the 50 characteristics of innovators and early adopters in their product categories and direct initial marketing efforts toward them.

marketers (n.): people whose work involves encouraging consumers to buy products

barrier (n.): problem that prevents people from doing something

pioneers (n.): someone whose actions are important in the early stages of something; other people build on their actions

saturation point (exp.): point at which nothing more can be added

© ERPI • Reproduction prohibited

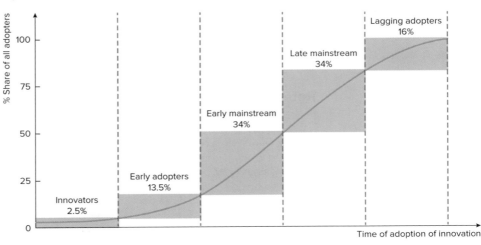

Figure 3.5 Adopter categories based on relative time of innovation adoption

Influence of Product Characteristics on Rate of Adoption

The characteristics of the new product affect its rate of adoption. Some products catch on almost overnight. For example, Apple's iPod, iPhone, and iPad flew off retailers'
55 shelves at an astounding rate from the day they were first introduced. Others take a longer time to gain acceptance. For example, the first high-definition televisions (HDTVs) were introduced in North America in the 1990s, but the proportion of households owning a high-definition set stood at only 12 percent by 2007. By the end of 2012, HDTV penetration was more than 75 percent (Nielsen Newswire, 2012).

60 Five characteristics are especially important in influencing an innovation's rate of adoption. For example, consider the characteristics of HDTV in relation to the rate of adoption:

- *Relative advantage* is the degree to which the innovation appears superior to existing products. HDTV offers substantially improved picture quality. This accelerated its
65   rate of adoption.

- ***Compatibility*** is the degree to which the innovation fits the values and experiences of potential consumers. HDTV, for example, is highly compatible with the lifestyle of the TV-watching public. However, in the early years, HDTV was not yet compatible with programming and broadcasting systems, which slowed adoption.

70 - Now, as high-definition programs and channels have become the norm, the rate of HDTV adoption has increased rapidly.

- ***Complexity*** is the degree to which the innovation is difficult to understand or use. HDTVs are not very complex. Therefore, as more programming has become available and prices have fallen, the rate of HDTV adoption has increased faster
75   than that of more complex innovations.

- *Divisibility* is the degree to which the innovation may be tried on a limited basis. Early HDTVs and HD cable and satellite systems were very expensive, which slowed the rate of adoption. As prices have fallen, adoption rates have increased.

- *Communicability* is the degree to which the results of using the innovation can be
80   observed or described to others. Because HDTV lends itself to demonstration and description, its use spread faster among consumers.

Other characteristics influence the rate of adoption, such as initial and ongoing costs, risk and uncertainty, and social approval. The new-product marketer must research all these factors when developing the new product and its marketing program.

(973 words)

References

Bunkley, N. (2009, February 5). Hyundai, using a safety net, wins market share. *New York Times*.

Nielsen Newswire. (2012, October 17). High definition is the new normal. Retrieved from http://www.nielsen.com/us/en/insights/news/2012/high-definition-is-the-new-normal.html

O'Leary, N. (2012, July 10). Chevy launches "love it or return it" promo. *Adweek*. Retrieved from www.adweek.com/news/advertising-branding/chevy-launches-love-it-or-return-it-promo-141772

Rogers, E. M. (2003). *Diffusion of innovations* (5th ed.). New York: Free Press.

Armstrong, G., Kotler, P., Trifts, V., Buchwitz, L., & Gaudet, D. (2017). *Marketing: An introduction* (Canadian 6th ed., pp. 216–218). Toronto: Pearson.

After You Read

C. Now that you have read the text, return to question 2 in Before You Read on page 71. Was your prediction correct? ☐ Yes ☐ No

D. Answer the following questions.

1 Put the following stages of the adoption process in order.

___4___ Interest

___5___ Adoption

___3___ Evaluation

___1___ Awareness

___2___ Trial

2 In the table, write the characteristics of each of the five adopter groups listed in the first column.

ADOPTER GROUP	CHARACTERISTICS
1 innovators	try new idea some risk
2 early adopters	idividual adopt much later
3 early mainstream	they adopt new idea before average person
4 late mainstream	majority people tried it
5 lagging adopters	adopt innovation only majority people when it becomes something traditional itself

E. As a class, brainstorm new products that have come on the market in the last five years. These will likely include new technologies (such as the Anki Cozmo robot or Apple TV), but also consider innovative services (such as online grocery purchasing or online newspaper subscriptions). Develop a list of at least ten new products or services.

_____

_____

_____

F. To show that you understand how product characteristics influence the rate of adoption, write the names of the products or services you brainstormed in task E in the table next to the product characteristics they best reflect. Some products may reflect more than one characteristic. If any of the characteristics in the left-hand column are not represented by an item you listed on the right, try to think of some products or services that demonstrate that particular characteristic. Discuss your answers with the class.

PRODUCT CHARACTERISTICS	PRODUCTS OR SERVICES THAT REFLECT THE CHARACTERISTICS
❶ relative advantage	
❷ compatibility	
❸ complexity	
❹ divisibility	
❺ communicability	

My Bookshelf > My eLab >
Exercises > Chapter 3 >
The Buyer Decision Process
for New Products

FOCUS ON
ACCURACY

Using Parallelism in Writing *Sme with each other*

The following sentences are taken from Reading 1. Look at them carefully and think about what they have in common.

> LINE 13–14: The product life cycle illustrates the process of introduction, growth, maturity and obsolescence in products.

> LINE 58–59: Recent examples are the mobile telephone, cable television and the personal computer. *2 words*

You may have noticed that these sentences list items.
Now take a closer look at how the items are listed.

In the first sentence, each item is a one-word noun used to name a stage in the product life cycle. You may also have noticed that the way this list is written creates a structure that helps the reader see the similarity of the listed items. This is called *parallelism*.

In the second sentence, each item is a two-word adjective + noun combination. The similarity of the grammatical structure, as well as its repetition, helps the reader understand the content of the sentence quickly. This sentence is also an example of parallel structure.

Here is another sentence that ends with a list of items. In this case, parallel structure is not used to list all the items. Underline the two items that don't fit the same pattern as the other three items.

> When considering a purchase, consumers can be influenced by their friends, family, culture, societal expectations, and financial situation.

You probably noticed that *friends*, *family*, and *culture* are one-word nouns while *societal expectations* and *financial situation* are two-word adjective + noun combinations. This is acceptable, but if you think further, you can improve the parallel structure of the sentence to help your readers understand the meaning more easily. There are two possibilities: you could list all the items either as one-word nouns or as two-word adjective + noun combinations. Try both to see which you like best:

a) One-word noun solution

   When considering a purchase, consumers can be influenced by their <u>friends, family, culture,</u> ~~societal expectations~~ society, and ~~financial situation~~ finances.

b) Two-word adjective + noun solution

   When considering a purchase, consumers can be influenced by their <u>*close* friends</u>, <u>*immediate* family</u>, <u>*ethnic* culture</u>, <u>societal expectations</u>, and <u>financial situation</u>.

Both of these sentences have strong parallel structures that help readers to understand content quickly. Which one do you prefer? Why?

You can see parallel structure across multiple sentences as well. In Reading 2, the authors list the stages in the adoption process. The writers describe the consumer action for each stage in the process. They start each sentence with, "The consumer + verb." Look at lines 11–17 on page 72 to see how parallelism can be used over multiple sentences.

You can also see parallel structure in business mottos. (A motto is a short phrase that expresses something memorable.) In Reading 2, the authors write about a sales campaign that Chevrolet launched to encourage consumers to buy cars. The campaign's motto was "Love It or Return It." You can see the parallel structure in this motto (verb + pronoun) and feel the rhythm as you say it. Can you think of other mottos that use parallel structure?

A. Improve the following sentences by using parallel structure whenever possible. Write the revised sentence on the lines below the original. Hints on how to create parallel structure in the first three sentences are in parentheses. (These sentences were adapted from Readings 1, 2, and 3.)

1 Adoption occurs when the consumer decides to make full and consistently regular use of the new product. (Match single-word adjectives.)

_____

_____

2 In the 1990s, only 12 percent of consumers owned a high-definition television; 75 percent owned a high-definition television in 2012. (Match the order of dates and percentages in the two clauses.)

_____

_____

3 The Attention to need, Interest in product, Desire, and Action model is probably among the oldest models in marketing (Match one-word nouns.)

_____

_____

4 Other characteristics influence the rate of adoption, such as initial and ongoing costs, risk and uncertainty, and social approval.

Other characteristics social approval

product cost, risk level, social approval

5 Eventually, the product will go into decline as competing products enter the market, or fashions change, or the market becomes saturated.

_____

_____

Patterns make find a word

My Bookshelf > My eLab >
Exercises > Chapter 3 >
Focus on Accuracy

WARM-UP ASSIGNMENT
Write a Short Process Essay

Write a short process essay to explain how one of these individuals moved through the stages of the adoption process (described in Reading 2) to buy these products. You may also want to refer to the stages of these products' life cycles and the characteristics that influence their rate of adoption.

• Fifteen-year-old Samuel Parker has been saving his paper route money for six months to buy a pair of the coolest basketball shoes. The shoes are new on the market. They are made of a new fabric that is very light and strong.

• Nineteen-year-old Xiaoshan Wu is an engineering student. She lives far away from the university campus and wants to buy a car. She wants a reliable second-hand car.

• Twenty-three-year-old Miguel Sanchez just graduated from university. He wants to buy a new cellphone; he would like the newest version of the iPhone because he has a Mac computer and he likes Apple products.

A process essay is written to explain how something is done—the steps or stages of a process. Like all essays, it has three sections: an introduction, a body, and a conclusion. The introduction ends with a thesis statement that includes the topic of the essay. The body of the essay outlines the steps in the process—generally, one step corresponds to one paragraph in a short process essay. Use parallel structure in your thesis and concluding statements, and in any other sentences that list items.

Refer to the Models Chapter (page 243) to see an example and to learn more about how to write a process essay.

> When you receive feedback from your teacher or your partners on this Warm-Up Assignment, you will have information that you can use to improve your writing.

READING ③   Adoption of Innovation

This reading presents several models that describe the adoption processes consumers move through before they decide to buy a new product. Next time you go to a store to buy something new, think about your decision-making process(es). What factors do you consider before you buy a new product?

VOCABULARY BUILD

A. The first column of the table lists some of the words that you will read in Reading 3. The second column gives the definitions. To help you remember the words, make a connection between the words and your own life to complete the third column.

WORDS	DEFINITIONS	MAKE A CONNECTION TO YOUR LIFE
❶ assume (v.)	think something is true although you don't have proof	Name something you assume: *I assume that my roommate is honest.*
❷ attribute (n.)	good or useful characteristic	Name an attribute of your best friend: *Chesta*
❸ evaluation (n.)	judgment about how good or useful something is	What is your evaluation of the latest product you purchased?
❹ hierarchy (n.)	system of organization in which people or things are ranked according to their importance	Name two hierarchies that you are part of:

WORDS	DEFINITIONS	MAKE A CONNECTION TO YOUR LIFE
5 implies (v.)	indicates something is true without actually saying it	What does high profit imply about a product?
		What does having many friends imply about a person?
6 obviously (adv.)	used to show that a fact is easily seen and clearly understood	What can you say about a product that sells well? *Obviously, the product …*
		What can you say about a product that requires a long adoption process?
7 logical (adj.)	seemingly reasonable	Name two things that seem logical to you:
		Name two things that seem illogical to you:
8 radically (adv.)	completely; in a big and important way	Name a radically new product that you would like to buy:
9 sequence (n.)	order in which steps should be completed	Name a sequence of events you are familiar with:

My Bookshelf > My eLab >
Exercises > Chapter 3 >
Vocabulary Review

Before You Read

So far in this chapter, you have twice been asked to consider the consumer adoption process for the purchase of products. Take a minute to review your initial thoughts in Gearing Up (page 61) and the more informed thinking you wrote about in the Warm-Up Assignment (page 77).

A. Now, working with a small group of students, consider whether the adoption processes you have written about could be improved. Could other models better reflect your buying behaviour? Brainstorm the steps in the adoption process that best reflect your own purchasing behaviour.

Does your model change depending on the product you purchase?
You will return to this question in After You Read.

While You Read

B. Continue applying your read smart skills to this reading. Skim Reading 3 and answer these questions.

1 Identify the two sections of the reading. How do you know where to divide the reading?

_____

_____

2 Looking specifically at the information in Table 3.6, identify where you have read similar information before.

_____

_____

3 Looking specifically at the models of the adoption and diffusion process, identify where you have read similar information before.

_____

_____

Identifying information that you are already familiar with should help you read this text more quickly.

Adoption of Innovation

The process of adoption of innovation has much more to do with communication throughout the population than with individual decision making. Each individual will make decisions using the processes already outlined for existing products; the main difference is that there will be many fewer sources of information about an innovative
5 product, since few people will have any experience of it as yet.

postulated (v.): suggested that something is true

Everett M. Rogers (1983) **postulated** that products would be adopted if they possessed most of the **attributes** shown in Table 3.6.

Table 3.6 Attributes necessary for adoption

ATTRIBUTE	EXPLANATION	EXAMPLES
Relative advantage	The product must have some advantage over the products already on the market. In other words, it must offer the consumer a better range of benefits than the existing solution.	Before the Sony Walkman was launched, the only way to listen to stereo-quality music was to carry a ghetto blaster on your shoulder. The Walkman replaced this cumbersome and anti-social device within a few years—and iPods have replaced the Walkman equally effectively.
Compatibility	The product must fit with the consumer's lifestyle.	Video on demand has become a popular service offered by cable TV companies, allowing people to watch TV shows or movies at times that suit them, rather than the broadcaster.
Complexity	The product must not be too complex for the consumer to understand.	Amazon's Kindle device was designed around the concept of being so simple to use that people would forget the device and simply enjoy reading the book. Kindle was designed to be as easy-to-use and intuitive as a paper book.

ATTRIBUTE	EXPLANATION	EXAMPLES
Trialability	Products that can be tried are more likely to succeed.	Whenever a motor manufacture launches a new vehicle, people are invited to test drive it.
Observability	The more observable the product, the quicker the diffusion process. If other potential consumers are able to see the product in use, this is bound to raise interest in it.	Part of the reason for Kindle's worldwide success is that it can clearly be observed in use. Likewise, new fashion ideas seem to catch on very quickly; this is due to the high level of product observability.

Models of the Adoption Process

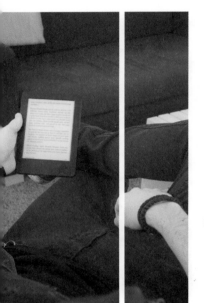

There have been several models of the adoption process, most of which **assume** a
10 somewhat complex process of assessing the new product. In the case of **radically**
new products (those that will alter the user's lifestyle), this may well be the case, but
since most products that are classified as new are, in fact, adaptations of existing
products, it might be safe to assume that consumers do not necessarily carry out a
lengthy **evaluation** of the type assumed by most researchers. Five adoption models
15 are shown in Figure 3.7.

The Attention, Interest, Desire, and Action (AIDA) model is probably among the oldest
models in marketing. It is commonly quoted when considering promotions, but it
applies equally well to adoption of innovation. The model is somewhat too simplistic,
however; it **implies** that the process is mechanical, without any conscious thought
20 on the part of the individual who adopts the product. There is also the view that the
model implies something being done *to* consumers (leading them through a process)
rather than something that is done *for* them (meeting a need).

The Adoption Process model includes some thought on the part of the customer. In
this case, becoming interested in the product leads to some serious evaluation before
25 trial and adoption. This model portrays adoption as a **sequence** which the individual
follows, using conscious thought and interaction with the product to come to the
adoption decision.

Figure 3.7 Adoption models

AIDA model

Attention → Interest → Desire → Action

Adoption Process model

Awareness → Interest → Evaluation → Trial → Adoption

Hierarchy of Effects model

Awareness   Knowledge   Liking   Preference   Conviction   Adoption →

Robertson model

Problem recognition | Awareness | Comprehension | Attitude | Legitimation | Trial | Adoption | Dissonance

Rogers model

Knowledge | Persuasion | Decision | Implementation | Confirmation

The **Hierarchy** of Effects model suggests that each stage of the process leads the customer closer to the decision—as each stage is passed, the individual is further up
30 the hierarchy and therefore becoming more committed. **Obviously**, an individual might drop out of the model at any stage, and thus the sale will not happen, but the model implies that people must normally pass through each stage in the correct order if a sale is to result. This is a suspect [assumption], since people are likely to skip stages or even buy the product
35 on impulse without any real evaluation at all.

Robertson's (1967) model is by far the most complex, seeking to break down the process into more stages. Robertson shows how the attitude is formed rather than simply [including] it in a category of "liking." This model
40 provides more of an insight into the internal workings of the adopter's mind, rather than simply describing behaviour.

Rogers (1983) includes the concept of persuasion in his model. Persuasion does not necessarily come from
45 outside, however; it may just as easily come from within the individual. Persuasion is clearly of interest to marketers, whether it is marketing-generated or whether it is produced socially via peer pressure (normative compliance).

The main feature that all of these models have in common is that they imply that
50 adoption of innovation is a linear process, following **logical** steps. This may or may not be true—individuals may follow a straight line, or they may be diverted by circumstances. This model also shows that innovations take a long time to be adopted. This means that it may be a year or more before a new product begins to show a return; this is implicit also in the shape of the product life cycle curve, where the
55 introduction phase shows a slow start. Often firms decide too early that a product is not succeeding and take it off the market before consumers have completed the evaluation process.

(921 words)

References

Robertson, T. S. (1967, January). The process of innovation and the diffusion of innovation. *Journal of Marketing*. 14–19.

Rogers, E. M. (1983). *Diffusion of innovation*. New York: Free Press.

Blythe, J. (2013). *Consumer behaviour* (2nd ed., pp. 309–312). London: Sage.

After You Read

C. In Reading 2 (page 71), you learned about product characteristics that influence the rate of adoption. In this reading, you see a similar group of characteristics (attributes).

1. To compare the lists from Readings 2 and 3, write the attributes from Reading 3 next to the characteristics from Reading 2 listed in the left-hand column of the table.

READING 2	READING 3
PRODUCT CHARACTERISTICS THAT AFFECT THE RATE OF ADOPTION	PRODUCT ATTRIBUTES NECESSARY FOR ADOPTION
1 relative advantage	The same
2 compatibility	Same
3 complexity	Same
4 divisibility	Trialibility
5 communicability	

2. Read the definitions of these characteristics and attributes carefully to determine if different words have different meanings. What differences do you notice?

_____

_____

_____

D. Why can we assume that most consumer adoption processes are relatively short?

___product is_____

_____

E. Working with a partner, consider the adoption process models in Figure 3.7 (page 81).

1. Which model seems to best describe your adoption process when you
   - buy dinner at a restaurant? ___Ada_____
   - buy a present for a friend? ___Heirarchy_____
   - rent an apartment with a roommate? ___Adoption Process____

2. What are the common features of these adoption process models? Do these models accurately reflect your adoption process?

   ___Aida_____

_____

_____

F. Working with a small group, develop a model that best reflects your own product adoption processes.

My Bookshelf > My eLab > Exercises > Chapter 3 > Adoption of Innovation

Writing Definitions

Below are four sentences from this chapter's readings that give definitions. Writing definitions is often required in academic writing. For this reason, it is useful to recognize typical sentence patterns that writers use for definitions.

Look at the following sentences and identify the shared characteristics and sentence structure. Some of the features are in bold to make them more obvious.

1. A **new product is** a good, service, or idea **that** some potential customers perceive as new.

2. The **adoption process is** the mental process **that** an individual follows from first learning about an innovation to final adoption.

3. **Innovators are** the first 2.5 percent of buyers **who** adopt a new idea.

4. **Compatibility is** the degree **to which** the innovation fits the values and experiences of potential consumers.

A. In the following table, the first sentence has been rewritten to show the common sentence structure for definition sentences. Follow the same pattern and rewrite sentences 2, 3, and 4.

	WORD TO BE DEFINED	TO BE (IS/ARE)	NOUN(S) OR NOUN PHRASE	RELATIVE PRONOUN	RELATIVE CLAUSE
1	A new product	is	a good, service, or idea	that	some potential customers perceive as new.
2 The	adoption	is	The mental process		
3					
4				to which*	

*to which: to is included before the relative pronoun which because it is part of the expression the degree to which, meaning "how much."

B. Working with a partner, write definition sentences for the following words from Reading 2. When you have finished, write your best sentence on the board.

← 1. An innovation is ___ creating or something that doesn't exist

2. The product life cycle is ___ is when you introduce a new product in the product market end when

3. Early adopters are ___ to be renewed

4. Lagging adopters are _____

My Bookshelf > My eLab >
Exercises > Chapter 3 >
Focus on Writing

Applying Knowledge to New Contexts

One of the characteristics of good academic writing is that it expresses new or unique knowledge. However, it can be hard for a writer to develop new knowledge. One practice that may help is applying existing knowledge to a new context. Often, thinking of how existing knowledge might apply, or not apply, to a new context generates some new or unique thoughts.

To practise applying existing knowledge to new contexts, start by reviewing all the processes and knowledge frameworks (i.e., consumer and product characteristics) that you learned about in this chapter.

A. Complete the table below to summarize what you've learned. Some of the information has already been added for you.

READING	PROCESSES AND KNOWLEDGE FRAMEWORKS
READING 1: INTRODUCTION TO INNOVATION	• *The Product Life Cycle*
READING 2: THE BUYER DECISION PROCESS FOR NEW PRODUCTS	• *Stages in the Adoption Process*
READING 3: ADOPTION OF INNOVATION	• *Several Models of the Adoption Process*

These frameworks were developed with reference to in-store purchasing, but these days, many purchases are made online. Online shopping is a new context. You can apply these processes and knowledge frameworks to see if they help you generate new thoughts. Ask yourself if the processes and knowledge frameworks accurately describe shopping in an online context or if they need to be revised or modified.

B. Work with another student to brainstorm how each of the processes or knowledge frameworks in the table above might need to be revised to reflect the online shopping context. Write notes on a separate page.

This critical thinking focus will help you write your Final Assignment.

FINAL ASSIGNMENT
Write a Longer Process Essay

For the purposes of this essay, assume that you are a marketing manager who must develop a campaign to encourage a specific adopter group through the stages of an adoption model to purchase a product online. You are writing this essay for your employer, the company owner.

ATTENTION
INTEREST
DESIRE
ACTION

A. Select a product from the list of new products that you developed with your partners in Reading 2, After You Read (task E, page 75). Identify the product's attributes that will contribute to its rate of adoption.

B. Select an adopter group (innovators, early adopters, early mainstream, late mainstream, or lagging adopters) you would like to write about. Write a definition of this adopter group that states their personal characteristics, age range, and influences (friends, family, society).

C. Develop a motto that will attract the specific adopter group to your product. (Try to use parallel structure in your motto).

D. Select a model of the adoption and diffusion process (AIDA, the Adoption Process model, the Hierarchy of Effects model, the Robertson model, or the Rogers model) that best reflects the process the adopter group would follow to buy your product.

E. Write your essay. Follow these guidelines:
- Use vocabulary from the readings to refer to product life cycles, adopter groups, product attributes, and adoption models.
- Write about the characteristics of the product that will influence (or are influencing) its rate of adoption.
- Write at least one definition sentence.
- Use parallel structure in your thesis and concluding statements, and in any other sentences that list items.

Refer to the Models Chapter (page 243) to see an example and to learn more about how to write a process essay.

Critical Connections

Practise your critical thinking skills by developing processes and knowledge frameworks to fit other contexts.

A. Select one of the options below or pick your own context. Try to describe a process that accurately reflects the new context.

① How people make friends; you could describe
- a friendship life cycle;
- the stages in the friend adoption process;
- different friend adopter groups;
- characteristics of friends that encourage adoption.

② How people decide which school to attend; you could describe
- a life cycle of the educational process;
- the stages in the school adoption process;
- different types of schools (or students);
- characteristics of schools that encourage adoption.

③ How people decide which career to pursue; you could describe
- a career life cycle;
- the stages in the career adoption process;
- different types of careers (or employees);
- characteristics of careers that encourage adoption.

B. Represent the processes and knowledge frameworks you have developed graphically in a figure, and present the figure to your class.

CHAPTER 4

The Social Impact of Marketing

There is no denying that most societies are consumer societies. And where there are products to sell, there is marketing: advertisements of all kinds are designed to persuade people to buy. We are exposed to dozens, hundreds, maybe even thousands of advertisements every day. Do you examine marketing materials carefully for information about products you would like to buy, or are you annoyed by the frequency of the advertisements? What are the effects of marketing on our society?

In this chapter, you will

- learn vocabulary related to the impacts of marketing;

- use expressions to represent cause and effect accurately;

- predict an author's opinion;

- concede and refute points to develop an argument;

- explore ways to introduce examples in a text;

- learn strategies to become an independent language learner;

- write cause and effect essays.

GEARING UP

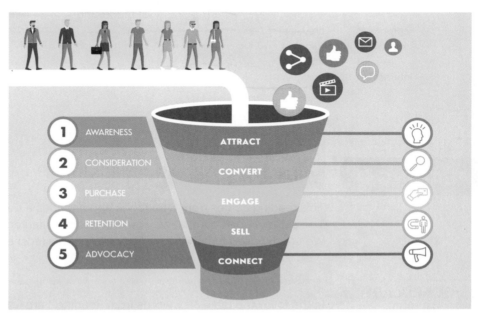

Most of us are consumers. Do you buy something every day? What do you purchase, and how frequently?

A. Complete the table below to list the products you buy in each category, and how frequently you buy each product. When you are finished, compare your answers with a classmate's.

PURCHASING HABITS		
CATEGORIES	**PRODUCTS**	**FREQUENCY**
food	*Starbucks coffee* *groceries*	*every day* *2 times per week*
electronics		
transportation (bus/subway/streetcar/car, etc.)		
household items		
gifts		
hobbies/sports		

B. With a classmate, discuss whether you think being a consumer has negative effects. Do you ever buy things you don't need? Why? Could you go a whole day without buying anything?

Below are the key words you will practise in this chapter. Check the words you understand, then underline the words you use. Highlight the words you need to learn.

abundance   function*   proliferation
billboards   goal*   promotion*
components*   logo   purchase*
consequence*   motto   reaction*
context*   process*   welfare*

nouns

impacts of marketing

verbs

assembled*   involves*
brainwashing   justified*
demonstrate*   obtain*
ensure*   purchase
exceed*   violating*
impose*

corporate*   prevalent
distorted*   psychological*
exempt   sustainable*
interactive*   traditional*

adjectives

* Appears on the Academic Word List

READING ❶   What Is Marketing?

This reading comes from a textbook and provides a definition of marketing. The authors point out that we are all experts at marketing; we have to be! We are exposed to hundreds of advertisements (ads) every day.

In the following table, key words from Reading 1 are listed in the first column, with their definitions in the second column. In the third column, answer each question with a sentence that connects the word to your own experience and shows that you understand the definition. The first one has been done for you.

KEY WORDS	DEFINITIONS	CONNECT TO YOUR OWN EXPERIENCE
❶ abundance (n.)	large quantity of something *more than enough*	What do you have an abundance of? *I have an abundance of books about marketing.*
❷ assembled (v.)	brought together for a particular purpose	What are some things that you assembled in the past?
❸ context (n.)	situation, events, or information that help you understand something	In what context are you likely to buy a lot of things?
❹ function (n.)	purpose or job that something has or does	What is the function of an advertisement?

KEY WORDS	DEFINITIONS	CONNECT TO YOUR OWN EXPERIENCE
⑤ goal (n.)	something you hope to achieve in the future *ambition*	What is a marketer's goal? *The marketers goal is to get more sales*
⑥ involve (v.)	include as a necessary part or result of something *In*	What does studying involve? *Studying involves a lot of effort*
⑦ motto (n.)	short sentence or phrase that expresses the goals or beliefs of a person, organization, or institution; slogan	What is the motto of a company from which you purchase goods? *The motto of the goods is We got it all for you*
⑧ obtain (v.)	get something through effort or skill	What can you obtain by developing a survey on consumer purchasing habits?
⑨ process (n.)	series of actions that are completed to achieve a result	What process did you follow to select your cellphone?
⑩ purchase (n.) purchase (v.)	something you buy formal word for *buy*	List the purchases (n.) you made in the last twenty-four hours.
⑪ traditional (adj.)	part of a belief or custom that has existed for a long time	When is it traditional for people to purchase (v.) gifts?

Before You Read

Where do you see ads? Do ads have an effect on you? Are you especially influenced by certain ads in certain locations or do you ignore all of them?

A. Working with a classmate, list all the places you see ads every day. Then place a star next to the locations of ads that influence your purchasing behaviour. Why do you find these ads so persuasive?

online ads _____

_____

While You Read

B. As you learned in Chapter 3, definitions are common in academic writing. When writers want to discuss something specific, they often start by defining it. There are four definitions in the following reading. While you read, underline each definition. When you have finished, check with a partner to verify that you have identified the same sentences.

What Is Marketing?

Marketing, more than any other business function, deals with customers. Although we will soon explore more detailed definitions of marketing, perhaps the simplest definition is this one: Marketing is managing profitable customer relationships. The twofold **goal** of marketing is to attract new customers by promising superior value
5 and to keep and grow current customer [numbers] by delivering satisfaction.

For example, McDonald's fulfills its "i'm lovin' it" **motto** by being "our customers' favourite place and way to eat" the world over, giving it nearly as much market share as its nearest four competitors combined. Walmart has become the world's largest retailer—the world's second-largest company—by delivering on its promise, "Save
10 Money. Live Better." Facebook has attracted more than a billion active web and mobile users worldwide by helping them to "connect and share" with the people in their lives (O'Brien, 2012).

Good marketing is critical to the success of every organization. Large for-profit firms, such as Google, Procter & Gamble, Toyota, and Microsoft, use marketing. But so do
15 not-for-profit organizations, such as universities, hospitals, museums, symphony orchestras, and even churches.

You already know a lot about marketing—it's all around you. Marketing comes to you in the good old **traditional** forms: You see it in the abundance of products at your nearby shopping mall and in the ads that fill your TV screen, spice up your magazines,
20 or stuff your mailbox. But in recent years, marketers have assembled a host of new marketing approaches: everything from imaginative websites and mobile apps to blogs, online videos, and social media. These new approaches do more than just blast out messages to the masses. They reach you directly, personally, and interactively. Today's marketers want to become a part of your life and enrich your experiences
25 with their brands—to help you *live* their brands.

Whether at home, at school, where you work, or where you play, you see marketing in almost everything you do. Yet there is much more to marketing than meets the consumer's casual eye. Behind it all is a massive network of people and activities competing for your attention and **purchases** …

30 ## Marketing Defined

What is marketing? Many people think of marketing as only selling and advertising. We are **bombarded** every day with TV commercials, catalogues, **spiels** from salespeople, and online **pitches**. However, selling and advertising are only the **tip of the** marketing **iceberg**.

35 Today, marketing must be understood not in the old sense of making a sale—"telling and selling"—but in the new sense of *satisfying customer needs*. If the marketer engages consumers effectively, understands their needs, develops products that provide superior customer value, and prices, distributes, and promotes them well, these products will sell easily. In fact, according to management **guru** Peter Drucker,
40 "The aim of marketing is to make selling unnecessary" (Kotler & Keller, 2012, p. 5). Selling and advertising are only part of a large *marketing mix*. The marketing mix is a set of marketing tools that work together to satisfy customer needs and build customer relationships.

bombarded (v.): subjected to too much of something, and too often

spiels (n.): speech or story used many times before, typically to persuade someone to buy something

pitches (n.): words used to persuade people to buy something (informal)

tip of the iceberg (exp.): small sign of a larger problem

guru (n.): expert

Broadly defined, marketing is a social and managerial **process** by which individuals
45 and organizations **obtain** what they need and want through creating and exchanging
value with others. In a narrower business context, marketing **involves** building
profitable, valuable exchange relationships with customers. Hence, marketing is the
process by which companies create value for customers and build strong customer
relationships in order to capture value from customers in return (American Marketing
50 Association, 2013).

(560 words)

References

American Marketing Association (2013, November). Retrieved from www.ama.org/AboutAMA/Pages/
   Definition-of-Marketing.aspx

Kotler, P. & Keller K. L. (2012). *Marketing management* (14th ed.). Upper Saddle River, NJ: Prentice Hall, 2012.

O'Brien, K. (2012, May 4). How McDonald's came back bigger than ever. *The New York Times Magazine*.
   Retrieved from http://www.nytimes.com/2012/05/06/magazine/how-mcdonalds-came-back-bigger-
   than-ever.html?pagewatned+all

———
Armstrong, G., Kotler, P., Trifts, V., & Buchwitz, L. (2017). *Marketing: An introduction* (6th Canadian ed., pp. 5–6).
   Toronto, ON: Pearson Education Canada.

After You Read

C. One of the purposes of this reading is to provide several definitions of marketing.
This reading gave three definitions for *marketing*, and one for *marketing mix*.

① In Chapter 3 (page 84), you learned that writers may use a sentence pattern
with an independent clause and a relative clause (e.g., x is a y that ...)
to provide a definition. Which of the four definitions in this reading follow(s)
a similar pattern?

> Managing profitebly costomers relationship

② Which of the three definitions of marketing makes the most sense to you?
Why? Which definition is most focused on money?

> satisfying costomers, marketing mix

D. Answer the following questions.

① In the second paragraph, there are several examples of companies
that fulfill the promise in their mottos. With a partner, think of several other
well-known companies and their mottos. Share this information with your
class. Do these companies fulfill the promises made in their mottos?

> Wallmart know for its low price compare
> to other groceries store

② In the reading, the authors write that new marketing approaches plan to
do more than simply provide information to consumers. New marketing
approaches aim to connect with consumers on a personal level. Have
you experienced any examples of these new marketing approaches?

> blogs influnce to the viewers

3 The authors suggest that marketing is more than just selling and advertising. What must a company do to satisfy customer needs?

_____

_____

_____

My Bookshelf > My eLab > Exercises > Chapter 4 > What Is Marketing?

FOCUS ON ACCURACY

Representing Cause and Effect Accurately

When you write cause and effect essays for your Warm-Up and Final Assignments, you will want to represent the causes and effects of marketing accurately. In English, and most likely in other languages you speak, you can use a wide range of expressions to express these ideas in interesting ways.

Consider this fact: every cause has an effect. The following expressions are grouped according to their grammatical similarities.

Use these expressions to show a causal relationship: *cause creates effect*.

	CAUSE	CREATES	EFFECT
1	Good marketing	causes creates generates produces	increased sales.
2	A strong digital advertisement	leads to results in brings about	increased consumer interest.
3	An advertisement that generates an emotional response in viewers	gives rise to is responsible for	increased company revenues.
4	A good product distribution plan	has an effect on has an impact on has an influence on has implications for	the company's success.

Use these expressions to show an immediate causal relationship: *cause quickly creates effect*.

	CAUSE	QUICKLY CREATES	EFFECT
5	Poorly designed advertisements	trigger set off	negative consumer response.

Use these expressions to show that the *cause is one of several things that create an effect.*

	CAUSE IS ONE OF SEVERAL THINGS THAT	CREATE	EFFECT
6	Coke's motto, "Taste the Feeling,"	influenced contributed to	Coke's success.
7	Pepsi's motto, "The Joy of Pepsi Cola,"	is a factor in plays a part in	Pepsi's success.

A. Based on the causes given below, complete the sentences with an effect. When you have finished, compare your sentences with a classmate's. Write your best sentences on the board for your class to read.

1 Nike's motto, "Just Do It," _____.

2 Failing to engage consumers effectively *can trigger negative feedback*

3 Successfully understanding consumer need _____.

4 Providing inferior value _____.

5 Advertising during a popular TV show _____.

Use these expressions to show that an *effect is created by a cause.*

	EFFECT	IS CREATED BY	A CAUSE
8	Unsuccessful marketing campaigns	are caused by are the result of are the outcome of arise from	failure to identify consumer need.

B. Based on the effects given below, complete the sentences with a cause. When you have finished, compare your sentences with a classmate's. Write your best sentences on the board for your class to read.

1 Successful marketing plans _____

2 Snapchat's success _____

3 Business failure _____

4 Unsatisfied consumers _____

5 Increased media interest _____

My Bookshelf > My eLab >
Exercises > Chapter 4 >
Focus on Accuracy

WARM-UP ASSIGNMENT

Write a Short Cause and Effect Essay

A cause and effect essay demonstrates the effect something (in this case, marketing materials) has on someone or something else (in this case, consumers).

A. For this assignment, select a company with a well-known motto or advertisement and write about the effect the company's marketing materials have on consumers. You may write about a successful or an unsuccessful marketing slogan or advertisement that you are familiar with.

B. Refer to the Models Chapter (page 245) to see an example and to learn more about how to write a cause and effect essay. Use some of the cause and effect expressions from Focus on Accuracy (page 94) to demonstrate the relationship between the marketing materials and their impact on consumers.

C. Include a definition of marketing in your introduction. Try to use parallel structure in your thesis and concluding statements and in any other sentences that list items.

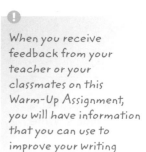

When you receive feedback from your teacher or your classmates on this Warm-Up Assignment, you will have information that you can use to improve your writing on the Final Assignment.

FOCUS ON CRITICAL THINKING

Predicting an Author's Opinion

As you read to understand more about a topic, you are probably reading for facts. However, you may notice that many authors provide not only facts, but also their own opinions on those facts. If you are not aware that authors may present both the facts and their opinions, you may not separate the facts from the opinions. As a result, you may not be able to think critically about the topic or form your own opinion.

Predicting an author's opinion should be one of the first things you think about as you prepare to read. You should consider who the author is, who the audience is, and what type of text it is. Once you know this, you will be in a good position to predict the author's opinion.

A. To predict author opinion in this chapter, begin by finding the references for Reading 1 (page 92), Reading 2 (page 100), and Reading 3 (page 113). Then answer the following questions.

Readings 1 and 2:

① What do you notice about the references for Readings 1 and 2?

_____

② What type of texts are Reading 1 and 2? What do you expect from this type of reading?

_____

_____

3 What would you expect the professions of the authors of Readings 1 and 2 to be?

_____

4 Did Reading 1 meet your expectations for this type of text?

_____

_____

Reading 2:

5 What is the title of Reading 2? Does this suggest the authors will present positive or negative information about the topic?

_____

_____

6 Despite the title, do you expect that the authors will represent marketing in a negative way?

_____

_____

7 Can you predict what the authors' opinions about marketing will be?

_____

_____

Reading 3:

8 Who is the author of Reading 3?

_____

_____

9 Search the Internet for information about Kalle Lasn. Based on what you find, can you predict what his opinion about marketing will be?

_____

_____

When you prepare to read any text, it is always a good idea to consider who the author is, who the audience is, and what type of text it is. Asking questions like these can help you predict the author's opinion about the topic. This information can help you develop your own opinion about the content of the reading.

READING ❷ Social Criticisms of Marketing

Some people believe that marketing has many negative social impacts. In this reading, the authors discuss some people's ideas about the effects of too much marketing.

<table>
<tr><td>VOCABULARY BUILD</td></tr>
</table>

Reading 2 includes verbs with specific meanings within the marketing context.

- These verbs show that people are unhappy with something (e.g., a company's product).

  ❶ Some consumers **claim** that companies design products that break easily.

  ❷ Some consumers **charge** that companies spend too much money on marketing.

  ❸ Some consumers **accuse** companies of unfairly raising prices to increase profits.

- These verbs show that companies disagree with these claims, charges, or accusations.

  ❶ These companies **refute** claims that they design products that break easily.

  ❷ These companies **counter** negative consumer claims by proving the strength of their products.

- This verb shows that companies agree with some of these claims, charges, or accusations.

  ❶ These companies **concede** that they spend a lot of money on marketing, but they insist that marketing enhances the value of their products.

A. Work with a partner. On a separate page, write a sentence using each of these verbs. When you have finished, exchange your sentences with another pair of students. Provide feedback on the sentences you now have, and return them to the original pair. When you receive feedback on your sentences, make corrections (if required).

B. Each key word appears in two sentences: first in a marketing context and then in a non-marketing context. Determine the common meaning and write a short definition (including the part of speech) for each word.

KEY WORDS	SENTENCES AND DEFINITIONS
❶ component	a) Consumers claim that companies make products with weak **components** that break quickly. b) Fish is a **component** of a healthy diet. *Definition: a part of something bigger (n.)*
❷ consequence	a) Companies concede that the **consequence** of poor marketing is decreased profits. b) Her university applications were submitted late. As a **consequence**, the universities rejected her application. Definition: _____

KEY WORDS	SENTENCES AND DEFINITIONS
❸ distorted	a) Companies accuse consumers of **distorted** accusations that make products sound worse than they are. b) Cellphone signals are **distorted** by tall buildings. Definition: _____
❹ ensure	a) Companies counter these consumer complaints by explaining that they must keep costs low to **ensure** their products are competitive. b) Hospitals hire enough doctors to **ensure** that they can see patients quickly. Definition: _____
❺ exceed ✗	a) Consumers accuse drug companies of increasing prices so drug costs **exceed** the consumer's ability to pay. b) If people drive too quickly, the speed of their vehicle **exceeds** the speed limit. Definition: _over or greater number_
❻ impose ✳	a) Companies concede that they are concerned about the environment; therefore, they **impose** rules on their production process to reduce their waste. b) In order to pay for public benefits, governments **impose** taxes on their citizens. Definition: _demand ~~for something~~_
❼ justified ✗ a/c	a) Drug companies counter consumer accusations by claiming high costs are **justified** by expensive research. b) Many people feel that overeating is **justified** during a vacation. Definition: _achieve_
❽ promotion	a) Consumers accuse companies of high-priced **promotion** campaigns that increase product costs. b) To reduce energy consumption, governments develop **promotion** materials that encourage people to turn down the temperature in their homes. Definition: _____
❾ sustainable	a) Consumers who are concerned about the environment claim that companies do not use **sustainable** marketing practices. b) Companies that build houses should follow **sustainable** building practices. Definition: _____
❿ violating _form of a verb_	a) Some consumers with children charge that companies are **violating** educational standards by advertising in schools. b) Criminals are convicted of **violating** the law. Definition: _____
⓫ welfare	a) Companies claim that they have an interest in the children's **welfare** too. b) Animal rights organizations are concerned about animal **welfare**. Definition: _____

Before You Read

A. With a partner, think of as many negative impacts of marketing as possible, and list them on a separate page. To help you, consider whether marketing has a negative impact on young people, old people, product costs, and businesses. When you are finished, write your list on the board, and compare your list with others.

While You Read

B. This excerpt is from a chapter in a marketing textbook. Answer the following questions to learn how the reading is organized. An understanding of text organization will help you to read faster.

1 Read the first paragraph and predict the section headings.

_____

_____

2 Read the second paragraph. Which of the points are used as headings in this reading?

_____

_____

3 Read the third paragraph and explain how the factors mentioned are used to organize the next six paragraphs.

_____

_____

4 How do these first three paragraphs act like a thesis statement for the reading?

_____

_____

5 The text under each subheading is divided into two parts based on content. Read the first sentence of each paragraph (starting with the section *High advertising and promotion costs*) and state the pattern that the text follows. This pattern repeats throughout the reading.

_____

_____

Social Criticisms of Marketing

Marketing receives much criticism. Some of this criticism is **justified**; much is not. Social critics claim that certain marketing practices hurt individual consumers, and society as a whole ... To be fair, it is not the practice of marketing itself that is bad or harmful—it's the way companies choose to implement it that matters. In most ways,
5 we all benefit greatly from marketing activities. However, like most other human [activities], marketing has its **flaws**.

flaws (n.): mistakes or weaknesses

Marketing's Impact on Individual Consumers

Consumers have many concerns about how well the marketing system serves their interests. Surveys usually show that consumers hold mixed or even slightly unfavourable
10 attitudes toward marketing practices. Consumer advocates, government agencies and other critics have accused marketing of harming consumers through high prices, deceptive practices, high-pressure selling, … unsafe products, and **planned obsolescence** … Such questionable marketing practices are not **sustainable** in terms of long-term consumer or business **welfare**.

planned obsolescence (n.): when a product is designed to break so it will soon have to be replaced

15 ### *High Prices*

Many critics charge that the marketing system causes prices to be higher than they would be under more "sensible" systems. Critics point to two factors: high advertising and **promotion** costs, and excessive markups.

High advertising and promotion costs

20 Modern marketing is accused of pushing up prices to finance heavy advertising and sales promotion. For example, a few dozen pills of a heavily promoted brand of pain reliever sell for the same price as a hundred pills of less promoted brands … Cosmetics, detergents, [and personal care products] include promotion and packaging costs that can amount to 40 percent or more of the manufacturer's price to the retailer. Critics
25 charge that much of the packaging and promotion adds only **psychological** value to the product rather than functional value.

Marketers respond that although advertising is expensive, it also adds value by informing potential buyers of the availability and merits of a product. Brand name products may cost more, but branding [promises] buyers … consistent quality.
30 Moreover, consumers can usually buy functional versions of products at lower prices. However, they *want* and are willing to pay more for products that also provide psychological benefits—that make them feel wealthy, attractive or special. Also, advertising and promotion are sometimes necessary, especially for marketers of products such as consumer electronics, cars, and personal care products—product
35 categories in which there exist many brands and many competitors. Otherwise, the firm would not be able to compete.

fallacy (n.): false belief or idea that people have; misconception

Though it may seem logical that advertising is expensive and therefore, if firms did no advertising the price of their products would go down, this is in fact a **fallacy**. Without advertising, sales would decrease; therefore, production would decrease. When fewer
40 products are manufactured, the price to manufacture each product goes up—and prices would go up correspondingly. When consumer activities in the UK called for more regulation in the advertising of children's toys, arguing that all toy advertising should be banned, economics researcher and journalist Chris Snowdon (2013) argued that the prohibition of advertising would lead to monopolistic markets and result in
45 higher prices for consumers.

Excessive Markups

Critics also charge that some companies mark up goods excessively. They point to the drug industry, where a pill [that costs] 5 cents to make may cost the consumer $2 to buy.

50 Marketers sometimes respond that consumers often don't understand the reasons for high markups. For example, pharmaceutical markups must cover the costs of purchasing, promoting, and distributing existing medicines, plus the high research

and development costs of formulating and testing new medicines—all of which are very expensive. The simple fact is that all companies are in business to offer something
55 of value to the market, and producing that market offering **involves** much more than just the costs of the manufacturing **process**.

Most businesses try to deal fairly with consumers because they want to build customer relationships and repeat business—it's simply not in their own best interests to cheat or mislead those customers. There are, of course, exceptions to the rule, and
60 when consumers perceive any abuse of marketing, whether it's false advertising or unfair pricing, they should report those abuses to their local Better Business Bureau [or equivalent].

Deceptive Practices

Marketers are sometimes accused of deceptive practices that lead consumers to
65 believe they will get more value than they actually do. *Deceptive practices* fall into three groups: pricing, promotion and packaging. *Deceptive pricing* includes practices such as falsely advertising "factory" or "wholesale" prices or a large price reduction from a [falsely] high retail list price. *Deceptive promotion* includes practices such as misrepresenting the products' features or performance or luring the customers to the
70 store for a bargain that is out of stock. *Deceptive packaging* includes exaggerating package contents through subtle design, using misleading labelling or describing size in misleading terms.

This may be true in some cases, but in Canada [for example], the Competition Bureau … prevents such practices. [Employees there] are alerted to instances of deceptive
75 marketing through consumer complaints, and they *do* take action. For example, they took Rogers Communications to court and charged the telecommunications giant with **violating** Canada's false advertising rules when it claimed that its Chatr cellphone service had "fewer dropped calls" than the competition. The Bureau charged that Rogers produced "false and misleading" ads and failed to back up its claims about
80 dropped calls with "adequate and proper tests"—and sought to **impose** a $10 million fine (Gray, 2013). The [Competition Bureau] also forced Bell Canada to stop making what the Bureau had concluded were misleading representations about the prices offered for its services—and required it to pay a penalty of $10 million, the maximum amount allowed under the Competition Act ("Bell Canada to pay," 2011).

85 High-Pressure Selling

Salespeople are sometimes accused of high-pressure selling that persuades people to buy goods they had not thought of buying. It is often said that insurance, real estate and used cars are *sold*, not *bought*. Salespeople are trained to be persuasive, and their companies reward them for reaching and **exceeding** their sales quotas.

90 However, there are laws that protect consumers from the dangers of being pressured into making a **purchase**. Ontario's Consumer Protection Act, for example, states that it is an "unconscionable representation" if "the consumer is being subjected to undue pressure to enter into a consumer transaction." In addition, the Act makes several provisions for "cooling-off periods"; that is, a period of time during which consumers
95 may change their mind about what they've purchased, and return it or get out of the deal with no penalty. And throughout Canada, there are many similar laws protecting consumers against high-pressure sales tactics.

Unsafe Products

Another criticism concerns poor product quality or **function**. One complaint
100 is that, too often, products are not made well and services are not performed well.
A second complaint is that many products deliver little benefit, or that they might
even be harmful.

Product problems are not usually caused by a company's indifference or other
improper behaviour—most manufactures *want* to produce quality goods. But problems
105 with product quality and safety do happen, and the way a company deals with them
can damage or help its reputation. Companies selling poor-quality or unsafe products
risk damaging their reputation, sustaining product liability suits, and having to pay
large awards for damages. Also, with the **ubiquity** of social media, once a problem
is discovered it is quickly made public; if a company doesn't take steps to respond,
110 its reputation is **at stake**. Today's marketers know that good quality results in customer
value and satisfaction, which in turn create sustainable customer relationships.

Planned Obsolescence

Critics have also charged that some companies practise *planned obsolescence*,
causing their products to become obsolete before they should actually need
115 replacement. They accuse some producers of using materials and **components** that
will break, wear, rust, or rot sooner than they should. And if the products themselves
don't wear out fast enough, other companies are charged with *perceived obsolescence*—
continually changing consumer concepts of acceptable styles to encourage more and
earlier buying. An obvious example is constantly changing clothing fashion.

120 Still others are accused of introducing planned streams of new products that make
older models obsolete, turning consumers into "serial replacers." Critics claim that
this occurs in the consumer electronics industries. If you're like most people, you
probably have a drawer full of yesterday's hottest technological gadgets—from mobile
phones and cameras to iPods and flash drives—now reduced to the status of **fossils**
125 (Suzuki, 2007; Guiltinan, 2009). It seems that anything more than a year or two old
is hopelessly out of date. For example, early iPods had non-removable batteries
that failed in about eighteen months, so that they had to be replaced. It wasn't until
unhappy owners filed a class action suit that Apple started offering replacement
batteries. Also, rapid new product launches—as many as three in one eighteen-month
130 period—made older iPod models obsolete ("Law targets obsolete products," 2013).

Marketers respond that consumers *like* style changes; they get tired of the old goods
and want a new look in fashion. Or they *want* the latest high-tech innovations, even
if the older models still work. No one has to buy a new product, and if too few people
like it, it will simply fail. Finally, most companies do not design their products to break
135 down earlier, since they don't want to lose customers to other brands. Instead, they
seek constant improvement to **ensure** that products will consistently meet or exceed
customer expectations.

Much of the so-called planned obsolescence is the working of the competitive and
technological forces in a free society—forces that lead to ever-improving goods and
140 services. For example, if Apple produced a new iPhone or iPad that would last ten
years, few consumers would want it. Instead, buyers want the latest technological
innovations (e.g., the newest phones, the fastest computers, the largest televisions).

ubiquity (n.): fact of
seeming to be everywhere

at stake (exp.): what is
lost if a plan of action
doesn't work

fossils (n.): animals or
plants that lived thousands
of years ago and are
encased in rock; reference
to extremely old things

Marketing's Impact on Society as a Whole

The marketing system has been accused of adding to several "evils" in society at
145 large. Advertising has been a special target of many of these accusations. [People claim
that advertising creates false wants and cultural pollution.]

False Wants and Too Much Materialism

Critics have charged that the marketing system urges too much interest in material
possessions, and that North Americans' love affair with worldly possessions is not
150 sustainable. Too often, people are judged by what they *own* rather than by who they
are. The critics view this "rampant consumerism" as the fault of marketing. Marketers,
they claim, stimulate people's desires for goods and create false wants and materialistic
models of the good life—a **distorted** interpretation of the "American Dream."

One such social critic group is Adbusters, which began in Vancouver in the mid-1980s
155 and has evolved into a highly effective social activist movement that spans the globe.
The organization's magazine now reaches over 120,000 people in forty countries
around the world, and its anti-consumption campaigns and **spoof ads** are getting
noticed. For example, consider Buy Nothing Day, an Adbusters-sponsored campaign
that began in 1992. The global event draws attention to the harmful effects of over-
160 consumption and not only asks consumers to stop shopping for twenty-four hours,
but also asks them to think about such questions as where their products originate
from, why they're making purchases, and what they do with their products after
purchase. Usually held the Friday after American Thanksgiving, the day has been
praised for drawing attention to issues such as how many resources consumers use
165 in developed versus developing countries (www.adbusters.org).

Another anti-consumerist activist is Annie Leonard, who founded The Story of Stuff
project with a twenty-minute online video about the social and environmental
consequence of America's love affair with stuff—"How our **obsession** with stuff is
trashing the planet, our communities, and our health." The video has been viewed
170 more than 11.7 million times online and in thousands of schools and community
centres around the world (storyofstuff.org).

Marketers respond that such criticism overstates the power of business to create needs.
People have strong defences against advertising and other marketing tools. Marketers
are most effective when they appeal to existing wants rather than when they attempt
175 to create new ones. Furthermore, people seek information when making important
purchases and often do not rely on single sources. Even minor purchases that may be
affected by advertising messages lead to repeat purchases only if the product delivers
the promised customer value. Finally, the high failure rate of new products shows that
companies are not able to control demand.

180 On a deeper level, our wants and values are influenced not only by marketers but
also by other social influences (e.g., family, peer groups, religion, cultural background,
and education). If [people] are highly **materialistic**, these values arise out of basic
socialization processes that go much deeper than what businesses and mass media
could produce alone.

185 Moreover, consumption patterns and attitudes are also subject to larger forces, such
as the economy. The 2008–2009 recession [reduced] materialism and overspending,
and caused consumers to re-evaluate their spending habits. Many observers predict

spoof (adj.) **ads**: ads that copy something serious to make it seem silly

obsession (n.): unhealthy interest in something that stops you from thinking about everything else

materialistic (adj.): concerned only with money and possessions

a new age of more sensible consumption. As a result, instead of encouraging today's more sensible consumers to overspend their means, most marketers are working to help them find greater value with less.

…

Cultural Pollution

Critics charge the marketing system with creating *cultural pollution*. Our senses are being constantly assaulted by marketing and advertising. Commercials interrupt television programs; pages of ads [overwhelm] magazines; **billboards** ruin beautiful scenery; junk emails fill our inboxes. Some feel that these interruptions continually pollute people's minds with messages of materialism, sex, power, or status.

And in the age of social media and mass electronics communications, consumer concerns about too many commercial messages have increased. Marketers must proceed with caution when planning strategies for advertising and promotion campaigns, because when consumers perceive that they are being bombarded with commercial messages, they become resentful. One study revealed that 75 percent of respondents reported they would resent a brand after being bombarded by emails. Although consumers are used to TV commercials and billboards, they are not yet used to advertising on their personal electronic devices, which they perceive as more intimate than mass media ("Survey reveals bombarding consumers," 2013).

Marketers respond to charges of "pollution" by attempting to target their communications as much as possible, so that only those consumers who are likely to be interested in the products or services will see the communications about them. People who buy fashion magazines, for example, rarely complain about the ads for fashion brands contained in them, nor do avid golfers complain about ads for the latest equipment in their golf magazines. "Junk mail" is only junk when we're not interested in it—that is, when it's not well targeted; but when coupons appear in our mailbox for stores or products we like (i.e., that are well targeted), we don't think of them as junk!

(2431 words)

References

Bell Canada to pay $10-million fine for misleading ads. (2011, June 28). Retrieved from http://www.ctvnews.ca/bell-canada-to-pay-10-million-fine-for-misleading-ads-1.663256

Gray, J. (2013, May 13). Rogers violated false-advertising rules with "fewest dropped-call" claims, court hears. *The Globe and Mail*. Retrieved from https://www.theglobeandmail.com/report-on-business/industry-news/the-law-page/rogers-violated-false-advertising-rules-with-fewest-dropped-call-claims-court-hears/article11897567/

Guiltinan, J. (2009, May). Creative destruction and destructive creations: Environmental ethics and planned obsolescence. *Journal of Business Ethics*, *89* (Supp. 1), 19–28.

Law targets obsolete products. (2013, April 22). Retrieved June, 2015 from https://www.connexionfrance.com/Planned-obsolescence-obsolete-products-iPod-washing-machine-printers-14655-view-article.html

Snowdon, C. (2013, April 11). Absurd Prohibition of Toy Advertising Will Lead to Higher Prices. [BBC Radio program]. Retrieved from https://iea.org.uk/in-the-media/media-coverage/absurd-prohibition-of-toy-advertising-will-lead-to-higher-prices

Survey reveals bombarding consumers with marketing results in brand resentment. (2013, January 15). Retrieved from https://www.prnewswire.com/news-releases/survey-reveals-bombarding-consumers-with-marketing-results-in-brand-resentment-186943651.html

Suzuki, D. (2007, March 15). We all pay for technology. *Niagara Falls Review*, p. A4.

Armstrong, G., Kotler, P., Trifts, V., & Buchwitz, L. A., & Gaudet, D. (2017). *Marketing: An introduction* (6th Canadian ed., pp. 83–90). Toronto, ON: Pearson.

After You Read

C. In the table below, take point-form notes to summarize the content of the reading. In the first column, "Conceding," list the social criticisms, or negative effects, of marketing presented by the authors. In the second column, "Refuting," outline how the authors address those negative claims. Some points have been added in the table to assist you.

CONCEDING	REFUTING
HIGH PRICES • *high advertising and promotion costs* • *excessive markups*	• *marketing adds value to a product* • *consumers like the value that marketing adds*
DECEPTIVE PRACTICES	
HIGH-PRESSURE SELLING • *force people to buy goods they don't want or need*	
MATERIALISM • *creating the need for false wants* • *Marketing can create a focus on material possessions.* • *Adbusters, and Annie Leonard*	
	• *Marketers don't want to bombard you with ads; they want to target their ads as much as possible.* • *People who are receptive to ads don't mind them.*

My Bookshelf > My eLab >
Exercises > Chapter 4 >
Social Criticisms of Marketing

D. When you have completed the table, compare your answers with those of two other students. Discuss your opinions about marketing. Why do you hold these beliefs? What points listed in the table most influence your opinions?

FOCUS ON WRITING

Conceding and Refuting

In Reading 2, you saw how the authors presented their beliefs about the usefulness of marketing by conceding their critics' views, and then refuting those views. You can follow this pattern when you write too. Giving opposing viewpoints first (you concede that the opposing view is worth thinking about), and then refuting the opposing views from your own perspective may help you to present your point of view more strongly. Presenting your own view last offers an added advantage, because your reader will be more likely to remember it.

In addition, the ability to concede and refute is important when you present ideas in academic writing or speech, because it is likely that someone will question you about those ideas. The questions may show that the person does not agree with you. If you can concede and then refute the questioner's point, you will be able to answer the question without sounding defensive or angry.

There are some key expressions you can use to achieve this.

A. Complete the following table with information from Reading 2 (page 100). The first six sections of the reading are listed in the first column. In the second column, write the key phrases the authors use to present the negative effects of marketing. These phrases are almost always in the topic sentence of each paragraph. In the third column, write the key phrases (again, from the topic sentences) that the authors use to move from the negative perspective to a more positive one.

SECTION OF READING	CONCEDE NEGATIVE EFFECT	REFUTE NEGATIVE EFFECT
❶ HIGH PRICES	*Many critics charge that …* *Modern marketing is accused of …*	*Marketers respond that …* *Though it may seem logical that … this is in fact a fallacy.*
❷ EXCESSIVE MARKUPS		
❸ DECEPTIVE PRACTICES *customers wont be loyal anymore and that will ruin your busnes*	*it against the law to*	
❹ HIGH-PRESSURE SELLING		
❺ UNSAFE PRODUCTS		
❻ PLANNED OBSOLESCENCE		

B. What types of sentence patterns are used to refute?

_____

_____

_____

C. Read the following statements. For each statement, write one or two sentences that concede the negative effect and then refute it.

1 Effective marketing costs too much money.

While it is true that companies must spend money to develop strong marketing plans (concede), without marketing, there would be no sales or profit (refute).

2 Pharmaceutical companies charge too much for their drugs.

_____

_____

_____

3 Companies deliberately develop products that will break so consumers have to buy these products more frequently.

_____

_____

_____

4 Companies change their packaging to promote new and improved products, but what the companies are really doing is reducing the size of the packages so consumers pay the same for less.

_____

_____

_____

My Bookshelf > My eLab >
Exercises > Chapter 4 >
Focus on Writing

FOCUS ON READING

Introducing Examples into a Text

In Reading 2, you observed how the authors introduced examples. In academic writing, it is important to include examples to support a point or provide more information. Authors use specific phrases or abbreviations to introduce examples:

- **for example**
- **e.g.,** = *exempli gratia,* which means "for example" in Latin
- **such as**
- **i.e.,** = *id est,* which means "that is" in Latin

A. Conventions dictate how to introduce examples in academic texts. The appropriate phrase or abbreviation to use depends on the position of the example in the sentence. Complete the table and answer the questions that follow to find out how these expressions are used. When you have finished, confirm your answers with the class.

[handwritten note in margin: it will be on quiz]

	READING 2 PHRASE OR ABBREVIATION	BEGINNING, MIDDLE, OR END OF SENTENCE?	IN PARENTHESES (YES OR NO)?
LINE 21	For example, a few dozen pills of a heavily promoted brand of pain reliever ...	*beginning*	*no*
LINE 66	Deceptive pricing includes practices such as falsely advertising "factory" or "wholesale" prices ...	*middle*	~~yes~~ no
LINE 76	For example, they took Rogers Communications to court ...	*beginning*	*no*
LINE 126	For example, early iPods had non-removable batteries that failed ...	*beginning*	*no*
LINE 141	... buyers want the latest technological innovations (e.g., the newest phones, the fastest computers, the largest televisions).	~~middle~~ *end*	*yes*
LINE 164	... the day has been praised for drawing attention to issues such as how many resources consumers use ...	~~end of sentence~~ *middle*	*no*
LINE 180	... our wants and values are influenced not only by marketers but also by other social influences (e.g., family, peer groups, religion, cultural background, and education).	~~beginning~~ *end*	*yes*
LINE 213	... when coupons appear in our mailbox for stores or products we like (i.e., that are well targeted), we don't think of them as junk!	*middle* ~~end of sentence~~	*yes*

B. Answer these questions about the information in the table above.

1 In which sentence position do the abbreviations *e.g.*, and *i.e.*, appear? What punctuation is used? Are they in parentheses?

_Line — 2,3__, Yes_____

2 In which sentence position is *such as* used to introduce examples? Is *such as* in parentheses? What punctuation is used?

_____middle or end   no parenthesis no punctatio_

3 When is *for example* used and with what punctuation?

_beginning w/ a comma_____

C. Fill in the blanks with the correct phrase or abbreviation to introduce the examples. Pay careful attention to punctuation.

In some contexts, ___Such as___ politics and public service announcements, negative advertising is common. ___For Example___, during many elections, the public can see and hear advertisements paid for by one political candidate that make another election candidate look unprepared for leadership. Similarly, public service announcements like ones that encourage people to stop smoking show the effects of too much smoking (___e.g___ wrinkled skin, lung disease, and death). However, in other contexts, advertising is always positive.

___For example___, Dove's Real Beauty marketing campaign was designed to encourage women to be confident in their looks. Dove finds real women (___i.e___ women who are both young and old) to feature in their advertisements. While people sometimes find negative advertisements amusing, they are usually happy when the ads are stopped (___i.e___ when an election is over). People are mostly attracted to positive advertising ___i.e Such as___ those advertisements for sports equipment, cars, and electronics.

READING 3 **Culture Jam**

In Reading 2, in the section "Marketing's Impact on Society as a Whole," the authors write about the activist organization Adbusters, which promotes Buy Nothing Day. The founder of that organization, Kalle Lasn, wrote a book about the effects of marketing called *Culture Jam: The Uncooling of America*. Read the excerpt from Lasn's book to learn more about his anti-materialistic viewpoint.

A. Working with a partner, answer the following questions about the key words in Reading 3. Use a dictionary if required.

> ~~billboards~~ brainwashing corporate demonstrate exempt
> interactive logo prevalent proliferation psychological reaction

1 What word refers to large advertising signs that people see along roads?

_____*billboards*_____

2 On billboards, we often see a small design that is an official company sign. What do we call that design? _____

3 What two words end in –*tion*, and what part of speech (noun, verb, adjective, adverb, etc.) are they? _____

4 What four other words can be turned into nouns by adding –*tion*?

_____

5 Which syllable is stressed in each of these words?

_____

6 This syllable stress pattern for words ending in –*tion* is consistent. To help you remember the rule, think of other words with the same ending and confirm that they follow the same pattern.

_____

7 Aside from the word *billboard*, what other word in the box is a compound word (composed of two shorter words)? _____

8 What does this word mean? _____

_____

9 What word means "related to the brain and behaviour"? _____

10 Complete this sentence with the best word from the box. If something is very common and easy to see everywhere,

it is _____ in the environment.

B. Fill in the blanks in the paragraph below with the best words from the box above. You may need to make some nouns plural or change them to the verb form, i.e., *proliferate* (v.) from *proliferation* (n.).

Along all the major roads, drivers can see _____ advertising

company products. Company _____ are everywhere; the

number of billboard advertisements continues to _____.

They are especially _____ along superhighways leading to

major cities. The billboards _____ that advertising must be

successful; if it were not successful, there would not be so many of them. For drivers and their passengers, it is impossible not to see the advertisements. The

billboards are designed to stimulate a _____ from people.

No one is _____ from the effects of advertising. There are

so many advertisements that people might believe that _____

marketing departments are _____ the population. The

advertisements are designed to encourage a _____
desire to buy products.

C. What one word from the box is not required to complete the paragraph above?

_____

What does that word mean?

_____

My Bookshelf > My eLab >
Exercises > Chapter 4 >
Vocabulary Review

Before You Read

A. Working in a small group, think about times when you have been annoyed
by marketing information; for example, by

- the content of an advertisement;
- the location of an advertisement;
- the way the information was delivered (e.g., by phone, email, or tweet).

Make a list of these cases on a separate page, and share them with the class.
What is the class's opinion about marketing?

B. Return to Focus on Critical Thinking (page 96). What was the author's opinion
about marketing that you predicted? Does your opinion of marketing match
the opinion you predicted Lasn would have about marketing?

_____

_____

_____

While You Read

C. Reading 3 is an excerpt from a popular book. As you read, think about how
the tone of this reading is different from that of Readings 1 and 2. How does the
author achieve this tone? Who is the audience for this text? How are the tone
and the audience connected?

_____

_____

_____

_____

_____

_____

_____

_____

_____

Culture Jam: The Uncooling of America

Advertisements are the most **prevalent** and toxic of the mental pollutants. From the moment your radio alarm sounds in the morning to the wee hours of late-night TV, microjolts of commercial pollution flood into your brain at the rate of about three thousand marketing messages per day. Every day, an estimated twelve billion display
5 ads, three million radio commercials, and more than 200,000 TV commercials are dumped into North America's collective unconscious.

Corporate advertising is the largest single **psychological** [experiment] ever undertaken by the human race. Yet for all of that, its impact on us remains unknown and largely ignored. When I think of the media's influence over years, over decades, I think of
10 those **brainwashing** experiments conducted by Dr. Ewen Cameron in a Montreal psychiatric hospital in the 1950s. The idea of the CIA-sponsored **"depatterning" experiments** was to give conscious, unconscious, or semiconscious people headphones, and flood their brains with thousands of repetitive "driving" messages that would alter their behaviour over time. Sound familiar? Advertising aims to do the same thing.
15 Dr. Cameron's **guinea pigs** emerged from the Montreal trials with serious psychological damage. It was a great scandal. But no one is saying [anything] about the ongoing experiment of mass media advertising. In fact, new guinea pigs voluntarily [subject themselves to advertisements] every day.

The **proliferation** of commercial messages has happened so steadily and relentlessly
20 that we haven't quite woken up to the absurdity of it all. No longer are ads confined to the usual places: buses, **billboards**, stadiums, anywhere your eyes can possibly come to rest is now a place that, in corporate America's view, can and ought to be filled with a **logo** or product message.

You reach down to pull your golf ball out of the hole and there, at the bottom of the
25 cup, is an ad for a brokerage firm. You fill your car with gas, there's an ad on the nozzle. You wait for your bank machine to spit out money and an ad pushing [banking services] scrolls by in the little window. You drive through the [countryside] and the view of the wheat fields is broken at intervals by enormous billboards. Your kids watch Pepsi and Snickers ads in the classroom. (The school has made the devil's
30 bargain of accepting free audiovisual equipment in exchange for [showing] these ads on "Channel One.") You think you've seen it all, but you haven't. An Atlanta-based marketing firm announces plans to send an inflatable billboard filled with corporate logos into geostationary orbit viewable every night like a second moon. British sprinter Linford Christie appears
35 at a press conference with little panthers replacing the pupils of his eyes, where his sponsor's logo has been imprinted on specially made contact lenses. New York software engineers **demonstrate** a program that turns your cursor into a corporate icon whenever you visit a
40 commercial site. A Japanese schoolboy becomes a neon sign during his daily two-hour subway commute by wearing a battery-powered vest promoting an electronics giant. Administrators in a Texas school district announce plans to boost revenues by selling ad space on the roofs
45 of the district's seventeen schools—arresting the attention of the fifty-eight million commercial jet passengers who

CIA (n.): Central Intelligence Agency, the US organization that collects and analyzes security data

"depatterning" experiments (n.): research that combined the use of drugs and electric shock therapy to change people's behaviour (these experiments were banned in the 1970s)

guinea pig (n.): animal sometimes used in medical lab experiments; calling people guinea pigs is a way of saying that they have no control over their own lives, like animals used in lab experiments

fly into Dallas each year. Kids tattoo their calves with swooshes. Other kids, at raves, begin wearing actual bar codes that other kids can scan, revealing
50 messages such as "I'd like to sleep with you." A boy named David Bentley in Sydney, Australia, literally rents his head to corporate clients, shaving a new ad into his hair every few weeks. "I know for sure that at least two thousand teenagers at my high
55 school will read my head every day to see what it says," says the young entrepreneur. "I just wish I had a bigger head." You pick up a banana in the supermarket and there, on a little sticker, is an ad for the new summer blockbuster at the multiplex.
60 ("It's **interactive** because you have to peel them off," says one ad executive of this new delivery system. "And people look at ten pieces of fruit before they pick one, so we get multiple impressions.") Boy Scouts in the UK sell corporate ad space on
65 their merit badges. An Australian radio station dyes its logo on two billion eggs. IBM beams its logo onto clouds above San Francisco with a scanning electron microscope and a laser. The image is visible from ten miles away. Bestfoods reveals plans to stamp
70 its Skippy brand of peanut butter onto the crisp [sand] of a New Jersey beach each morning at low tide, where it will push peanut butter for a few hours

before being washed away by the waves. (The company is widely commended for its environmental responsibility.) Coca-Cola strikes a six-month deal with the Australian
75 postal service for the right to cancel stamps with a Coke ad. A company called VideoCarte installs interactive screens on supermarket carts so that you can see ads while you shop. (A company executive calls the little monitors "the most powerful micromarketing medium available today.")

A few years ago, marketers began installing ad boards in men's washrooms on college
80 campuses, at eye level above the urinals. From their perspective, it was a brilliant idea: where else is a guy going to look? But when I first heard that this was being done, I was incensed. One of the last private acts was being co-opted. "What's been the **reaction** on campus?" I asked the reporter who told me the story. "Not much reaction," he said. It became apparent, as these ad boards began springing up in bars and restaurants,
85 and just about anywhere men stand to pee, that not only did guys not share my outrage, they actually welcomed a little diversion while nature took its course.

This flood of psycho-pollution is spreading all around us, and we love every minute of it. The adspeak means nothing. It means worse than nothing. It is "anti-language" that, whenever it runs into truth and meaning, destroys them.

90 There is nowhere to run. No one is **exempt**, and no one will be spared.

(1017 words)

Lasn, K. (1999). *Culture jam: The uncooling of America* (pp. 18–21). New York, NY: Eagle Brook, Williams Morrow and Company, Inc.

After You Read

D. Answer the following questions.

1 In the first two paragraphs, Lasn makes two powerful comparisons that clearly indicate the topic of the reading and his opinion on the topic.

a) In the first sentence, what does Lasn compare advertisements to? Do you believe this is a useful comparison?

_____

_____

b) In the second paragraph, what does Lasn compare decades of exposure to corporate advertising to? What do you think of this comparison?

_____

_____

_____

2 What is Lasn really angry about?

_____

_____

3 What is the purpose of paragraph 4? Why did Lasn present this information in this way?

_____

_____

_____

_____

_____

4 What advertising locations mentioned in paragraph 4 do you find most objectionable? Can you think of any other inappropriate locations?

_____

_____

5 Why is Lasn upset about ads in men's college and university washrooms? Is there advertising in the washrooms at your school?

_____

_____

6 Do you find Lasn's final sentence powerful? How does the style in this sentence contrast with his writing in the very lengthy paragraph four?

_____

_____

_____

My Bookshelf > My eLab > Exercises > Chapter 4 > Culture Jam

E. What do you think about Lasn's argument that marketing is evil? Do you agree? Discuss this with a classmate, and then with your class.

Learning Independently

It is difficult to study in an academic context in a second language. You must constantly struggle with course content, which is always complex, as well as language uncertainty. Furthermore, you may have little time to improve your English and successfully complete your degree or diploma. Not only do you need to learn English to accomplish your goals, you also need to learn English fast.

In the same way that a coach helps an athlete, your instructors and professors will help you. However, you must complete some of your training on your own. Consider yourself an academic athlete struggling to achieve a difficult goal. Think about the number of hours that you dedicate to studying English in one week. If you are limited to class time and homework periods, you may not be progressing as quickly as you would like. If you believe that your English skills should be progressing faster, think about how you can learn independently.

The following key tips help language learners improve their success and learn quickly.

- Practise, assessing your own strengths and weaknesses.
- Make plans to help improve your weakest language skills.
- Remain positive—even when faced with frustration.
- Know that what you do outside the classroom is as important to language learning as what you do inside the classroom.
- Understand that you don't have to sit in the library or the classroom to learn a language.

A. In a group of four or five students, discuss ways that you can practise and improve language skills on your own. Write the ideas in your notebook.

B. When you have finished, combine your best ideas with those from other student groups, and discuss them with your teacher. Some ideas are included here to help you.

What you can do to improve your vocabulary skills

- Make a list of words and store them in a mobile electronic device. Colour code different parts of speech. As you wait for class to begin or the bus to come, review the words on the list—often at first, then less often as you learn them.
- Subscribe to a free online "word a day" service.

What you can do to improve your reading skills

- Read in English whatever you like to read in your own language: mystery novels or sports magazines, or the entertainment, business, technology, or travel news on a news app.
- Scan the Internet and newspapers for information that interests you.

What you can do to improve your writing skills

- Use the writing tutorial services available to all students on campus.
- Read a short news item several times; then hide it and rewrite the item. When you have finished, compare your version with the original.

Think about your language strengths and weaknesses. Decide which areas you want to improve, and then make a plan. If you learn independently, you will soon notice an improvement.

FINAL ASSIGNMENT

Write a Cause and Effect Essay

Write a cause and effect essay to answer this question: What are the effects of marketing on individuals and society?

A. Start with an introduction and a thesis statement that lists your main points. Provide a definition of marketing in your introduction.

B. In the body of your essay, use the concede and refute pattern to express your ideas. (Depending on your point of view, you may concede the negative effects of marketing and refute with positive effects, or you may concede the positive effects of marketing and refute with the negative effects.)

C. Use parallel structure where needed. Provide examples to support your points. Choose accurate vocabulary to express the cause and effect relationships you write about.

Refer to the Models Chapter (page 245) to see an example and to learn more about how to write a cause and effect essay.

Critical Connections

To practise thinking critically about and predicting an author's opinion, and to develop your conceding and refuting skills, follow the steps below.

A. Select a marketing-related topic that you would like to know more about. Here are some possible topics:

- Phone marketing
- High-pressure selling
- Online advertisements
- Customer surveys
- Customer reviews of a specific product

B. Search online (or in the library, in books, or in newspapers) to find an article about the topic. (Your teacher may also bring in some articles for you to think about.) Consider who the author of the article is and the type of writing, and predict the author's opinion. Then read the text to determine if your prediction was correct.

C. Using information from the article you have just read, and working with a small group of students, list the positive and negative effects of your chosen topic. Once your list is complete, take turns conceding a negative point, and refuting with a positive one.

TOPIC:	
POSITIVE POINTS	NEGATIVE POINTS

CHAPTER 5
The Science of Nutrition

It seems many people are concerned about their diets these days. Do you have friends who are vegetarian (no meat), vegan (no animal products), or pescatarian (no meat, but fish)? Do you know people who follow low-fat, high-carbohydrate, or high-protein diets? Have you ever tried adding muscle, losing weight, or both? Do you believe that it's healthy to eat gluten-free (no wheat) or lactose-free (no milk or dairy), or practise intermittent fasting (not eating for most of the day)? Do you eat chia seeds (or other "superfoods") or drink herbal teas to enjoy their nutritional benefits? How can you know what diet is best?

In this chapter, you will

- learn vocabulary about diet and nutrition;
- compare and contrast using conjunctions;
- consider the academic perspective;
- recognize the structure of compare/contrast texts;
- quote and reference to avoid plagiarism;
- evaluate information based on prior knowledge;
- write compare/contrast essays.

GEARING UP

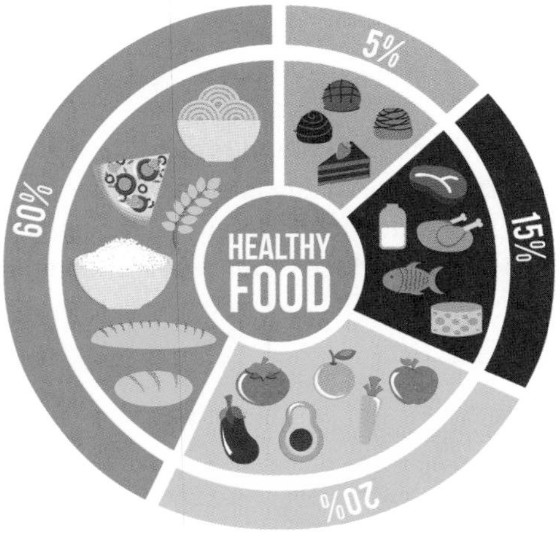

A. Look at the illustration above. The plate is divided into pieces that represent the percentage of food you might eat from each food group every day to achieve a healthy diet. Do you agree that these percentages represent a healthy diet? How could the plate be divided differently to represent other healthy diets?

_____

_____

_____

B. With a small group of students, discuss all the reasons why people change their diets. When you are finished, list the reasons below. Then, next to each reason, list some common dietary changes that people may make in response to these reasons.

REASONS	DIETARY CHANGES
• _to lose weight_	• _follow a low-fat or low-carbohydrate diet_

Below are the key words you will practise in this chapter. Check the words you understand, then underline the words you use. Highlight the words you need to learn.

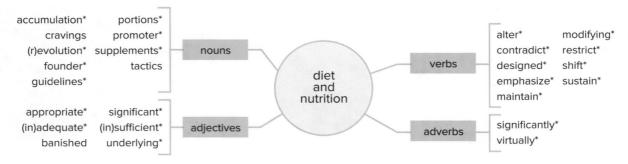

nouns
- accumulation*
- cravings
- (r)evolution*
- founder*
- guidelines*
- portions*
- promoter*
- supplements*
- tactics

adjectives
- appropriate*
- (in)adequate*
- banished
- significant*
- (in)sufficient*
- underlying*

diet and nutrition

verbs
- alter*
- contradict*
- designed*
- emphasize*
- maintain*
- modifying*
- restrict*
- shift*
- sustain*

adverbs
- significantly*
- virtually*

* Appears on the Academic Word List

READING ❶   Understanding Healthy Body Weight

The most common reason to make dietary changes is probably to lose weight. But what exactly is a healthy weight? This reading defines what a healthy weight is and acknowledges that this may not match societal expectations. The reading also introduces four types of common diets.

In the following exercises, explore key words from Reading 1.

A. When we want to say that people eat specific foods as part of a particular diet or program, we use the following verbs with the noun *diet* or *program*.

VERBS	NOUNS
be on	a diet
follow	a program
stick to	

When we describe a diet, we often use these adjectives that collocate with the word *diet* or *program*.

DESCRIPTIONS	ADJECTIVES	NOUNS
to describe an *extreme* diet (not much food)	crash	diet
	starvation	program
	strict	
to describe a diet *low* in a specific nutrient	low-calorie	
	low-carbohydrate (carb)	
	low-fat	
	low-protein	
to describe a diet *high* in a specific nutrient	high-calorie	
	high-carbohydrate (carb)	
	high-fat	
	high-protein	

© **ERPI** • Reproduction prohibited

DESCRIPTIONS	ADJECTIVES	NOUNS
to describe a *moderate* diet	balanced reasonable sensible	diet program
to describe a *specific* diet	gluten-free lactose-free vegan vegetarian	

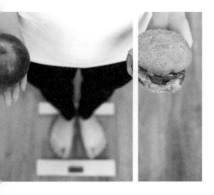

Using the verbs, nouns, and adjectives in the tables above, describe what diet you would try for these reasons:

a) To gain weight, people might ____*follow a high-fat (or high-carbohydrate) diet*____.

b) To lose weight, people might _____

c) To lose weight in a hurry, people might _____

d) To keep their weight stable, people might _____

e) To avoid eating meat, people might _____

f) To avoid eating dairy products, people might _____

g) To avoid eating wheat products, people might _____

B. Read each sentence and, using context clues, fill in the blank with the best word from the word box.

> appropriate   designed   emphasize   maintain   promoter
> restrict   significant   supplements   sustain

1. Some crash diets require people to severely _____ the amount of food they eat.

2. If people follow a diet that restricts specific nutrients, they may need _____ to make sure their bodies get all the vitamins and minerals they need.

3. When a person chooses a diet, it is best to select the most _____ diet for his or her age, height, build, and health.

4. Many people do well on diets when they first try them; however, they have difficulty trying to _____ the diet over the long term.

5. Some diets are supported by famous celebrities who serve as _____ for the diets.

6. If these food restrictions last too long, there are _____ risks to long-term health.

7. The best diet is the one that has been especially _____ for an individual.

8. People should stick to a sensible diet that they can _____ over time.

9. Nutritionists _____ that there is no single diet that works for everyone.

Before You Read

A. Foods are made of nutrients such as carbohydrates, fats, proteins, vitamins, and minerals. To understand this reading, it is important to understand which foods are made up of mostly carbohydrates (carbs for short), fats, or proteins. In the table below, write the foods from the list under the most appropriate nutrient group. (Note: some foods are made of more than one nutrient.)

> beans, beef, bread, butter, canola oil, cereal, cheese, chicken, coconut oil, cookies, corn, crackers, cream, ~~eggs~~, fish, fruit, fruit juice, hamburger, lard, noodles, nuts, ~~olive oil~~, pork, potatoes, ~~rice~~, salad dressing, tofu, whole milk

CARBOHYDRATES (CARBS)	FATS	PROTEINS
• nutrients that contain sugar and starch to heat the body and provide energy	• oily and greasy nutrients that don't dissolve in water	• nutrients that provide energy for growth and repair
• *rice*	• *olive oil*	• *eggs*

While You Read

B. Read the definition of a healthful weight and the descriptions of four common diets. After reading the description of each diet, write short notes in the chart that follows. These notes will help you recognize the similarities and differences between the different diets.

Understanding Healthy Body Weight

As you begin to think about achieving and **maintaining** a healthful weight, it's important to make sure you understand what a healthful body weight is … We can define a healthful weight as [meeting] all the following [criteria]:

- A weight that is **appropriate** for your age and physical development
5 - A weight that is based on your genetic background and family history of body shape and weight
- A weight that you can achieve and **sustain** without severely [**restricting**] your food intake or constantly dieting
- A weight that is compatible with normal blood pressure, **lipid** levels, and **glucose**
10 tolerance
- A weight that promotes good eating habits and allows you to participate in regular physical activity
- A weight that is acceptable to you

As you see, a healthful weight is not one at which a person must be extremely thin
15 or overly muscular. In addition, there is no one body type that can be defined as healthful. Thus, achieving a healthful body weight should not be dictated by the latest fad or society's expectations of what is acceptable.

lipid (n.): one of several types of fatty substances in living things

glucose (n.): natural sugar found in fruits and other foods; chemical formula $C_6H_{12}O_6$

Diets Focusing on Macronutrient Composition May or May Not Work

macronutrients (n.): important nutrients (carbohydrates, fats, or proteins) that are required in large quantities in the diet

20 Many weight-loss diets encourage increased consumption of certain **macronutrients** and restrict the consumption of others. Provided here is a brief review of [four types of] diets and their general effects on weight loss and health (Prentice et al., 2006).

Diets High in Carbohydrate and Moderate in Fat and Protein

Nutritionally balanced high-carbohydrate, moderate-fat and protein diets typically 25 contain 55 to 60 percent of total energy intake as carbohydrate, 20 to 30 percent of total energy intake as fat, and 15 to 20 percent of energy intake as protein. These diets include Weight Watchers, Jenny Craig, others that follow the general guidelines of the Dietary Approaches to Stop Hypertension (DASH Diet), and the USDA Food Guide. All of these diet plans **emphasize** that weight loss occurs when energy intake 30 is lower than energy expenditure. The goal is gradual weight loss, or about 1 to 2 lb (0.4–0.9 kg) of body weight per week. Typical suggested energy deficits are between 500 and 1000 kcal per day. Regular physical activity is encouraged.

To date, these types of low-energy diets have been researched more than any others. A substantial amount of high-quality scientific evidence (from randomized control 35 trials) indicates that they may be effective in decreasing body weight—at least initially. In addition, the people who lose weight on these diets may improve their blood lipid levels and decrease their blood pressure. However, recently published results from a randomized controlled trial following almost 50,000 US women for seven years indicate that, contrary to established beliefs, this type of diet does not result in 40 **significant** long-term weight loss or reduce the risks for breast and colorectal cancers or cardiovascular disease (Prentice et al., 2006; Beresford et al., 2006; Howard, Manson, et al., 2006; Howard, Van Horn, et al., 2006). Many limitations affected the study findings, however, and more research needs to be done before we are able to determine the long-term effectiveness of higher-carbohydrate diets on weight loss and disease risks.

HIGH-CARBOHYDRATE DIETS	NOTES
percentage of nutrients that come from carbohydrates, fat, or protein	
examples of this type of diet	
details of diet	
attitude to physical exercise	
benefits	
disadvantages	

45 *Diets Low in Carbohydrate and High in Fat and Protein*

Low-carbohydrate, high-fat and protein diets cycle in and out of popularity on a regular basis. By definition, these types of diets generally contain about 55 percent to 65 percent of total energy intake as fat and most of the remaining balance of daily energy intake as protein. Examples include Dr. Atkins' Diet Revolution, the Carbohydrate
50 Addict's Diet, and Protein Power. These diets minimize the role of restricting total energy intake on weight loss. They instead advise participants to restrict carbohydrate intake, proposing that carbohydrates are addictive and that they cause significant overeating, insulin surges leading to excessive fat storage, and an overall metabolic imbalance that leads to obesity. The goal is to reduce carbohydrates enough to cause
55 ketosis, which will decrease blood glucose and insulin levels and can reduce appetite.

Countless people claim to have lost substantial weight on these types of diets. Although quality scientific studies are just beginning to be conducted, the current limited evidence suggests that individuals following them, in both free-living and experimental conditions, do lose weight. In addition, it appears that those people who lose weight
60 may also experience positive metabolic changes similar to those seen with higher-carbohydrate diets.

So are low-carb diets effective? A recent review of all the published studies of these diets resulted in the conclusion that low-carb diets are just as effective, and possibly more effective, in promoting weight loss and reducing cardiovascular disease risk for
65 a period of up to one year (Hession, Rolland, Kulkarni, Wise, & Broom, 2009). However, the authors conclude that long-term health benefits of this type of diet are unknown at this time, and more research is needed.

LOW-CARBOHYDRATE DIETS	NOTES
percentage of nutrients that come from carbohydrates, fat, or protein	
examples of this type of diet	
details of diet	
attitude to physical exercise	
benefits	
disadvantages	

Low-Fat and Very-Low-Fat Diets

Low-fat diets contain 11 to 19 percent of total energy as fat, whereas very-low-fat diets
70 contain less than 10 percent of total energy as fat. Both of these types of diets are
high in carbohydrate and moderate in protein. Examples include Dr. Dean Ornish's
Program for Reversing Heart Disease and the New Pritikin Program. These diets do
not focus on total energy intake but emphasize eating
foods higher in complex carbohydrates and fibre.
75 Consumption of sugar and white flour is very limited.
The Ornish Diet is vegetarian, whereas the Pritikin Diet
allows 3.5 oz (99 g) of lean meat per day. Regular physical
activity is a key component of these diets.

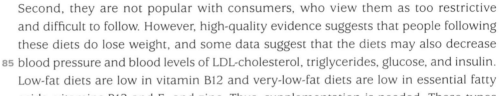

Data are limited on the effectiveness of these programs
80 for two reasons. First, they were not originally **designed**
for weight loss but to decrease or reverse heart disease.
Second, they are not popular with consumers, who view them as too restrictive
and difficult to follow. However, high-quality evidence suggests that people following
these diets do lose weight, and some data suggest that the diets may also decrease
85 blood pressure and blood levels of LDL-cholesterol, triglycerides, glucose, and insulin.
Low-fat diets are low in vitamin B12 and very-low-fat diets are low in essential fatty
acids, vitamins B12 and E, and zinc. Thus, supplementation is needed. These types
of diets are not considered safe for people with diabetes who are insulin dependent
(either type 1 or type 2) or for people with carbohydrate-malabsorption illnesses.

LOW-FAT DIETS	NOTES
percentage of nutrients that come from carbohydrates, fat, or protein.	
examples of this type of diet	
details of diet	
attitude to physical exercise	
benefits	
disadvantages	

90 *Fad Diets*

Unfortunately, many dieters are drawn to fad diets ... Beware of fad diets! They are simply what their name implies—fads that do not result in long-term, healthful weight changes. Although fad diets enjoy short-term popularity, most will "die" within a year, only to be born again as a "new and improved" fad diet. The goal of the person or
95 company designing and marketing a fad diet is to make money. How can you tell if the program ... qualifies as a fad diet?

gimmick (n.): trick intended to attract attention (used to show disapproval)

Fad diets are weight-loss programs that enjoy short-term popularity and are sold based on a marketing **gimmick** that appeals to the public's desires and fears. In addition, the goal of the person or company designing and marketing the diet is not
100 to improve ... health but to make money. How can you tell if a program ... is a fad diet? Here are some [obvious] signs:

- The **promoters** of the diet claim that the program is new, improved, or based on some new discovery; however, no scientific data are available to support
105 these claims.

- The program is [known] for its ability to result in rapid weight loss or body-fat loss, usually more than 2 lb (0.9 kg) per week, and may claim that weight loss can be achieved with little or no physical exercise.

110 - The diet includes special foods and **supplements**, many of which are expensive and/or difficult to find or can be purchased only from the diet promoter. Common recommendations for these diets include avoiding certain foods, eating only a special combination of
115 certain foods and including magic foods in the diet that "burn" fat and speed up metabolism.

- The diet includes a rigid menu that must be followed daily or allows only a few, select foods each day. Alternatively, the diet focuses on one macronutrient group (such as protein) and
120 severely restricts the others (such as carbohydrate and fat). Variety and balance are discouraged, and certain foods (such as all dairy products or all foods made with refined flour) are entirely forbidden.

- Many fad diets identify certain foods and/or supplements as critical to the success of the diet and usually claim that these substances can cure or prevent a variety
125 of health ailments or that the diet can stop the aging process.

flourish (v.): develop well and be successful

In a world in which many of us feel we have to meet a certain physical standard to be attractive and "good enough," fad diets **flourish**, with millions of people trying one each year (Manore, Meyer, & Thompson, 2009). Unfortunately, the only people who usually benefit from them are marketers, who can become very wealthy
130 promoting programs that don't work.

(1480 words)

FAD DIETS	NOTES
percentage of nutrients that come from carbohydrates, fat, or protein.	
examples of this type of diet	
details of diet	
attitude to physical exercise	
benefits	
disadvantages	

References

Beresford, S. A., Johnson, K. C., Ritenbaugh, C., Lasser, N. L., Snetselaar, L. G., Black, H. R., ... Anderson, G. L. (2006). Low-fat dietary pattern and risk of colorectal cancer: The Women's Health Initiative Randomized Controlled Dietary Modification Trial. *JAMA, 295*, 643–654.

Hession, M., Rolland, C., Kulkarni, U., Wise, A., & J. Broom. (2009). Systematic review of randomized controlled trials of low-carbohydrate vs. low-fat/low-calorie diets in the management of obesity and its comorbidities. *Obes Rev, 10*(1), 36–50.

Howard, B. V., Manson, J. E., Stefanick, M. L., Beresford, S. A., Frank, G. Jones, B., ... Radabough, R. J. (2006). Low-fat dietary pattern and weight change over 7 years: The Women's Health Initiative Randomized Controlled Dietary Modification Trial. *JAMA, 295,* 39–49.

Howard, B. V., Van Horn, L., Hsia, J., Manson, J. E., Stefanick, M. L., Wassertheil-Smoller, S., ... Kuller, L. H. (2006). Low-fat dietary pattern and risk of cardiovascular disease: the Women's Health Initiative Randomized Controlled Dietary Modification Trial. *JAMA, 295,*655–666.

Manore, M. M., Meyer, N. L., & Thompson, J. (2009). *Sport nutrition for health and performance* (2nd ed.). Champaign, IL: Human Kinetics.

Prentice, R. L., Caan, B., Chlebowski, R. T., Patterson, R., Kuller L. H., Ockene, J. K., ... Margolis, K. L. (2006). Low-fat dietary pattern and risk of invasive breast cancer: The Women's Health Initiative Randomized Controlled Dietary Modification Trial. *JAMA, 295*, 629–642.

Thompson, J., & Manore, M. (2016). *Nutrition for life* (4th ed., pp. 251, 266–270). USA: Pearson.

After You Read

C. To check your comprehension of the four types of common diets, compare the notes you wrote in the charts above with a classmate's notes.

D. Answer the following questions.

1 Check the characteristics of a healthy weight, as defined in this reading.
- ☐ A weight at which you are extremely thin
- ☐ A weight that is right for your age and genetics
- ☐ A weight that means you must constantly restrict what you eat
- ☐ A weight that makes you look good, but means you often feel hungry
- ☐ A weight at which you have energy to exercise
- ☐ A weight at which you don't have to diet all the time
- ☐ A weight at which you feel comfortable
- ☐ A weight you can maintain through daily fasting
- ☐ A weight that allows you to eat with friends and family

2 Check the characteristics of a fad diet, as defined in this reading.
- ☐ A diet that promotes sustainable eating habits
- ☐ A diet that may require expensive supplements
- ☐ A diet that promises you will lose more than 5 pounds a week
- ☐ A diet that is new and improved
- ☐ A diet that allows you to eat a wide range of healthy foods
- ☐ A diet that focuses on a single macronutrient
- ☐ A diet that restricts the foods you can eat
- ☐ A diet that does not include exercise

3 Do you think the authors support diets that can make people extremely thin or muscular? Why do you think this?

_____

_____

My Bookshelf > My eLab >
Exercises > Chapter 5 >
Understanding Healthy
Body Weight

FOCUS ON ACCURACY

Comparing and Contrasting Using Conjunctions

A. Using your notes from the charts in Reading 1, and working with a partner or a small group of classmates, discuss the similarities and differences between the four common diets. To help you express your ideas clearly, use your knowledge of conjunctions (summarized below) and varied sentence structure (Focus on Writing, Chapter 2, page 34).

TYPES OF CONJUNCTIONS	TO EXPRESS SIMILARITY	TO EXPRESS CONTRAST
subordinate	as/just as	although/even if/even though/though/whereas/while
coordinate	and	but yet
adverbial	likewise similarly	however nevertheless
IN ADDITION TO CONJUNCTIONS		
	compared to/with in comparison parallel to	in contrast to as opposed to unlike

B. Write four sentences to demonstrate the similarities and differences between various diets. Show your sentences to a classmate or to your teacher. Check to make sure that your use of conjunctions and sentence structure is correct.

Example: *While high-carbohydrate diets require people to reduce their calorie intake, low-carbohydrate diets only involve restricting carbohydrate intake.*

1 _____

_____

2 _____

_____

3 _____

_____

4 _____

_____

My Bookshelf > My eLab >
Exercises > Chapter 5 >
Focus on Accuracy

FOCUS ON
WRITING

Considering the Academic Perspective

When you use the academic perspective in formal speaking or writing, you should always be *objective*. This means that you just present the facts. Your *subjective* experiences and opinions—based on feelings and emotions instead of facts—are less relevant.

Sometimes, your instructors may ask you to speak or write about a personal experience or to express an opinion; in these cases, it is acceptable to write about yourself and what you think. However, as you progress in your post-secondary education, you will be asked to read and summarize other types of sources. These assignments will be based on objective information, and you will no longer be able to use your experiences or opinions to support your statements.

Avoiding the personal perspective in academic writing isn't difficult if you know how to revise subjective sentences to make them objective. Look at the following examples.

PERSONAL PERSPECTIVE/ FIRST PERSON/SUBJECTIVE	ACADEMIC PERSPECTIVE/ THIRD PERSON/OBJECTIVE
I think that following a fad diet can be harmful for dieters.	Following a fad diet can be harmful for dieters.
In my opinion, macronutrient diets work for some people, but not for others.	Macronutrient diets work for some people, but not for others.
Once I went to see a nutritionist, and she really helped me understand that my poor diet was reducing my energy levels.	Nutritionists can help people understand how poor diet may be related to other health problems. For example, following a low-fat diet may reduce energy levels.
I always follow the Weight Watchers diet because I think the weekly meetings are helpful for behaviour modification.	Many people who follow the Weight Watchers diet benefit from weekly meetings that support behaviour modification.
I know tons of people who are trying fad diets.	Millions of people try fad diets every year (Thompson & Manore, 2016).

Reference: Thompson, J., & Manore, M. (2016). *Nutrition for life* (4th ed., p. 270). USA: Pearson.

A. Convert these sentences from a subjective to an objective perspective. Use information from Reading 1 (page 122) if required.

1 I never believed a nutritionist could help me feel better until I went to see one.

_____

_____

2 In my opinion, low-carb diets can help people lose weight.

_____

_____

3 I was hoping to lose weight quickly by following the Tea x 12 diet, but it didn't work for me at all.

_____

_____

4 Like more and more people these days, I don't eat as well as I should.

_____

_____

5 My nutritionist suggests I follow a low-carb diet, so I don't have to count calories, just reduce the amount of carbs I eat.

_____

_____

My Bookshelf > My eLab > Exercises > Chapter 5 > Focus on Writing

WARM-UP ASSIGNMENT
Write a Short Compare and Contrast Essay

When you receive feedback from your teacher or your classmates on this Warm-Up Assignment, you will have information that you can use to improve your writing on the Final Assignment.

A. Write a short compare and contrast essay. In order to keep the essay relatively short, review the four common diets in Reading 1 (page 122) and select two of them. Decide whether you will write about their similarities or their differences.

B. In a compare and contrast essay, you must organize and explain the similarities or differences that you identify. Like other essays, compare and contrast essays have an introduction (that includes a thesis) and a conclusion (that contains a concluding sentence). The body of a compare and contrast essay can be organized in either block or point-by-point style. Refer to the Models Chapter (page 248) to see examples and to learn more about each style of compare and contrast essay.

C. Be sure to write from an academic perspective. Use conjunctions accurately, and use parallel structure when required.

READING ❷ Of Bananas and Cavemen

The authors of this reading compare and contrast two very different extreme diets: the Primal Blueprint and the 30 Bananas a Day diet. Although these diets are distinct, the authors discover that they are similar in a number of ways.

VOCABULARY BUILD

In the following exercises, explore key words from Reading 2.

A. There are several words to refer to people who follow diets. You will read these words in Reading 2 and use them to complete the Final Assignment.

People who follow a diet or program can be called

- *adherents*
- *proponents*
- *converts*
- *followers*
- *community members*
- *dieters*

Adherents of specific diets can also be named according to the diet; for example, *vegetarians*, *vegans*, or *fruitarians*.

To practise using these words, write sentences about dieters who would most likely eat the following foods. The first example has been completed for you.

FOODS DIETERS EAT	SENTENCES
carrots, peas, and beans	*Adherents of a vegetarian diet will eat carrots, peas, and beans.*
fish, meat, eggs, and cheese	
bananas, apples, and kiwis	
bread, pasta, and rice	
vegetables and fruit, but no meat, fish, or dairy.	

B. Read the sentences with key words in both columns. Write your own sentence for each key word in the second column.

SENTENCES ADAPTED FROM READING 2	ADDITIONAL EXAMPLES OF KEY WORDS
1 Followers of the Primal Blueprint believe that excess carbohydrate consumption leads to fat **accumulation** and overeating.	The **accumulation** of money is an important step toward any major purchase.
2 Occasional short bursts of intense exercise such as sprinting or weightlifting along with **adequate** sleep are also recommended to best imitate the habits and presumed health of early humans.	The professor was pleased that the quality of the students' work was more than **adequate**.
3 When met with research or guidelines that **contradict** their views, both Primal Blueprint and fruitarian community members employ parallel tactics to discredit those sources.	In many cultures, it is considered rude to **contradict** older people.
4 The **founder** of the Primal Blueprint diet is Mark Sisson, a former professional marathoner and triathlete who started the website Mark's Daily Apple in 2006.	Bill and Melinda Gates are the **founders** of the Bill and Melinda Gates Foundation, which works toward improving equity for all.
5 Fruitarians also rely on **evolution** to justify their diet's healthfulness, but they place the dietary target several million years further in the past.	The **evolution** of the Apple computer is well documented in history.
6 High-carbohydrate diets include Weight Watchers, Jenny Craig, others that follow the general **guidelines** of the Dietary Approaches to Stop Hypertension (DASH Diet), and the USDA Food Guide.	All large companies have **guidelines** about employee rights and responsibilities.
7 Against the background of constantly **shifting** nutritional advice and the belief that health is a personal responsibility in which most individuals are failing, a space is created in which online fad diets emerge.	In a large lecture hall, it can be difficult for an instructor to maintain students' **shifting** attention.
8 Community members of both diets employ **tactics** to discredit non-adherents by claiming they are mindless consumers who eat whatever they find in grocery stores.	Governments list the terrible diseases that smoking can cause on cigarette packages. These shock **tactics** are designed to prevent people from smoking.
9 According to fruitarianism, eating a diet that consists primarily or exclusively of raw fruits will ... ensure **sufficient** protein and fat intake.	If students complete all the assignments, that is **sufficient** effort for them to pass the course.
10 These **underlying** beliefs lead adherents to feel that they have (re)discovered the "one food truth."	There is an **underlying** assumption that it is easier for people to learn an additional language when they are young.

Before You Read

A. In small groups, discuss what you know about extreme diets. Are you familiar with any extreme diets or any "superfoods" (e.g., chia seeds) that you think are too extreme? Do you believe they help people achieve their weight goals? Do you think the extreme diets are completely different, or do they have some similarities?

B. When you have finished your group discussion, share the most interesting points with the rest of your class.

While You Read

C. This reading is divided into sections, indicated by the headings. While you read, do the following:

- Write *I* next to the heading that contains the introductory paragraph(s).
- Write *D* next to the heading(s) containing paragraphs that show the differences between the two diets.
- Write *S* next to the heading(s) containing paragraphs that show similarities.
- Write *C* next to the heading containing the concluding paragraph(s).

Of Bananas and Cavemen: Unlikely Similarities between Two Online Food Communities

starkly (adv.): unpleasantly clear and impossible to avoid

1. This chapter compares two increasingly popular online food communities—the primal diet and fruitarianism. The dietary beliefs of these groups are **starkly** oppositional: where the primal diet [avoids] carbohydrates in favour of animal fats and proteins, fruitarians are vegans who believe that a healthy diet consists primarily of carbohydrates
5 sourced from raw fruit. However, … these differences are largely superficial and **belie** underlying similarities in each group's logics, **tactics** and motivations.

belie (v.): show that something cannot be true

[The Primal Blueprint]

Paleolithic (adj.): from the Stone Age (time when humans used stone tools and weapons)

2. Largely an offshoot of Loren Cordain's (2010) Paleo Diet, the Primal Blueprint diet is based on specific interpretations of **Paleolithic** humans' dietary and physical habits.
10 Its **founder**, Mark Sisson, is a former professional marathoner and triathlete who started the website Mark's Daily Apple in 2006 in order to publicize his *Primal Blueprint* for dietary and lifestyle choices. Dietary supplements and Sisson's self-published books are available for purchase through the website, and dietitians, gym trainers, or enthusiasts can pay for access to additional educational materials and
15 modules that, upon completion, certify them as "Primal Blueprint Experts." Sisson is a celebrity voice within the evolutionary health community with a sizable following: his Twitter feed has more than 95,000 followers, and his site's online forums are home to more than 204,400 members (as of May 2016).

3. Primal Blueprint followers believe that the healthiest diet derives the majority of its
20 calories from proteins and fats, preferably from animal sources (Sisson, 2011). Adherents argue that these foods not only provide nutrients critical to muscle formation, organ function, balanced hormone levels, and appropriate blood sugar levels but also yield higher **satiety** than a diet rich in carbohydrates. They suggest that carbohydrate intake, particularly grains, sugars, and starchy vegetables, should
25 be minimized in order to better regulate blood sugar levels. Moreover, followers believe that excess carbohydrate consumption leads to fat **accumulation**, insulin

satiety (n.): feeling of fullness or having had enough of something

resistance, and overeating. The Primal Blueprint views the standard American diet, with its wide base of carbohydrate-heavy grains, as the leading contributor to rising obesity and chronic disease rates. The primal diet does not recommend completely

30 eliminating carbohydrates; rather generous servings of leafy, low-carb greens are encouraged for their nutrient and fibre content. Smaller quantities of fruit and certain low-glycemic plants, such as wild rice or lentils, are also permitted, especially if one is exercising heavily.

4. Adherents believe that outdoor physical activity should be a daily occurrence.
35 Occasional short bursts of intense exercise such as sprinting or weightlifting along with **adequate** sleep are also recommended to best imitate the habits and presumed health of Paleolithic humans (Sisson, 2008). Furthermore, intermittent fasting (IF) —which ranges from skipping a meal to a full day's fast—is promoted among some adherents. Periodic deprivation through IF is understood to allow the body to burn
40 some of its own fat reserves, speeding weight loss ...

5. [On the Primal Blueprint diet] calorie counting is de-emphasized; instead, new members are encouraged to get in touch with their appetite [signals] and to eat until satiated. Trusting one's own bodily signals is [considered] the most natural way to make food choices and, when followed alongside the Primal Blueprint's general
45 [**guidelines**], should result in fat loss and overall improved health ...

30 Bananas a Day

6. Fruitarianism is a subset of raw veganism, and many adherents refer to their specific diet as high-carb, low-fat raw veganism (HCLFRV) (www.30bananasaday.com). Although there are multiple varieties of fruitarianism, this [group] focuses on the
50 viewpoints popular within the 30 Bananas a Day community and promoted by the website's founders, Leanne "Freelee" Ratcliffe, also known as "the Banana Girl," and Harley "Durianrider" Johnstone. Freelee and Harley both run a variety of social media accounts, including on YouTube, Instagram, Facebook, and Twitter, as well as their own personal blogs. On 30 Bananas a Day alone, there are over 30,600 current
55 members, while Freelee and Harley's main YouTube channel each have more than 130 million views (as of May 2016). Through these social media outlets, Harley and Freelee sell their own ebooks, logo-bearing merchandise, and an iPhone application.

7. Like raw vegans, fruitarians [avoid] animal products and generally avoid cooked foods. Some raw food proponents argue that high temperatures destroy the beneficial
60 enzymes, vitamins, and minerals present in raw plants (Cousens, 2003). Others suggest that cooked foods contain chemical by-products that are toxic to the body (Graham, 2006). However, even though raw vegans may eat plant-based fats and proteins such as those found in avocados, nuts, and sprouted seeds or legumes, many fruitarians explicitly avoid consuming ... fats and protein (www.30bananasaday.com).

65 8. Instead, many fruitarians follow a version of the 80/10/10 plan outlined by Douglas Graham (2006) and [rely] heavily on research findings popularized in *The China Study* (Campbell & Campbell, 2004), which claims correlations between meat eating, cancer, and a variety of chronic diseases. The 80/10/10 diet recommends that 80 percent of an individual's daily caloric intake should come from carbohydrates, 10 percent
70 from proteins, and 10 percent from fats (Graham, 2006). Moreover, according to fruitarianism, eating a diet that consists primarily or exclusively of raw fruits will ... ensure **sufficient** protein and fat intake (www.30bananasaday.com). For example, a large raw banana provides about 1.5 grams of protein and a little less than 0.5 grams

of fat (www.30bananasaday.com) … Moreover, based largely on *The China Study*,
75 many fruitarians further argue that eating too much protein actually increases one's
risk for chronic diseases, particularly cancer (Campbell & Campbell, 2004).

9. Heavy carbohydrate consumption, especially from the sugars found in raw fruits,
is believed to be key to weight loss and good health. Many fruitarians encourage
relatively high caloric intakes … around 2500 to 3000 calories daily … A key
80 fruitarian [belief] is the harmfulness of calorie restriction. When new diet converts
express concerns with their bodies' responses to the HCLFRV meal plan, veteran
community members frequently suggest insufficient calorie consumption as the
primary [problem] … Low carbohydrate consumption is seen as a path to
depression, fatigue, and weight gain (www.30bananasaday.com).

85 ## [The Logic of Mainstream Nutrition Science Is Contradictory]

10. … As dissimilar as their specific diets are, the **underlying** logic of both fruitarianism
and the primal diet reveals a shared distrust of not only conventional dietary
standards but also the very position that mainstream nutritional science holds
in society … The standard American diet is characterized by high intakes of fatty
90 meats and refined carbohydrates as well as added sugars, fats, and sodium. Such
a diet has been variously linked with an increased risk of obesity, diabetes, and
cardiovascular disease and stroke (Grotto & Zied, 2006).Yet, despite increasing
concern over health consequences of a standard American diet, available
nutritional information on preferable alternatives is notoriously unclear. Scientific
95 and popular experts alike acknowledge that healthy eating advice ranges from
complex to contradictory. Marion Nestle describes how, for many people, choosing
what to eat for their daily meals "feels like walking through a minefield" (Nestle,
2006, p. 4). As more nutrition studies are conducted, new discoveries are made
and old knowledge is challenged, leaving many consumers feeling simultaneously
100 **bombarded** by information and lost when it comes to actual decision-making …

bombarded (v.): subjected
to too much of something,
and too often

11. Popular media's treatment of diet-related disease further aggravates public anxiety
about health eating: get it exactly right, they warn, or else. Panic-driven metaphors
make frequent reference to a "diabetes time bomb," the "war on obesity," and
"epidemics" of cardiovascular disease, cancer and stroke. These metaphors have
105 been abundantly effective at [increasing] public concern … They … work in part
because they touch a moral nerve, tapping into notions of responsibility—that
being healthy is an individual duty (Wright, 2009). Internalizing these messages,
individuals focus their energies toward constant self-discipline of behaviour and
body. Today, this frequently takes the form of stringent attention to one's exercise
110 habits, weight, and dietary choices.

12. Against this background—constantly **shifting**
nutritional advice and the belief that health is a
personal responsibility in which most individuals are
failing— a space is created in which online [fad diets]
115 emerge. Online forums offering clearly articulated
doctrines coupled with supportive communities are
especially well positioned to thrive. As different as the
fruitarian and primal [diets] are, … both are [logical
results] of the current state of nutritional science and
120 wider cultural [conversation] about health.

[Questioning Research as a Tactic]

13. When met with research or guidelines that **contradict** their views, [both Primal Blueprint and fruitarian community] members employ parallel tactics to discredit those sources. Members quickly point out methodological problems [of studies
125   that offer negative evidence], such as [small] sample sizes and the unreliability of nutritional self-reporting, or questions [about] funding sources. Fruitarians, for example, readily dismiss research funded by meat and dairy organizations, and individuals often post such studies specifically to [ask for] help in **debunking** them. When primal dieters encounter research that finds negative health effects
130   associated with high-protein, low-carbohydrate diets, community members suggest that study participants consumed soybeans or processed meat, not the "right" kind of protein. Importantly, however, the mistrust that these communities hold toward mainstream nutritional science does not result in the complete rejection of peer-reviewed research. Rather, both groups rely heavily on favourable
135   scientific evidence and frequently ask for advice on how to use science to convince non-adherents (www.30bananasaday.com).

debunking (v.): showing that an idea is false

14. … Since each community believes that its diet represents the single best approach to eating, individuals who do not follow [their
140   rules] are necessarily also failing in their moral duty to safeguard health. Community members [of both diets employ tactics to discredit] non-adherents by claiming they are mindless consumers who eat whatever
145   they find in grocery stores, believe food labels without hesitation, and fail to question federal dietary guidelines …

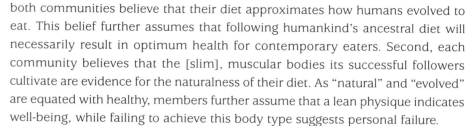

[Evolution as Motivation]

15. … [Followers of both the Primal Blueprint
150   and the 30 Bananas a Day diets are motivated by similar beliefs to explain] the superiority of their preferred diet. First, members from both communities believe that their diet approximates how humans evolved to eat. This belief further assumes that following humankind's ancestral diet will
155   necessarily result in optimum health for contemporary eaters. Second, each community believes that the [slim], muscular bodies its successful followers cultivate are evidence for the naturalness of their diet. As "natural" and "evolved" are equated with healthy, members further assume that a lean physique indicates well-being, while failing to achieve this body type suggests personal failure.

160 16. The primal diet begins with the assumption that most people living in high-income countries have abandoned the dietary habits of hunter-gatherers. Primal Blueprint adherents trace the origins of this shift back around 10,000 years to the Neolithic Revolution, when humans began to practise a more settled, agricultural lifestyle. They suggest that this shift [initiated] harmful changes to human lifestyles,
165   including increased [sedentary behaviour,] a decline in dietary diversity, and greater reliance on cultivated grains … [P]rimal dieters blame this mismatch for increased chronic disease, obesity, and mortality rates (www.marksdailyapple.com/forum).

17. Fruitarians also rely on **evolution** to justify their diet's healthfulness but throw the dietary target several million years further in the past. For fruitarians, the most appropriate diet is the one practised by humanity's closest living relatives: the great apes. According to fruitarians, the genetic and anatomical similarities between humans and apes demonstrate that [humans] are, above all, [fruit eaters]. For example, fruitarians argue that human teeth are most similar to those of [fruit-eating] mammals as [humans] lack large canines and exhibit molars useful for processing plant material … [F]ruitarians argue that human physiology still reflects an earlier, superior [fruit-eating habit]. Moreover, they believe that insufficient time has elapsed for humans to adequately adapt to any other diet, thus explaining the rise in chronic disease rates (www.30bananasaday.com).

[Logic, Tactics, and Motivations]

180 18. The fruitarian and primal diet communities discussed here have developed as parallel responses to contemporary cultural pressures. These pressures include … linking individual moral responsibility to health, media-fueled public anxiety regarding diet-related illness, and an ever-shifting landscape of official nutritional advice. The virtue that individuals feel in achieving the slim physique currently popular… merges with the satisfaction they derive from following the diet humans evolved to consume. Together, these underlying beliefs lead adherents to feel that they have (re)discovered the "one food truth." Moreover, the presumed simplicity, constancy, and naturalness of eating the diet humans were designed to eat offers followers an empowering alternative to mainstream dietary advice. While radically different dietary rules prevent them from sharing a meal, these communities ultimately share [similar logic, tactics, and motivations].

(2063 words)

References

Campbell, T. C., & Campbell, T. M. (2004). *The China study: The most comprehensive study of nutrition ever conducted and the startling implications for diet, weight loss and long-term health*. Dallas, TX: BenBella Books.

Cordain, L. (2010). *The paleo diet: Lose weight and get healthy by eating the foods you were designed to eat* (Revised ed.). Hoboken, NJ: Wiley.

Cousens, G. (2003). *Rainbow green live-food cuisine*. Berkeley, CA: North Atlantic Books.

Graham, G. (2006). *The 80/10/10 diet: Balancing your health, your weight, and your life in one luscious bite at a time*. Key Largo, FL: FoodnSport.

Grotto, D., & and Zied, E. (2006). The standard American diet and its relationship to the health status of Americans. *Nutrition in Clinical Practice, 25*(6), 603–612.

Foucault, M. (1977). *Discipline and punish: The birth of the prison*. New York, NY: Vintage.

Nestle, M. (2006). *What to eat*. New York, NY: North Point Press.

Sisson, M. (2011, November 3). Introducing the new primal blueprint food pyramid. *Mark's Daily Apple*. Retrieved from http://www.marksdailyapple.com/introducing-the-new-primal-blueprint-food-pyramid

Sisson, M. (2008, June 4). Definitive guide: The primal blueprint. *Mark's Daily Apple*. Retrieved from http://www.marksdailyapple.com/definitive-guide-primal-blueprint

US Department of Agriculture, Agricultural Research Service, Nutrient Data Laboratory. USDA national nutrient database for standard reference, Release 28. (2016). Retrieved from https://iapreview.ars.usda.gov/Services/docs.htm?docid=8964. Accessed September, 2015.

Wright, J. (2009). Biopower, biopedagogies and the obesity epidemic. In J. Wright & V. Harwood (Eds.), *Biopolitics and the "obesity epidemic": Governing bodies* (pp. 1–14). New York, NY: Routledge.

Maxfield, A. & Rissing, A. (2017). Of bananas and cavemen: Unlikely similarities between two online food communities. In K. Cargill (Ed.), *Food cults: How fads, dogma, and doctrine influence diet* (pp. 141–155). London, UK: Rowman & Littlefield.

After You Read

D. In small groups, compare which headings you placed the letters *I, D, S,* and *C* next to in the reading. Do you all agree? Confirm your letter placement with the class. Underline the sentence in the introductory paragraph that contains the thesis, and discuss your answer with the class.

E. Read each statement and indicate whether it is true or false. If a statement is false, write a true statement below it.

STATEMENTS	TRUE	FALSE
1 The Primal Blueprint diet is not popular. *The Primal Blueprint diet is popular, as demonstrated* *by the number of online followers.*		✓
2 Followers of the Primal Blueprint diet eat mostly protein and fat from meat.		
3 Adherents of the Primal Blueprint diet believe exercise is not important.		
4 Fasting has no place in the Primal Blueprint diet.		
5 Proponents of the Primal Blueprint diet think you should eat until you feel full.		
6 The 30 Bananas a Day diet is popular.		
7 Converts to the 30 Bananas a Day diet eat mostly raw protein.		
8 Proponents of the 30 Bananas a Day diet suggest people eat a small amount of fruit every day.		

STATEMENTS	TRUE	FALSE
9 The authors believe that both diets are similar because they are extreme responses to the contradictory nutritional evidence provided by mainstream nutrition science.		
10 Adherents of both diets may like the clear rules that these diets provide.		
11 The followers of both diets refuse to accept scientific evidence that doesn't support their diet rules.		
12 Online community members of both diets believe that health is a shared responsibility.		
13 Both diet communities are motivated to eat the way they believe their ancestors did in the past.		
14 The authors believe that the two diets are more different than they are similar.		

F. If you had to follow either the Primal Blueprint or the 30 Bananas a Day diet, which one would you choose, and why?

_____

_____

_____

G. Discuss this question with a partner or a small group. Do you believe that there is "one food truth" for everyone? Why?

My Bookshelf > My eLab >
Exercises > Chapter 5 >
Of Bananas and Cavemen

Recognizing a Compare and Contrast Text

The table below outlines (almost completely) the structure of Reading 2. The section headings are listed in the left column, and the purpose/topic of the paragraphs in each section is listed in the right column. Most of the right-hand column is complete; however, there are a few blanks to fill in next to some paragraph numbers.

A. Read the purpose/topic statements in the box below, and write them into the table in the best spot. When you are finished, you will have a complete outline of Reading 2.

> **Missing Purpose/Topic Statements**
> - Adherents of both diets distrust mainstream nutrition science.
> - Calorie counting; eat more carbs to lose weight.
> - Importance of exercise and fasting
> - Members of both diets believe they follow the evolutionary diet humans followed in the past.
> - Non-members are failing their moral duty to optimize their health.

SECTIONS	PURPOSE/TOPIC OF PARAGRAPH
❶ Of Bananas and Cavemen	PARAGRAPH 1: Introduction
❷ The Primal Blueprint	PARAGRAPH 2: Founder of Primal Blueprint diet PARAGRAPH 3: Description of diet PARAGRAPH 4: PARAGRAPH 5: Calorie counting; eat until full
❸ 30 Bananas a Day	PARAGRAPH 6: Founders of the 30 Bananas a Day diet PARAGRAPH 7: Description of diet PARAGRAPH 8: Description of diet PARAGRAPH 9:
❹ The Logic of Mainstream Nutrition Science Is Contradictory	PARAGRAPH 10: PARAGRAPH 11: Popular media suggests health is a personal responsibility. PARAGRAPH 12: These social conditions encourage online fad diets.
❺ Questioning Research as a Tactic	PARAGRAPH 13: Followers of both diets ignore negative research or guidelines. PARAGRAPH 14:
❻ Evolution as Motivation	PARAGRAPH 15: PARAGRAPH 16: Primal Blueprint adherents believe humans mostly ate meat. PARAGRAPH 17: Fruitarians believe humans mostly ate plants.
❼ Logic, Tactics, and Motivations	PARAGRAPH 18: These diet communities are similar in their logic, tactics, and motivations.

B. Look carefully at the outline in the table, then read the sentences below. Fill in the blank with the word that best completes each sentence.

① The first paragraph of the reading is the _____ and contains the thesis.

② Sections 2 and 3 describe the two diets. These two sections illustrate the _____ between the two diets. These two sections are organized like a _____ style compare and contrast essay.

③ Sections 4, 5, and 6 show the _____ between the two diets.

④ Section 7 is the _____ of the reading and repeats the thesis.

Academic
Survival Skill

Quoting and Referencing to Avoid Plagiarism

Copying another person's words or ideas is called *plagiarism*, and is an academic offence. As there are serious penalties for plagiarism, it should be of significant concern for students and instructors alike.

Generally, there are two types of plagiarism:
- Copying another person's *words*
- Copying another person's *ideas*

Providing in-text citations and references for other people's words and ideas is one way to avoid plagiarizing. When you give a reference, you let the reader know who wrote or spoke the original words or who developed the ideas.

You have seen in-text citations and references before; in fact, there are a number of them in this book. In-text citations and references are the paper equivalents of embedded electronic links. They allow the reader to find the original source.

- In-text citations (found in the body of a text) briefly identify the original author of the words or ideas you are writing about and the date on which the work was published, without interrupting the flow of the reading. For each in-text citation, you need to provide complete information about the publication in a reference section at the end of a text or a bibliography.

- References should provide enough detail so that readers can easily find the source of the words or ideas you are writing about.

Citing and referencing words and ideas accurately can be challenging. There are a number of different citation and referencing styles, such as

- American Psychological Association (APA);
- Modern Languages Association (MLA);
- Institute of Electrical and Electronics Engineers (IEEE).

Each style demands that citation and reference elements be placed in a specific order with unique punctuation.

You can find guidelines for MLA and IEEE referencing in My eLab Documents.

The in-text citation and reference examples in the following section are formatted according to American Psychological Association (APA) requirements. As APA format is widely used in several academic disciplines, this style of citing and referencing will be useful for many students.

In-Text Citations

Here are some examples of in-text citations from Reading 2 where a writer uses another writer's words.

LINE	IN-TEXT CITATIONS	CHARACTERISTICS
LINES 96–98	Marion Nestle describes how, for many people, choosing what to eat for their daily meals "feels like walking through a minefield" (2006, p. 4).	• short quotation • use of quotation marks • author name in the text • date and page number at the end in parentheses

Here are some examples of in-text citations where a writer uses another writer's ideas.

LINE	IN-TEXT CITATIONS	CHARACTERISTICS
LINES 34–37	Adherents believe that outdoor physical activity should be a daily occurrence. Occasional short bursts of intense exercise such as sprinting or weightlifting along with adequate sleep are also recommended to best imitate the habits and presumed health of Paleolithic humans (Sisson, 2011).	• *not* a quotation • ideas are paraphrased • author and date in parentheses at end
LINES 59–60	Some raw food proponents argue that high temperatures destroy the beneficial enzymes, vitamins, and minerals present in raw plants (Cousens, 2003).	• page number *not* included, likely because this idea is a main idea of the original author and repeated in more than one place

A Note on Referencing Another Writer's Ideas

Here are some general guidelines to help you avoid plagiarizing another person's ideas.

Writing about information that is considered general knowledge in your field is *not* considered plagiarism.

Example: Over the last two decades, advice from nutrition scientists has been contradictory, first suggesting people reduce their fat intake, and later advising people to eat more fat.

This isn't considered copying because it presents a widely known fact in the field of nutrition science. Many researchers have agreed that this is true, and many people have written about it in a variety of ways.

You must learn information that is common knowledge in your field. You will learn which ideas are widely known as you continue to study. If you aren't sure, you should reference the information to be certain to avoid plagiarizing.

Writing about a specific idea without providing a reference to explain its origins is considered plagiarism. Specific ideas are usually an author's unique idea, the results of research, or a statistic.

Example: In *The China Study*, Campbell (2004) links meat eating to several diseases such as cancer and chronic cardiovascular disease.

This requires a reference because it discusses the results of specific research.

References
Here are some basic examples of how to cite source materials according to APA style. Your sources should be listed in alphabetical order, according to the authors' last names.

BOOK	
Last name, First Initial., & Last name, First Initial. (Year). *Book title: Subtitle* (Edition) [if other than the 1st]. Place: Publisher.	Smolin, L., & Grosvenor, M. (2010). *Nutrition: Science and applications* (2nd ed.). Hoboken, NJ: Wiley.

CHAPTER IN A BOOK WITH AN EDITOR	
Author's Last name, First Initial., & Last name, First Initial. (Year). Chapter title. In Editor's First Initial. Last Name (Ed.), *Book title* (pp. #–#). Place: Publisher.	Maxfield, A., & Rissing, A. (2017). Of bananas and cavemen: Unlikely similarities between two online food communities. In K. Cargill (Ed.), *Food cults: How fads, dogma, and doctrine influence diet* (pp. 141–155). London, UK: Rowman & Littlefield.

ARTICLE IN A JOURNAL OR MAGAZINE WITHOUT A DIGITAL OBJECT IDENTIFIER (DOI)	
Last name, First Initial. (Year). Article title. *Journal/Magazine Title, Volume* (Issue number), page numbers [inclusive: the page numbers of the entire article].	Nogales-Gadea, G., Santalla, A., Arenas, J., Martin, M. A., Moran, M., & Lucia, A. (2017). Low versus high carbohydrates in the diet of the world-class athlete: Insights from McArdle's disease. *The Journal of Physiology, 595*(9), 2991–2992.

ARTICLE IN AN ACADEMIC JOURNAL WITH A DIGITAL OBJECT IDENTIFIER (DOI)	
Last name, First Initial., & Last name, First Initial. (Year). Article title. *Journal Title, Volume* (Issue number), page number(s). doi:	Nurul Adilah, Z., & Mohd Redzwan, S. (2017). Effect of dietary macronutrients on aflatoxicosis: A mini-review. *Journal of the Science of Food and Agriculture, 97*(8), 2277–2281. doi:10.1002/jsfa.8234

ARTICLE IN A NEWSPAPER	
Author's Last Name, First Initial. (Year, Month Day). Article title. *Newspaper Title*, Section & page number.	Parker, W. (2017, October 27). High fat diets promote weight loss. *The Record*, C7.

ARTICLE IN AN ONLINE NEWSPAPER	
Author's Last Name, First Initial. (Year, Month Day). Article title. *Newspaper Title*. Retrieved from URL of article's homepage	Siddiqi, M. (2017, November 6). Everybody's eating alone. *The Globe and Mail*. Retrieved from https://beta.theglobeandmail.com/life/food-and- wine/dining-with-a-group-is-better-for-our-health-so-why-is-is-everybody-eatingalone/article36845476/

A. With a classmate, write a reference for each of the following items on a separate page:

- this book or another book that you have with you
- a newspaper article provided by your teacher or one that you can find online
- a magazine or academic journal article provided by your teacher or one that you can find online

B. When you have finished, your teacher may ask you to write your references on the board. Compare your references with those of other students. Make sure to use correct punctuation.

Evaluating Information

One way to develop your critical thinking skills is to apply information you already know (from reading or listening to texts, or through personal experience) to new information. When you consider new information in relation to information you already know, you can make decisions about the new information: is it similar to what you already know; can you categorize it based on what you already know; do you think it is useful, interesting, or remarkable in some way?

In this chapter, you can use information from Reading 1 to evaluate information in Readings 2 and 3.

A. Go back to Reading 1, page 126, lines 90–130, which define fad diets. Review that information, and then use it to evaluate the two diets described in Reading 2 (page 133). Here are some questions that you might ask yourself in order to think critically about information in Reading 2.

   1 In what ways are the Primal Blueprint and the 30 Bananas a Day diets fad diets?

   2 What do the founders of these diets promise their community members?

   3 Do diet adherents have to spend money for supplements on these diets?

   4 In what ways are the diets *not* fad diets?

   5 The high-carbohydrate, low-carbohydrate, and low-fat diets described in Reading 1 are presented as sensible (i.e., not fad diets). Do you think they share characteristics of fad diets? Why?

   6 Would you recommend either of the two diets described in Reading 2 to a friend?

   7 Would you recommend any of the three diets described in Reading 1 (high-carb, low-carb, low-fat) to a friend?

B. Now you are ready to use information from Readings 1 and 2 to evaluate the information in Reading 3.

READING ③   Losing Weight, Gaining Life

The South Beach Diet is a well-known diet developed by cardiologist Arthur Agatston in 2003. This reading is an excerpt from his book, *The South Beach Diet: the Delicious, Doctor-Designed, Foolproof Plan for Fast and Healthy Weight Loss.* The diet is named for the glamorous South Beach area in Miami, Florida.

VOCABULARY BUILD

In the following exercises, explore key words from Reading 3.

A. Determine the meaning of each word from the reading context. Write a definition for each key word in the second column of the table below. When you have finished, confirm your answers with a classmate.

KEY WORDS	DEFINITIONS	WORD FORMS
1 alter (v.) (line 69)	*change*	alternative/alternate/alternatively
2 banished (adj.) (line 48)		ban/banish
3 cravings (n.) (line 28)		crave
4 modifying (v.) (line 41)		modification/modified
5 portions (n.) (line 6)		
6 significantly (adv.) (line 69)		significance/signify/significantly
7 virtually (adv.) (line 28)		virtual

B. With a partner, write all the other forms of the key words in the table below. Use the third column of the table above for information, as well as a dictionary if required.

Word Forms

NOUNS	VERBS	ADJECTIVES	ADVERBS
alternative	alter *alternate*	*alternative*	*alternatively*
		banished	
craving			
	modify(ing)		
portion(s)			
significance			significantly
			virtually

C. To demonstrate your knowledge of word meaning and form, write no more than two sentences that contain some form of the seven key words.

_____

_____

_____

_____

_____

_____

My Bookshelf > My eLab >
Exercises > Chapter 5 >
Vocabulary Review

Before You Read

A. Review the information in Focus on Critical Thinking (page 144). Remind yourself of everything you know about healthy weight, sensible diets, and fad diets.

While You Read

B. As you read, think critically about the text and evaluate this diet based on your existing knowledge. Do you believe this diet is a fad diet?

Losing Weight, Gaining Life

The South Beach Diet is not low carb. Nor is it low fat. The South Beach Diet teaches you to rely on the right carbs and the right fats—the *good ones*—and enables you to live quite happily without the bad carbs and the bad fats. As a result, you're going to get healthy and lose weight—somewhere between eight and thirteen pounds in
5 the next two weeks alone. Here's how you'll do it.

> You'll eat normal-size [**portions**] of meat, chicken, turkey, fish, and shellfish.
>
> You'll have plenty of vegetables. Eggs. Cheese. Nuts.
>
> You'll have salads with real olive oil in the dressing.
>
> 10 You'll have three balanced meals a day, and it will be your job to eat so that your hunger is satisfied. Nothing undermines a weight-loss plan more than the distressing sensation that you need more food. No **sane** eating program expects you to go through life feeling discomfort. You'll be urged to have snacks in the mid-morning and mid-afternoon,
> 15 whether you need to or not. You'll have dessert after dinner.
>
> You'll drink water, of course, plus coffee or tea if you wish.

For the next fourteen days you *won't* be having any bread, rice, potatoes, pasta, or baked goods. No fruit, even. Before you panic: you'll begin adding those things back into your diet again in two weeks. But for right now, they're off limits. No candy, cake,
20 cookies, ice cream, or sugar for two weeks, either. No beer or alcohol of any kind. After this phase you'll be free to drink wine. It's beneficial for a variety of reasons. Not a drop during the first two weeks, however.

Now, if you're the kind of person who lives for pasta or bread or potatoes, or if you believe that you can't get through a day without feeding your sweet tooth (three or
25 four times), let me tell you something: you're going to be shocked at how painlessly two weeks will pass without these foods. The first day or two may be challenging; but once you weather that, you'll be fine. It's not that you'll have to fight your urges— during the first week the **cravings** will **virtually** disappear. I say this with such confidence only because so many overweight people who have already succeeded
30 on this program tell me so. The South Beach Diet may be new to you, but it has existed for several years—long enough to have helped hundreds of people lose weight easily and keep it off.

So that's Phase 1, the strictest period.

After two weeks of that, you will be somewhere between 8 and 13 pounds lighter
35 than you are today. Most of that weight will come off your midsection, so right away you'll notice the difference in your clothes. It will be easier to zip your jeans than it's been for some time. That [jacket] will close without a bulge.

---

sane (adj.): normal or reasonable

But this will be just the noticeable difference. You won't be able to see that during those two weeks, you'll also have changed yourself internally. You will have corrected the 40 way your body reacts to the very foods that made you overweight. There's a switch inside you that has been turned on. Now, simply by **modifying** your diet, you'll have turned it off. The physical cravings that ruled your eating habits will be gone, and they'll stay away for as long as you stick with the program. The weight loss doesn't happen because you're trying to eat less. But you'll be eating fewer of the foods that created 45 those bad old urges, fewer of the foods that caused your body to store excessive fat.

As a result of *that* change, you will continue losing weight after the fourteen-day period ends, even though by then you will have begun adding some of those **banished** foods back into your life. You'll still be on a diet, but if 50 it's bread that you love, you'll have bread. If it's pasta, you'll reintroduce that. Rice or cereal, too. Potatoes. Fruit will definitely be back.

Chocolate? If it makes you feel good, sure. You will have to pick and choose which of these [pleasures] you permit 55 yourself. You won't be able to have all of them, all of the time. You'll learn to enjoy them a little differently than before—maybe a little less enthusiastically. But you will enjoy them again soon.

That's Phase 2.

60 You'll remain in that phase and continue losing weight until you reach your goal. How long it takes depends on how much you need to lose. In Phase 2, people lose, on average, a pound or two a week. Once you hit your target, you'll switch to an even more [generous] version of the program, which will help you to maintain your ideal weight.

That's Phase 3, the stage that lasts the rest of your life. When you get to that point, 65 you'll notice that this plan feels less like a diet and more like a way of life. You'll be eating normal foods, after all, in normal-size **portions**. You can then feel free to forget all about the South Beach Diet, as long as you remember to live by its few basic rules.

As you're losing weight and altering how your body responds to food, a third change will be taking place. This one will **significantly alter** your blood chemistry, to the 70 long-term benefit of your cardiovascular system. You will improve invisible factors that only cardiologists and heart patients worry about. Thanks to this final change, you will substantially increase your odds of living long and well—meaning you will maintain your health and vitality as you age.

You may start on the South Beach Diet hoping just to lose weight. If you adopt it and 75 stay with it, you will surely accomplish that much. But you'll also do a lot more for yourself: all of it very good. I'm not exaggerating when I say this diet can, as a fringe benefit, save your life.

(997 words)

Agatston, A. (2003). *The South Beach Diet: the delicious, doctor-designed, foolproof plan for fast and healthy weight loss* (pp. 3–5.). (n.p.): Rodale.

After You Read

C. Do you believe the South Beach Diet is a reasonable, sensible diet, or do you believe that it is a fad diet? Why? Discuss your evaluation of the reading with your class.

_____

_____

D. In this reading, there are some sentences that make the South Beach Diet sound quite sensible, and others that make it sound like a fad diet. Read the sentences below, and put a check mark in the appropriate box if you think they describe a sensible or a fad diet. When you have finished, compare your answers with a classmate.

SENTENCES	SENSIBLE	FAD
❶ … you're going to get healthy and lose weight—somewhere between 8 and 13 pounds in the next two weeks alone.		
❷ You'll have three balanced meals a day, and it will be your job to eat so that your hunger is satisfied.		
❸ For the next fourteen days you _won't_ be having any bread, rice, potatoes, pasta, or baked goods. No fruit, even.		
❹ … let me tell you something: you're going to be shocked at how painlessly two weeks will pass without these foods.		
❺ It's not that you'll have to fight your urges—during the first week the cravings will virtually disappear.		
❻ There's a switch inside you that has been turned on. Now, simply by modifying your diet, you'll have turned it off.		
❼ In Phase 2 people lose, on average, a pound or two a week.		
❽ That's Phase 3, the stage that lasts the rest of your life. When you get to that point, you'll notice that this plan feels less like a diet and more like a way of life.		
❾ I'm not exaggerating when I say this diet can, as a fringe benefit, save your life.		

My Bookshelf > My eLab >
Exercises > Chapter 5 >
Losing Weight, Gaining Life

E. Now that you have completed task D, has your evaluation of the South Beach Diet changed? What is your opinion now? Discuss this with your class. Has the class's opinion changed? Why?

FINAL ASSIGNMENT

Write a Compare and Contrast Essay

A. Write a compare and contrast essay to explain the similarities and differences between two diets. Choose two from those described in Reading 1 (high-carbohydrate, low-carbohydrate, or low-fat), Reading 2 (Primal Blueprint or 30 Bananas a Day diet), or Reading 3 (South Beach Diet).

As an alternative, you could choose one of the diets described in Reading 1, 2, or 3, and another diet that you know about.

B. Use academic perspective in your essay. Quote and refer to information from the chapter readings, using appropriate in-text citations and references. Refer to the Models Chapter (page 248) to see an example and to learn more about how to write a compare and contrast essay.

Critical Connections

To gain further practice in critical thinking, select a different diet to evaluate. The following are some examples that you can research online. You can use one of these diets for this activity, or find a different one.

Atkins Diet	Jenny Craig Diet	6:1 Diet
Clean Eating Diet	Mayo Clinic Diet	Teatox diets
Cut Diet	Mediterranean Diet	TLC Diet
Flexitarian Diet	Ornish Diet	Volumetrics Diet
Green Juice Diet	Red Wine Diet	Weight Watchers

A. Once you have decided on a diet, evaluate its nutritional information. Do you believe the diet is a macronutrient diet or a fad diet? Explain why.

B. You can use the questions in task A of Focus on Critical Thinking (page 144) to help you develop your thinking. Use a similar process of applying information from one source to information from another source to generate new ideas and achieve greater understanding of the new information.

CHAPTER 6
Digital Currencies

Bitcoin is the best known of the many digital currencies that are used these days, and its use is growing. Developed by the mysterious Satoshi Nakamoto, the bitcoin blockchain uses clever new technology that allows people to transfer money without using a bank. Bitcoin became popular during the 2008 global financial crisis, and appears to offer some advantages over government-regulated currencies. However, it may also have some unintended disadvantages. Have you used bitcoin (or any other digital currencies such as ethereum, dash, or nubits) to buy or sell anything? Would you use bitcoin?

In this chapter,
you will

- learn vocabulary related to digital currency and banking;

- learn how to paraphrase and reference to avoid plagiarism;

- annotate readings to help you remember information;

- write accurate conditional sentences;

- learn how to avoid problems with writing in the third-person academic perspective;

- contextualize new information;

- paraphrase a paragraph and write a cause and effect essay that includes a paraphrase.

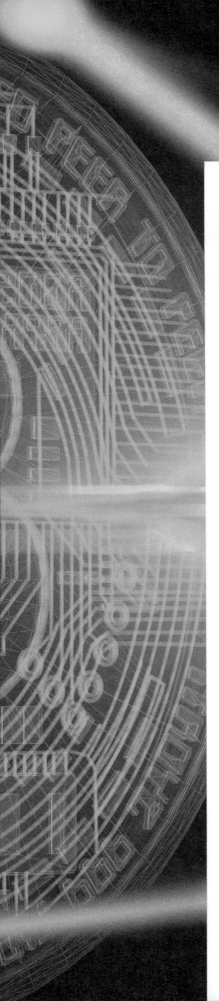

GEARING UP

Let us assume that there are two kinds of payment for work: cash payments, and money that is deposited directly into your bank account. Which method would you prefer? Why? What is the most common payment method in your community?

A. Working with a small group, list the advantages of cash payments and direct deposit payments in the table. When you have finished, discuss your ideas with the class.

ADVANTAGES OF CASH PAYMENTS	ADVANTAGES OF DIRECT DEPOSIT PAYMENTS TO YOUR BANK
• *you can be paid quickly*	• *you don't have to carry around cash*

B. Now, imagine a world in which no one had bank accounts. Money could be earned, transferred, and spent without the need for a bank account. Discuss with your class how your world be different. What advantages and disadvantages would there be? Would you be happy in this new world?

The world that digital currencies promise is one in which money is not tied to personal identification information or location. Throughout this chapter, we will consider what the world would be like if everyone used a digital currency like bitcoin.

Below are the key words you will practise in this chapter. Check the words you understand, then underline the words you use. Highlight the words you need to learn.

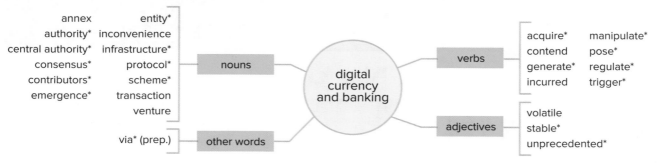

nouns

annex   entity*
authority*   inconvenience
central authority* infrastructure*
consensus*   protocol*
contributors* scheme*
emergence*   transaction
               venture

other words

via* (prep.)

digital currency and banking

verbs

acquire*   manipulate*
contend   pose*
generate*   regulate*
incurred   trigger*

adjectives

volatile
stable*
unprecedented*

* Appears on the Academic Word List

READING ❶ Digital Cash for a Digital Age

This reading demonstrates the power of digital currency. In this case, the author describes the benefits of a currency that is earned, distributed, and spent in ways that don't require personal identification.

In this chapter, *Bitcoin* (with a capital letter) is used to refer to the Bitcoin technology. When referring to the actual money, use *bitcoin* (with a small letter). Of course, at the beginning of a sentence, the first letter is always capitalized.

In this reading, you will see the word *annex* used as a noun multiple times. An annex usually refers to a separate building that has been added to a larger building. In this case, the word implies a protected space for creative people to work. You will see the word used in the names of two businesses: the **Film Annex** (an online site for people interested in movies) and the **Women's Annex** (a company that promotes education for women in Afghanistan).

A. Working with a partner, look at how the key words in bold are used in the following sentences. For each, fill in the part of speech in the parentheses: n. for noun; v. for verb; adj. for adjective. When you have finished, check your answers with a partner.

risk danger

❶ The Film Annex is a business **venture** (___*n.*___) that was founded by Francesco Rulli.

donor, grantor, patron, giver

❷ The many young women who write movie reviews and commentary for the Film Annex are **contributors** (_____) to the business.

worry, difficulty

❸ It is an **inconvenience** (_____) to send small amounts of regulated currency around the world because it is expensive and difficult.

provoke

❹ Francesco Rulli **incurred** (_____) high banking fees when he sent money to the people who **contributed** (_____) **to** the Film Annex.

project/plan of action

❺ People who don't understand how bitcoins are made and distributed believe they are a **scheme** (_____) to trick people out of their money.

6 The fact that the price of bitcoins is **volatile** (_____) adds to that impression.

7 Bitcoin's price **volatility** (_____) is **inconvenient** (_____). Its price keeps rising and falling, so it is hard to know how much a bitcoin will buy from day to day.

8 In the end, Ahmadi's persistence and her quality **contributions** (__n__) to the Film Annex earned her money.

B. Using the sentences above, write the different forms of the key words in the table below. Use context clues in the sentences to write a definition for each form of the word.

KEY WORDS	DEFINITIONS
1 *venture (n.)*	*business activity that may be risky*
2 *contributors (n.)* *contributed (v.)*	
3 *inconvenience (n.)*	
4 *incurred (v.)*	
5 *scheme (n.)*	
6 *volatile (adj.)*	

Before You Read

A. In this text, you will read about three people and three businesses. To help you keep the personal identities and business functions separate, scan the text, then match the name of the person or business in the first column to the appropriate description in the second column. When you are finished, compare your answers with a classmate's.

NAME OF PERSON / BUSINESS		DESCRIPTION
1 Parisa Ahmadi	_____	a) company that develops software, founded by Roya Mahboob
2 Roya Mahboob	_____	b) online American arts group that supports new filmmakers and uses social media to post movie reviews
3 Francesco Rulli	_____	c) organization that supports digital literacy classes for women in Afghanistan, co-founded by Roya Mahboob
4 Film Annex	_____	d) teenager in Afghanistan who was a top high school student
5 Women's Annex	_____	e) entrepreneur and founder of the Film Annex
6 Afghan Citadel Software Company	_____	f) businesswoman, CEO of Afghan Citadel Software Company

While You Read

B. This text alternates the story of Parisa Ahmadi with information about the Film Annex and bitcoin. As you read, write PA in the margin next to each paragraph that tells the story of Parisa Ahmadi, and write FA&B next to paragraphs that provide information about the Film Annex and bitcoin.

C. When you have finished, review your answers on your own by reading all the paragraphs about Parisa Ahmadi one after the other. If you have labelled the paragraphs correctly, you will have her complete story without reading (much) about the Film Annex and bitcoin.

Digital Cash for a Digital Age

> "Money won't create success; the freedom to make it will."
> - Nelson Mandela

_PA_

1. Even though Parisa Ahmadi was in the top of her class at the all-girls Hatifi High School in Herat, Afghanistan, her family was initially against her enrolling in classes
5   being offered by a private **venture** that promised to teach young girls Internet and social-media skills—and even pay them for their efforts. "Here in Afghanistan a woman's life is limited by her room's walls and school," she wrote in an email. In Afghanistan, girls are not exposed to the Internet, not at home and not at school. That's the way it might have stayed, too, if Ahmadi hadn't persisted. She was a top
10   student, and she wanted to take even more classes. In her mind, that was reason enough. She pressed her family, by her own admission, "a lot."

2. The venture backing these classes is the Film Annex, a US-based arts group that uses social media and an online site to pay the three hundred thousand bloggers and filmmakers who **contribute** their work. Film Annex ended up in Afghanistan

15 [through] its direct affiliation with the Women's Annex, a digital literacy program set up in conjunction with Afghan businesswoman Roya Mahboob, which now educates fifty thousand girls in schools across Afghanistan. Mahboob is something of a celebrity; named one of the one hundred most influential people in the world by *Time* magazine, she runs a software company called Afghan Citadel, is one of the

20 few female chief executive officers (CEOs) in Afghanistan, and has made education for Afghani women her central cause. The Women's Annex sets up its classrooms in local high schools, and the classes are taught by women. Because of this last feature, Ahmadi's family finally [agreed] and let her sign up.

_____ 3. Ahmadi started taking classes in 2013. She and her classmates were learning

25 about the World Wide Web, social media, and blogs. A movie lover who also loved to write about the movies that moved her, she began posting on a blog, and its members responded positively to her reviews, earning her the first real income of her young life.

_____ 4. Still, one of the other things most girls don't have in Afghanistan is a bank account.

30 If the Afghani teen ever had any money, she had to transfer it into her father's or brothers' bank accounts, and that's simply the way it is for most girls where she lives. In this sense, she was lucky—for many women from her background, male family members block them from access to their funds and treat the money as their own.

_____ 35 5. The Film Annex's New York-based founder, Francesco Rulli, aware of the difficulty faced by women like Ahmadi and frustrated by the transaction costs he incurred in sending relatively small amounts of money around the world, implemented a sweeping change to the Film Annex's payment system. He would pay his bloggers in bitcoin, the digital currency that had seemed to come out of nowhere in 2013,

40 with a small, fiercely dedicated band of tech-minded, **libertarian-leaning** digital **utopians** acting as its standard-bearers, and swearing to anybody who'd listen that it was going to change the world.

libertarian-leaning (adj.): believing that people should live without any government control

utopian (n.): someone who believes in a perfect world

_____ 6. Rulli … soon [understood bitcoin and] the advantages it could have for people like Ahmadi, who was one of the more than seven thousand young Afghani

45 women listed as paid **contributors** to the Film Annex. Bitcoins are stored in digital bank accounts or "wallets" that can be set up at home by anyone with Internet access. There is no trip to the bank to set up an account, no need for documentation or proof that you're a man. Indeed, bitcoin does not

50 know your name or gender, so it allows women in **patriarchal** societies, at least those with access to the Internet, to control their own money. The importance of this cannot be overstated. These women are building something that is theirs, not their fathers' or brothers'.

55 While not a [complete solution], this blast of cutting-edge, twenty-first-century technology offers real promise as a way to help [give some financial freedom to women in these countries].

patriarchal (adj.): ruled or controlled by men

_____ 7. Many Film Annex contributors in the United States,

60 the United Kingdom, Italy, and other rich countries grumbled about the **inconvenience** of the digital

currency. Few businesses, online or otherwise, accepted it for payment, and to many the whole thing seemed

dodgy (adj.): seeming to be false or dishonest

65 **dodgy**. The complaints aren't unique to Film Annex contributors; to many people bitcoin seems like a ... scam, some **scheme** to [steal money from] fools. Moreover, Ahmadi [struggles]

70 with the same issues related to bitcoin that her peers in other countries had grumbled about, in particular that the options for spending it are still limited, especially in an economy as underdeveloped as Afghanistan's. To deal with such

75 problems, the Film Annex set up an e-commerce site in 2014 allowing its members to trade bitcoins for gift cards from global sites such as Amazon that will ship to Kabul, Herat, and other Afghan cities. In effect, Film Annex is creating its own self-enclosed bitcoin economy ...

_____ 8. Ahmadi used her bitcoins to buy a new laptop. Only a few years ago, this would

80 have been impossible. She credits bitcoin with "teaching us how to be independent and how to decide by our own, and best of all, how to stand on our own feet."

appendage (n.): something that is connected to a larger or more important thing

It's allowed her to [think about] a future in which she isn't merely an **appendage** to the men in her life, a future in which she can chart her own course. "I see myself an educated and active female doctor in the future," she said.

_____ 85 9. You don't typically read stories like Ahmadi's in press coverage of bitcoin. Most of it has focused on the roller-coaster ride of what's seen as a suspect monetary concept. Ask people on the street what they know about bitcoin, and if they can answer anything at all, they'll likely cite the most prominent of those press reports. They'll say something about drug dealers who were busted using bitcoin on the

90 illicit Silk Road website. Or they'll refer to **volatile** price movements and utter the word "**bubble**." Or they might recall the sudden [disappearance] of a large number

bubble (n.): term used to refer to a rapid and significant increase in prices (e.g., of assets or shares) followed by a collapse in value

of bitcoins from a thing with the [strange] name of Mt. Gox, knowing little more than that it was a [little known] online exchange in Tokyo. Perhaps they know of the search for Satoshi Nakamoto, the shadowy figure who created bitcoin.

_____ 95 10. All of these elements of the circus sideshow that has arisen around bitcoin are both colourful and important to understanding its story. But to dismiss it as a **con**

con (n.): trick used to get someone's money or make them do something

because of them is to turn your back on something that may well change your life. Bitcoin is a groundbreaking digital technology with the potential to radically change the way [individuals] conduct banking and commerce, and to bring billions

100 of people from the emerging markets into a modern, integrated, digitized, globalized economy. If it works—and that's still a big if—an awful lot of things that today seem like part of the natural state of the world are going to look as old-fashioned as [the] printing press.

(1218 words)

Vigna, P., & Casey, M. (2015). *The age of cryptocurrency: How bitcoin and digital money are challenging the global economic order* (pp. 1–4). New York, NY: St. Martin's Press.

After You Read

D. Decide whether the following statements are true or false. For each false statement, write a true statement below it. When you are finished, compare your answers with a classmate's.

STATEMENTS	TRUE	FALSE
1 Parisa Ahmadi is a top student in Afghanistan who is driven to pursue further education in a country that does not fully support the education of women. _____ _____	*True*	
2 Ahmadi was able to learn about the Internet through courses offered by the Film Annex, owned by Roya Mahboob. _____ Francisco _____ _____	✗	✓
3 Because women can't have bank accounts in Afghanistan, the money Ahmadi earned was paid to her father, who withheld the money from her. _____ _____ _____		✓
4 Rulli paid bloggers with bitcoin to reduce the large transaction costs that were required to transfer small amounts of money around the globe. _____ _____	✓	
5 From the very beginning, the bloggers were happy to be paid with bitcoin. _____ _____	✓	✓
6 Rulli established a virtual marketplace where bloggers exchange bitcoin for gift cards with which they can purchase products from large international companies. _____ _____	✓	
7 Many people believe that bitcoin is used by drug dealers, or its value is too volatile, or it could be stolen somehow. _____ _____		
8 As a result, it is likely that bitcoin will soon lose its value and the people who do use it will return to using regulated currencies. _____ _____		

E. Answer the following questions. Then discuss the answers with your class.

1 Why do you think the author of this text alternated between writing about Parisa Ahmadi and presenting more technical information about bitcoin?

_____

_____

_____

_____

2 Now that you have completed the first reading, what do you think about bitcoin? Would you use it tomorrow? Why?

_____

_____

_____

My Bookshelf > My eLab >
Exercises > Chapter 6 >
Digital Cash for a Digital Age

Exam

FOCUS ON READING

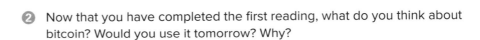

Annotating Readings

Reading in an additional language can be rewarding, but it can also be difficult and time consuming. Usually, once you have made the effort and taken the time to read an academic text, you don't want to have to read it again when you study for a test or exam. How can you remember what you have read and review it quickly to help you prepare for an exam? One solution to this challenge is to annotate your texts as you read.

Annotating texts means taking notes as you read. You may already do this. If so, discuss with your class what you do as you read to annotate the text.

Common text elements to annotate

- Main points and important ideas
- Points in a list or argument
- Key words
- Unfamiliar words
- Concepts you don't understand
- Elements you have questions about
- Aspects that remind you of something else you have read
- Your own opinion about what the author has written

Common annotation techniques

- Highlight (possibly in colours)
- Underline
- Circle
- Create an outline of the reading so the organization is clear in your mind.
- Write in point form in the margins of the text.

Annotating is a unique process; your annotations may not look the same as your partner's, but they are essential to help you review information quickly. You will practise annotating the next reading.

Frequently Asked Questions from the Bitcoin Website

This reading is from the bitcoin website. Written in a Frequently Asked Questions format (question and answer), the text responds to all the practical questions people have about bitcoin currency.

VOCABULARY BUILD

Explore key words from Reading 2 while you build your knowledge of synonyms—an important strategy for developing your paraphrasing skills.

A. Read the sentences in column one. For each bold word or phrase, write the best synonym from the box in the second column; then think of at least one more synonym. When you are finished, you will have at least two synonyms for each key word or phrase. Confirm your answers with your class.

(handwritten: Exam)

| agreement | business deal | government control | influence | ~~obtain~~ |
| plan of action | set of rules | steady | | |

(handwritten: how identify key word in a text)

SENTENCES WITH KEY WORDS OR PHRASES	SYNONYMS
❶ How does one **acquire** bitcoins?	*obtain, get, gain, earn*
❷ Bitcoin is the first decentralized peer-to-peer payment network that is powered by its users with no **central authority.**	*agre·*
❸ Bitcoin can only work correctly with a complete **consensus** among all users.	consent, agreement
❹ No central authority or developer has any power to **manipulate** the system to increase their profits.	handle or control operate, employ, utilize
❺ The Bitcoin **protocol** is designed in such a way that new bitcoins are created at a fixed rate.	agreement, Treaty ritual, procedure Conversion
❻ No one knows what the demand for bitcoins will be. This means the bitcoin price is not **stable.**	sturdy, fixed, steady firm
❼ Each **transaction** is protected by digital signatures corresponding to the sending addresses, allowing all users to have full control over sending bitcoins from their own Bitcoin addresses.	

Before You Read

A. If you were going to use bitcoin tomorrow to pay for a new computer, what questions would you have about the digital currency? With a small group of students, brainstorm a list of questions to which you would need answers before you used bitcoin.

B. Once you have finished, skim Reading 2 to identify which of your questions it asks and answers. Which of your questions are the same as the ones in Reading 2?

While You Read

C. In order to remember information from Reading 2, annotate the text as you read. Remember, the aim is to be able to simply reread your annotations (rather than the full text) when you want to review.

Frequently Asked Questions from the Bitcoin Website

1. What is Bitcoin?

Bitcoin is a consensus network that enables a new payment system and a completely digital money. It is the first decentralized peer-to-peer payment network that is powered by its users with no **central authority**. From a user perspective, Bitcoin is
5 pretty much like cash for the Internet. Bitcoin can also be seen as the most prominent triple-entry bookkeeping system in existence.

2. Who created Bitcoin?

Bitcoin is the first implementation of a concept called *cryptocurrency*, which was first described in 1998 by Wei Dai on the cypherpunks' mailing list, suggesting the idea
10 of a new form of money that uses cryptography to control its creation and **transactions**, rather than a central authority. The first Bitcoin specification and proof of concept was published in 2009 in a cryptography mailing list by Satoshi Nakamoto. Satoshi left the project in late 2010 without revealing much about himself. The community has since grown exponentially with many developers working on Bitcoin.

15 Satoshi's anonymity often raised unjustified concerns, many of which are linked to misunderstanding of the open-source nature of Bitcoin. The Bitcoin **protocol** and software are published openly and any developer around the world can review the code or make their own modified version of the Bitcoin software. Just like current developers, Satoshi's influence was limited to the changes he made being
20 adopted by others and therefore, he did not control Bitcoin. As such, the identity of Bitcoin's inventor is probably as relevant today as the identity of the person who invented paper.

3. Who controls the Bitcoin network?

Nobody owns the Bitcoin network, much like no one owns the technology behind
25 email. Bitcoin is controlled by all Bitcoin users around the world. While developers are improving the software, they can't force a change in the Bitcoin protocol because all users are free to choose what software and version they use. In order to stay compatible with each other, all users need to use software **complying** with the same rules. Bitcoin can only work correctly with a complete **consensus** among all users.
30 Therefore, all users and developers have a strong incentive to protect this consensus.

complying (v.): obeying a command or rule

4. How does Bitcoin work?

From a user perspective, Bitcoin is nothing more than a mobile app or computer program that provides a personal Bitcoin wallet and allows a user to send and receive bitcoins with them. This is how Bitcoin works for most users.

ledger (n.): book in which a business's expenses and revenues are recorded

35 Behind the scenes, the Bitcoin network is sharing a public **ledger** called *the block chain*. This ledger contains every transaction ever processed, allowing a user's computer to verify the validity of each transaction. The authenticity of each transaction is protected by digital signatures corresponding to the sending addresses, allowing all users to

have full control over sending bitcoins from their own
40 Bitcoin addresses. In addition, anyone can process transactions using the computing power of specialized hardware and earn a reward in bitcoins for this service. This is often called *mining*.

5. Is Bitcoin really used by people?

45 Yes. There are a growing number of businesses and individuals using Bitcoin. This includes brick and mortar businesses like restaurants, apartments, law firms, and popular online services such as Namecheap, WordPress, and Reddit. While Bitcoin remains a
50 relatively new phenomenon, it is growing fast. At the end of August 2013, the value of all bitcoins in circulation exceeded US$1.5 billion with millions of dollars worth of bitcoins exchanged daily.

6. How does one acquire bitcoins?

55 • Receive as payment for goods or services.

• Purchase bitcoins at a Bitcoin exchange.

• Exchange bitcoins with someone near you.

• Earn bitcoins through competitive mining.

7. How difficult is it to make a Bitcoin payment?

60 Bitcoin payments are easier to make than debit or credit card purchases, and can be received without a merchant account. Payments are made from a wallet application, either on your computer or smartphone, by entering the recipient's address and the payment amount, and pressing send. To make it easier to enter a recipient's address, many wallets can obtain the address by scanning a QR [quick response] code or
65 touching two phones together with NFC [near-field communication] technology.

8. What are the advantages of Bitcoin?

• *Payment freedom* – It is possible to send and receive bitcoins anywhere in the world at any time. No bank holidays. No borders. No bureaucracy. Bitcoin allows its users to be in full control of their money.

70 • *Choose your own fees* – There is no fee to receive bitcoins, and many wallets let you control how large a fee to pay when spending. Higher fees can encourage faster confirmation of your transactions. Fees are unrelated to the amount transferred, so it's possible to send a hundred thousand bitcoins for the same fee it costs to send one bitcoin. Additionally, merchant processors exist to assist
75 merchants in processing transactions, converting bitcoins to **fiat** currency and depositing funds directly into merchants' bank accounts daily. As these services are based on Bitcoin, they can be offered for much lower fees than with PayPal or credit card networks.

• *Fewer risks for merchants* – Bitcoin transactions are secure, irreversible, and do
80 not contain customers' sensitive or personal information. This protects merchants from losses caused by fraud or fraudulent chargebacks, and there is no need for Payment Card Industry (PCI) compliance. Merchants can easily expand to

fiat (adj.) currency: government supported money

new markets where either credit cards are not available or fraud rates are unacceptably high. The net results are lower fees, larger markets, and fewer administrative costs.

- *Security and control* – Bitcoin users are in full control of their transactions; it is impossible for merchants to force unwanted or unnoticed charges as can happen with other payment methods. Bitcoin payments can be made without personal information tied to the transaction. This offers strong protection against identity theft. Bitcoin users can also protect their money with backup and encryption.

- *Transparent and neutral* – All information concerning the Bitcoin money supply itself is readily available on the block chain for anybody to verify and use in real time. No individual or organization can control or **manipulate** the Bitcoin protocol because it is cryptographically secure. This allows the core of Bitcoin to be trusted for being completely neutral, **transparent** and predictable.

9. What are the disadvantages of Bitcoin?

- *Degree of acceptance* – Many people are still unaware of Bitcoin. Every day, more businesses accept bitcoins because they want the advantages of doing so, but the list remains small and still needs to grow in order to benefit from network effects.

- *Volatility* – The total value of bitcoins in circulation and the number of businesses using Bitcoin are still very small compared to what they could be. Therefore, relatively small events, trades, or business activities can significantly affect the price. In theory, this **volatility** will decrease as Bitcoin markets and the technology matures. Never before has the world seen a start-up currency, so it is truly difficult (and exciting) to imagine how it will play out.

- *Ongoing development* – Bitcoin software is still **in beta** with many incomplete features in active development. New tools, features, and services are being developed to make Bitcoin more secure and accessible to the masses. Some of these are still not ready for everyone. Most Bitcoin businesses are new and still offer no insurance. In general, Bitcoin is still in the process of maturing.

10. How are bitcoins created?

New bitcoins are generated by a competitive and decentralized process called *mining*. This process involves individuals who are rewarded by the network for their services. Bitcoin miners are processing transactions and securing the network using specialized hardware and are collecting new bitcoins in exchange.

[Because bitcoin is a triple-entry bookkeeping system, it requires three records of each transaction. The first two people who record a transaction are the buyer and the seller. However, before the money can change "wallets," a third person must approve the transaction. This third person records the transaction (cryptographically) and is rewarded by a small fee, paid in bitcoins. These people are mining bitcoins. Once the third person recognizes the transfer, the money can change wallets.]

The Bitcoin protocol is designed in such a way that new bitcoins are created at a fixed rate. This makes Bitcoin mining a very competitive business. When more miners join the network, it becomes increasingly difficult to make a profit and miners must seek efficiency to cut their operating costs. No central authority or developer has any power to control or manipulate the system to increase its profits. Every Bitcoin node in the world will reject anything that does not comply with the rules it expects the system to follow.

Bitcoins are created at a decreasing and predictable rate. The number of new bitcoins
130 created each year is automatically halved over time until bitcoin issuance halts completely
with a total of twenty-one million bitcoins in existence. At this point, Bitcoin miners
will probably be supported exclusively by numerous small transaction fees.

11. Why do bitcoins have value?

Bitcoins have value because they are useful as a form of money. Bitcoin has the
135 characteristics of money (**durability**, portability, **fungibility**, scarcity, divisibility, and
recognizability) based on the properties of mathematics rather than relying on physical
properties (like gold and silver) or trust in central authorities (like fiat currencies).
In short, Bitcoin is backed by mathematics. With these attributes, all that is required
for a form of money to hold value is trust and adoption. In the case of Bitcoin, this
140 can be measured by its growing base of users, merchants, and start-ups. As with all
currency, bitcoins' value comes only and directly from people willing to accept them
as payment.

12. What determines bitcoin's price?

The price of a bitcoin is determined by supply and demand. When demand for bitcoins
145 increases, the price increases, and when demand falls, the price falls. There is only
a limited number of bitcoins in circulation and new bitcoins are created at a predictable
and decreasing rate, which means that demand must follow this level of inflation
to keep the price **stable**. Because Bitcoin is still a relatively small market compared
to what it could be, it doesn't take significant amounts of money to move the market
150 price up or down, and thus the price of a bitcoin is still very volatile.

13. Can bitcoins become worthless?

Yes. History is littered with currencies that failed and are no longer used, such as
the German mark during the Weimar Republic and, more recently, the Zimbabwean
dollar. Although previous currency failures were typically due to hyperinflation of a
155 kind that Bitcoin makes impossible, there is always potential for technical failures,
competing currencies, political issues, and so on. As a basic **rule of thumb**, no
currency should be considered absolutely safe from failures or hard times. Bitcoin
has proven reliable for years since its inception and there is a lot of potential for
Bitcoin to continue to grow. However, no one is in a position to predict what the future
160 will be for Bitcoin.

(1814 words)

_____
Bitcoin Project (2017). Frequently asked questions. Retrieved from https://bitcoin.org/en/faq

durability (adj.): ability
to remain in good
condition after
a lot of use

fungibility (adj.):
exchangeability

rule of thumb (exp.):
general principle that
is good to follow

After You Read

D. Compare your annotations with a partner's. Although your annotations will be
different, it should be interesting to compare the main points. Use the comparison
to confirm that you successfully annotated the main points. Share your opinion
about Bitcoin with your partner. Do you have similar or differing opinions?

E. Still working with your partner, answer the following questions, referring only
to your annotations. (The numbers in parentheses refer to the questions in
the reading where you can find the answers.)

1 What are the main characteristics of Bitcoin? (questions 1 to 4)

_____

_____

_____

2 Who uses bitcoins, and how do they acquire them? (questions 5 and 6)

_____

_____

_____

3 List the advantages and disadvantages of bitcoins in the table below. (questions 7, 8, 9)

ADVANTAGES	DISADVANTAGES
• *Bitcoin payments are easy to make.*	

4 To demonstrate your understanding of questions 10 to 13 in the reading, indicate if the statements below are true or false. When you are finished, compare your answers with a partner's.

STATEMENTS	TRUE	FALSE
a) The process of creating bitcoins is called mining.	✓	
b) The people who "mine" bitcoins acquire them by processing transactions for a fee (paid in bitcoins).		
c) The Bitcoin protocol can be hacked and manipulated for profit.		
d) The Bitcoin protocol is controlled by a central bank.		
e) The number of bitcoins is infinite.		
f) Bitcoins have value because people accept them as a form of exchange for goods and service.		
g) The value of a bitcoin is determined by supply and demand.		
h) The value of a bitcoin is stable.		
i) Bitcoins will continue to hold their value; they are a reliable investment.		

My Bookshelf > My eLab >
Exercises > Chapter 6 >
Frequently Asked Questions

Avoiding Plagiarism by Paraphrasing

As you now know, copying another person's words or ideas is called *plagiarism*, and it is considered an academic "crime." In Chapter 5, you learned why plagiarism is a serious concern and how you can avoid it by providing references for quoted information. You can also avoid plagiarism by paraphrasing. However, even if you choose to paraphrase another person's words or ideas, you will still need to provide an in-text citation and reference your source.

Although you may use quotations to express specific ideas, it is best to use your own words in your written assignments. Expressing another person's ideas in your own words is called *paraphrasing*.

Here are the characteristics of a good paraphrase:

- The paraphrase has the same meaning as the original text.
- The paraphrase is roughly the same length as the original writing.
- The paraphrase rephrases the original words and structures, except for technical words or very common words ("public domain" words).

The following techniques will help you paraphrase successfully. Usually, you will use more than one technique.

Use appropriate synonyms.

Examples:

money	→ currency	earn money	→ make money
organization	→ institution	backing a cause	→ supporting an issue
volatile	→ unstable	sweeping change	→ complete overhaul

Some words, such as the names of specific people, countries, and religions, and scientific terms, cannot be changed.

Change the sentence type.

Ask yourself, "What sentence structure is used in the original writing?" Once you have answered this question, you can change the sentence structure to avoid plagiarism.

Original source (single independent clause + prepositional phrase)
Bitcoin is a groundbreaking digital technology with the potential to radically change the way individuals conduct banking and commerce.

Change the sentence structure to independent clause + dependent clause + phrase.
Individuals could radically change the way they conduct banking and commerce if they used Bitcoin, the groundbreaking digital technology.

Add appropriate synonyms.
People can completely overhaul their banking and business transactions if they adopt Bitcoin, the innovative digital currency.

Change the voice from active to passive, or from passive to active.

Original source (active voice)
In Afghanistan, the Women's Annex offers classes on social media
and the Internet to independent-minded young women.

Change to passive voice.
In Afghanistan, classes on social media and the Internet are offered
to independent-minded young women by the Women's Annex.

Add appropriate synonyms.
In Afghanistan, social media courses are taught by the Women's Annex
to support the digital education of aspiring teenage girls.

Change the parts of speech.

Change nouns to verbs, adjectives to adverbs, verbs to adjectives,
adjectives to nouns, and so on.

Original source
The Film Annex's founder (n.), Francesco Rulli, aware (adj.) of the difficulty (n.)
faced by women like Ahmadi and frustrated (adj.) by the transaction costs
he incurred in sending relatively small amounts of money around the world,
implemented (v.) a sweeping change to the Film Annex's payment system.

Change the parts of speech wherever possible.
Francesco Rulli founded (v.) the Film Annex. He had an awareness (n.) of how
difficult (adj.) it was for women like Ahmadi, and a frustration (n.) with the high
transaction costs he incurred sending relatively small amounts of money around
the world, so he decided to implement (v.; infinitive form) a sweeping change
to the Film Annex's payment system.

Add appropriate synonyms.
Francesco Rulli established the Film Annex. He realized how hard it was
for women like Ahmadi, and how expensive it was to send comparatively
insignificant amounts of currency across borders, so he took action to
completely overhaul the way the Film Annex paid its contributors.

Change the sentence structure and voice (from active to passive).
The Film Annex was established (passive) by Francesco Rulli. He realized
how hard it was for women like Ahmadi, and how expensive it was to send
comparatively insignificant amounts of currency across borders, so the way
the Film Annex paid its contributors was completely overhauled (passive).

Quick tips to help you paraphrase successfully.

• You must understand the original writing before you try to paraphrase it.

• You may need to use more than one technique to paraphrase well.

• When you have finished your paraphrase, check to make sure that
it makes sense.

A. With one or two partners, paraphrase the following sentences in writing.

1 Although many people are skeptical that bitcoin will hold its value, other people believe it will completely overhaul national and international banking systems.

_____

_____

2 The Film Annex set up an e-commerce website; consequently, its contributing bloggers can purchase gift cards for products sold by large retailers.

The film owner has created on e-commerce website so that contributing bloggers can now buy gift cards for goods offered by big retailers

B. Compare your answers with those of other students. Identify the paraphrasing techniques that work particularly well. Why do they work so well?

WARM-UP ASSIGNMENT
Paraphrase a Paragraph

Using the techniques you have just learned, on a separate page, paraphrase the following two paragraphs from Reading 2. You will include these paraphrases in the cause and effect essay you will write for the Final Assignment.

1. Bitcoin is a consensus network that enables a new payment system and a completely digital money. It is the first decentralized peer-to-peer payment network that is powered by its users with no central authority. From a user perspective, Bitcoin is pretty much like cash for the Internet. Bitcoin can also be seen as the most prominent triple-entry bookkeeping system in existence.

2. Bitcoin payments are easier to make than debit or credit card purchases, and can be received without a merchant account. Payments are made from a wallet application, either on your computer or smartphone, by entering the recipient's address and the payment amount, and pressing send. To make it easier to enter a recipient's address, many wallets can obtain the address by scanning a quick response (QR) code or touching two phones together with near-field communication (NFC) technology.

Bitcoin Project (2017). Frequently asked questions. Retrieved from https://bitcoin.org/en/faq

> When you receive feedback from your teacher on this Warm-Up Assignment, you will have information that you can use to improve your writing.

Writing Conditional Sentences

Conditional sentences are useful when you want to predict possible outcomes in the face of uncertainty. They include an *if-clause* and a *main clause*. The likelihood of the outcome in the main clause depends on the condition expressed in the if-clause.

IF-CLAUSE (CONDITION)	MAIN CLAUSE (OUTCOME)
If people use bitcoins,	their value will increase.

There are three types of conditional sentences.

First conditional: a possibility in the present or future

These sentences show that the condition is possible.

IF + PRESENT TENSE	WILL + SIMPLE FORM
If people reject bitcoins,	their value will decrease.
	the currency will not succeed.

IF + PRESENT TENSE	CAN + SIMPLE FORM
If people mine bitcoins consistently,	they can earn a significant amount of currency.
	they can spend the money on anything they want.

Second conditional: unlikely present or future

These sentences show that the condition is unlikely.

IF + PAST TENSE	WOULD + SIMPLE FORM
If only criminals used Bitcoin,	regular people would refuse to use the currency.
	the currency would not be popular.

IF + PAST TENSE	COULD + SIMPLE FORM
If governments and banks adopted Bitcoin,	everyone could use the currency for all financial transactions.
	people could not avoid taxes by using bitcoins.

Third conditional: impossible past

These sentences show that the condition is impossible because the time for action has already passed.

IF + PAST PERFECT TENSE	WOULD HAVE + PAST PARTICIPLE
If the fees for bitcoin transactions had been high,	fewer people would have understood the benefits of the currency.
	people would not have adopted the currency so quickly.

IF + PAST PERFECT TENSE	COULD HAVE + PAST PARTICIPLE
If Satoshi Nakamoto had revealed his true identity,	the police could have arrested him.
	reporters could not have written so many stories.

A. Complete the following sentences by writing a main clause corresponding to the if-clause. The verb tense in the if-clause is provided (in parentheses) for the first four sentences.

① (present) If you send money to someone in another country,
you can save transaction fees by sending bitcoins.

② (past perfect) If Wei Dai had not written about cryptocurrency in 1998,
_____

③ (present) If people have a positive experience with bitcoins,
no one will ~~used~~ cash.

④ (past) If someone wanted to control the bitcoin network,
_____

⑤ If merchants want to avoid high transaction fees,
_____

⑥ If the Film Annex had not used bitcoins to pay Parisa Ahmadi,
_____

⑦ If more businesses use Bitcoin, I ~~would~~ will established my own
Business
_____ past

⑧ If employers began to pay their employees with bitcoins,
I will be more productive, it would be ~~unconditionally~~
under pay
their employe

⑨ If bitcoin payments were more complicated to make,
_____

⑩ If Nakamoto had known in advance about Bitcoin's success,
_____

My Bookshelf > My eLab > Exercises > Chapter 6 > Focus on Accuracy

---

FOCUS ON WRITING

Writing in the Third Person

Most academic writing is in the third person and the present tense because
- an academic perspective (third person) is needed to show objectivity (see Chapter 5, page 129); and
- academic writing discusses facts or repeated actions (present tense).

Writers may choose to use the third-person *singular* perspective (*he, she, it, everybody, anyone, nothing*) or the third-person *plural* perspective (*they*).

If you use the third-person singular perspective, you may have problems with a) subject-verb agreement in the present tense, and b) pronoun-antecedent agreement.

Subject-verb agreement in the present tense

Remember to add *–s* or *–es* to a verb in the present tense to agree with a third-person singular subject. Subject-verb agreement must also be respected in relative clauses.

PROBLEM: Often students forget to make verbs agree with third-person singular subjects.

SOLUTION: Switch to a third-person plural perspective.

SINGULAR SUBJECT / PRESENT TENSE	PLURAL SUBJECT / PRESENT TENSE
A *merchant receives* bitcoins for goods or services.	*Merchants receive* bitcoins for goods or services.
Fear of price volatility *prevents* many people from investing in bitcoins. (Problem: subject separated from its verb by a phrase)	*Fears* of price volatility *prevent* many people from investing in bitcoins.
Extensive media coverage, which *increases* awareness of bitcoin price volatility, often *does not report on* the real benefits of digital currencies. (Problems: no plural form of *media coverage, and verbs in both clauses must agree with subject*)	*Extensive media reports,* which *increase* awareness of bitcoin price volatility, often *do not reflect* the real benefits of digital currency.
Investors want all possible *information* that *relates* to Bitcoin before they invest in it. (Problem: no plural form of *information*)	Investors want all possible *facts* that *relate* to Bitcoin before they invest in it.

Pronoun-antecedent agreement with the third-person singular

Remember to make pronouns agree in number and gender with their antecedents (corresponding nouns).

PROBLEM: Using singular pronouns can be awkward, or can exclude either males or females.

SOLUTION: Switch to a third-person plural perspective.

SINGULAR SUBJECT/PRESENT TENSE	PLURAL SUBJECT/PRESENT TENSE
A bitcoin *investor* may think *he or she* is well informed about bitcoin value, but *he or she* may be mistaken and lose *his or her* money. (Problem: awkward)	Bitcoin *investors* may think *they* are well informed about bitcoin value, but *they* may be mistaken and lose *their* money.
A bitcoin *user* may realize the benefits *she* receives by using digital currency, and *she* may try to use the currency more often. (Problem: excludes male bitcoin users)	*Bitcoin users* may realize the benefits *they receive* by using digital currency, and *they* may try to use the currency more often.

Of course, it isn't always possible to switch to a third-person plural subject. In those cases, you can look for these specific errors (subject-verb agreement and pronoun-antecedent agreement) once you have completed a draft of the writing.

 Exam

A. Revise the following sentences to eliminate problems that occur when writing in the third-person *singular* perspective. Change these sentences to the third-person *plural* perspective to correct the problems.

1. A new bitcoin investors should be well informed about digital currency so she *they are* isn't surprised by price volatility.

   A new bitcoin _____

   _____

2. A *people* person who mine bitcoins will earn fees for approving transactions between two other people.

   _____

   _____

3. An advantages of bitcoins that reduce the cost of banking include low transaction fees.

   _____

   _____

4. The developer of bitcoins was *were* very smart. He or she *They* created a decentralized currency of exchange that his or her *Their* colleagues could develop further.

   _____

   _____

5. A young woman who live in a patriarchal society can earn and keep bitcoins because Bitcoin does not have a central authority that requires proof that she is a man. *They are*

   _____

   _____

My Bookshelf > My eLab > Exercises > Chapter 6 > Focus on Writing

FOCUS ON CRITICAL THINKING

Contextualizing Information

Often, when we read about a new topic (especially in our second or additional languages), we automatically accept what we read. After all, understanding the new information is difficult enough; it requires even more effort to question that information. However, the ability to question information is a useful academic skill because it allows us to understand the material more deeply and develop our own opinions about it.

One way to question new information is to contextualize it, or place it in a larger context. For example, you may read about a zoo purchasing rare animals and trying to breed them. This is interesting in itself, but if you ask why the zoo does this, you may also learn that the animals are endangered, and that the zoo is attempting to preserve the species. The larger context is the zoo's concern for endangered species, which motivates it to try to save the animals.

▶

It is possible to place almost any new information in a larger context to reveal why people do what they do, or why things are the way they are. We can use this approach to contextualize information about Bitcoin as well. For example, we might ask, "Why is Bitcoin so popular now?" The answer will reveal why Bitcoin exists, explain what problems Bitcoin solves, and outline the conditions that have led to Bitcoin's success.

A. Here are some statements about Bitcoin's unique characteristics. First with a partner, then with your class, discuss the larger context that makes these characteristics important.

1 Bitcoin does not need a central authority to control it.

2 There are (almost) no fees to use bitcoins to complete a transaction.

3 There is a limited number of bitcoins.

Finding the larger context for Bitcoin can help you understand the underlying problems that Bitcoin solves. Contextualizing information about Bitcoin will prepare you for the Final Assignment.

READING ③ The Rise of Bitcoin

This reading explains the global circumstances that encouraged Satoshi Nakamoto to develop Bitcoin. It also lists the reasons why Bitcoin has continued to attract global attention.

VOCABULARY BUILD

A. Read the sentences and match the key words to their definitions.

SENTENCES		DEFINITIONS
❶ Many millennials (people born between 1980 and 2000) had to **contend with** high unemployment and scarce economic opportunities at a time when they were establishing their careers.	_____	a) something that exists as a single unit or business
❷ The **emergence** of digital natives and smart cities has generated even more interest in the development of cryptocurrency.	_____	b) existed in a way that might have caused problems; presented
❸ For the first time, governments realized the decentralized nature of this currency creates great problems for any central authority that intends to control an **entity.**	_____	c) causing an event or situation to happen very quickly
❹ Digital currency continues to **generate** interest among those who are uncomfortable with the national currencies of some central governments.	_____	d) deal with (e.g., something unpleasant or difficult)
❺ The technology that is developed in cyberspace will be of great interest in countries that spend billions preparing their **infrastructure** for a digital economy.	_____	e) process of beginning to be visible or known

SENTENCES		DEFINITIONS
6 Never before has technology invention attracted so much attention and **posed** so many challenges as it involves international finance, monetary systems, and innovative financial technology with cybersecurity.	_____	f) basic systems and structures a country or organization requires to run (i.e., banking systems, roads, buildings, etc.)
7 There are too many participants in Bitcoin for anyone to effectively monitor and **regulate** the currency single-handedly.	_____	g) by means of, through
8 The financial market crash started in the United States and soon spilled over to Europe and Asia, thereby **triggering** the global financial crisis in a time-compressed manner.	_____	h) produce or cause
9 Governments responded to the financial crisis with **unprecedented** monetary policy expansion and fiscal stimulus which caused high inflation.	_____	i) control an activity or a process through rules
10 The white paper by Satoshi Nakamoto first appeared on the Internet **via** the Cryptography Mailing List in November 2008.	_____	j) never done or known before

My Bookshelf > My eLab >
Exercises > Chapter 6 >
Vocabulary Review

Before You Read

A. Bitcoin became popular after the global financial crisis of 2008. Read the following statements, and check the ones you understand. Discuss the statements you don't understand with your class. Understanding this information will help you with Reading 3.

STATEMENTS ABOUT MONETARY POLICY AND BITCOIN	I UNDERSTAND
1 The global financial crisis began in the United States, but it quickly became a global concern.	☐
2 Initially, governments responded to the crisis by printing more money (called quantitative easing). When governments print more money, the prices of assets increase. This is inflation.	☐
3 Bitcoins are limited in number. This means there can be no quantitative easing with bitcoins. As a result, bitcoins do not encourage inflation.	☐
4 Governments regulate their national currencies. This means they control the supply of money and work with the banks to manage financial transactions. Governments tax financial transactions. For example, in many countries, employers pay their employees by depositing money in their bank accounts. Governments tax that money.	☐
5 As governments don't regulate Bitcoin, they cannot tax bitcoin transactions.	☐
6 The global financial crisis led to many social movements that push governments and banks to be more financially inclusive. Members of these social movements believe financial policy should encourage more equitable distribution of money among wealthy and less wealthy people.	☐
7 People who have less money may not have bank accounts. Bankers refer to these people as "unbanked." Bitcoin allows for cheap financial transactions (no banking fees) that are unregulated (not taxed). This suggests that "unbanked" people may be able to participate more in the economy using bitcoins as a currency for exchange.	☐

While You Read

B. Using the techniques you learned in Focus on Reading (page 158), annotate this text as you read.

The Rise of Bitcoin

The year 2008 has left a deep and lasting impression on the millennial [generation, those people who were] born in the early 1980s to early 2000s. It was the year of the financial market crash that started in the United States and soon spilled over to Europe and Asia, thereby **triggering** the global financial crisis in a time-compressed
5 manner. While governments responded with **unprecedented** monetary policy expansion and fiscal stimulus, many millennials had to **contend with** high unemployment and scarce economic opportunities at a time when they were establishing their careers. But few realize their lives have been shaped not only by happenings on Wall Street and Main Street but also by technology. They will remember 2008 as the
10 beginning of the peer-to-peer decentralized cryptocurrency called the Bitcoin protocol. The **white paper** by Satoshi Nakamoto first appeared on the Internet **via** the Cryptography Mailing List in November 2008 ... after the global financial crisis [had begun, making] a significant contribution to the world without actually being published in an academic journal.

white paper (n.): official governmental report explaining ideas and plans before they become law

15 Since then, the white paper ... has **generated** a lot of interest [for a wide range of reasons]. First, the timing of the release was a direct response to a crisis of confidence in reserve currency, and there was no better time than 2008. Faced with an era of disquiet and gradual loss of trust in the fiat currency system introduced in 1971, as well as the prospect of massive printing of money known as quantitative easing, the
20 white paper offers a set of feasible alternative solutions to those who have little faith in a centralized monetary system. Cryptocurrency was first introduced in the early 1990s by academic entrepreneur David Chaum in the form of eCash and DigiCash. The National Security Agency released an analytic report of great significance on the same subject over the Internet in 1996. But few in the financial world paid much
25 attention to the development of cryptocurrency until the global financial crisis. It only caught the attention of many financial experts when successive quantitative easings pushed up asset prices [and caused high inflation.] ... Cryptocurrency, a special class of digital currency, continues to generate interest among those who are uncomfortable with the national currencies of some central governments [that are struggling with]
30 huge liability, rather than backed by assets.

Second, the white paper of Satoshi was the first paper that proposed a distributed monetary system and challenged the central authority that controlled money supply. The proposed system was designed to address some of the issues that a centralized system could not. In particular, control was decentralized and the supply of money
35 was predetermined. Given the open-source nature of the Bitcoin protocol, there are too many participants for anyone to effectively monitor and **regulate** [the currency] single-handedly. For the first time, governments realized the decentralized nature [of this system] poses great problems for anyone who intends to regulate a legal **entity** or small number of entities, let alone to hold them responsible for any wrongdoing.

40 Third, there are a lot of unanswered questions about the Bitcoin system, thus creating curiosity among those who follow its development. In particular, the identity of the creator or group of creators of Bitcoin remains a mystery. While there have been

many attempts to uncover the mystery surrounding Mr. Nakamoto, including at least one hacker who
45 claimed to know the identity of Mr. Nakamoto after gaining access to his email account, Mr. Nakamoto's identity is still unknown to the public. The mysterious nature surrounding Bitcoin has generated even more following. The community remains amazed at the
50 foresight of the creator(s) and respects the reason for remaining **under the radar**.

under the radar (exp.): unknown or unnoticed

in the spotlight (exp.): in a position to receive a lot of attention (especially from the media)

Fourth, the Bitcoin invention has put regulators **in the spotlight**. Any attempt to regulate the cryptocurrency protocol has proved to be extremely
55 difficult. However, regulators have managed to study the issues carefully … and have focused on the areas of consumer protection, anti-money laundering, and counterterrorist financing. The balance between regulation and entrepreneurship has proved to be most challenging to achieve. This has therefore attracted a lot of
60 attention from tax authorities, central bankers, and [police]. Never before has technology invention attracted so much attention and **posed** so many challenges as it involves international finance, monetary systems, and innovative financial technology with cybersecurity.

Fifth, the income and wealth inequality of the world has risen rapidly since the
65 quantitative easings. [… Now,] governments are focusing on financial inclusion. Bitcoin provides a cheap form of payment system and that possibility has put cryptocurrency **in the limelight** as an alternative payment system. Organizations such as the Bill and Melinda Gates Foundation have made payment systems one of their priorities, together with the Maya Declaration initiated by the Alliance for Financial Inclusion.
70 We can see that Bitcoin will share the limelight with those serving the 2.5 billion unbanked [people] and attract the attention of those who are engaged in impact investing as advocated by the Global Impact Investing Network. Both financial inclusion and impact investing are areas of great interest and cryptocurrency is in the right space.

in the limelight (exp.): in a position to receive a lot of attention (especially from the media)

75 Sixth, cryptocurrency has contributed to innovation, and we have seen many interesting developments. It is said that the best brains are [working] in cryptocurrency because it is not only a currency but also a form of programmable money. The developers will be able to program in a way to serve the intended purpose. These innovations include smart accounting, smart contracts, crowdsourcing, crowdfunding, crypto-
80 equity, and many other [applications] that can change the way business is done and managed. The consensus ledger, digital register, and Blockchain are an emerging class of technology for the future. It is likely that there will be acceleration in the development of Bitcoin 2.0, blockchain 2.0, and sidechains, with new development only limited by our imagination.

85 Seventh, the **emergence** of digital natives and smart cities has generated even more interest in the development of cryptocurrency. Cities such as Singapore will [be entirely] connected to the digital world, with projected growth coming from the digital economy. Its citizens will be natives of the digital world. The technology that is developed in cyberspace will be of great interest in these countries that spend millions

90 or billions in getting their **infrastructure** [ready] for a digital economy. Incentives for start-ups will get more interesting and the majority of the investment will certainly be focused on cybersecurity and connectivity, and that will involve investment in encryption, financial cryptography, decentralized storage, and mobile payments. Cryptocurrency will of course be of great interest given that it will lead innovation in 95 secure payments, decentralized ledgers, and encryption technology.

(1143 words)

Chuen, D. L. K. (2015). Preface and acknowledgements. In D. L. K. Chuen (Ed.), *Handbook of digital currency: Bitcoin, innovation, financial instruments, and big data* (pp. xxi–xxiii). Amsterdam, Netherlands: Academic Press, Elsevier.

After You Read

C. Working with a partner, use your annotations to complete the table with the main points from the reading.

POINTS	REASONS FOR BITCOIN'S SUCCESS
INTRODUCTION	*The global financial crisis created the conditions where a digital currency could be successful.*
FIRST	
SECOND	
THIRD	
FOURTH	
FIFTH	
SIXTH	
SEVENTH	

D. Answer the following questions on your own.

1 Who is the author of this reading? Where does the author come from? How do you know?

_____

_____

_____

2 What is the social problem that Bitcoin (and other digital currencies) may solve?

_____

_____

_____

My Bookshelf > My eLab >
Exercises > Chapter 6 >
The Rise of Bitcoin

FINAL ASSIGNMENT

Write a Cause and Effect Essay

A. Write a cause and effect essay to answer the following question:
If all people used bitcoins, what would the world be like?

As you know from Chapter 4, a cause and effect essay demonstrates the effect something (in this case, a global change from fiat to digital currency) has on someone or something else (in this case, how people and governments respond to change).

B. In your essay,

- refer to all three readings in this chapter;
- include the paraphrases of the two paragraphs you completed for the Warm-Up Assignment (page 167). Be sure to provide a citation of the original work and a full reference in your Works Cited section;
- include at least two conditional sentences to express possible outcomes in uncertain circumstances;
- use some of the vocabulary from Chapter 4 (page 94) to help you express cause and effect relationships;
- use the third-person plural to demonstrate an academic perspective.

Refer to the Models Chapter (page 245) to see an example and to learn more about how to write a cause and effect essay.

Critical Connections

There are many different digital currencies in circulation today; some of them are listed here.

- Litecoin (LTC)
- Ethereum (ETH)
- Zcash (ZEC)
- Dash
- Ripple (XRP)
- Monero (XMR)

A. Select one of these digital currencies (or another one that you are interested in), and read about it online. Try to discover the larger context in which this currency was developed. As you know, Bitcoin solved certain existing problems. What problems led to the invention of the currency you chose?

B. Here are some questions to help guide your thinking:

- Who developed the currency?
- Where is the currency used?
- Who uses the currency?
- What do people buy with the currency?
- What conditions created a need for the currency?
- What problems does the currency solve?
- What problems does the currency solve that Bitcoin does not?

CHAPTER 7
The Internet of Things

Have you noticed that the advertisements you see on the Internet are always related to your interests? How does the Internet know what you like and select advertisements to match? The Internet of Things (IoT) is the term used to describe *machine-to-machine* (or M2M) communication that allows this to happen. The advantages of the IoT are significant and range from personal benefits (like tracking your health information to warn you if your health is at risk) to city-wide benefits (like coordinating traffic lights to reduce traffic congestion). However, with the benefits come risks. For example, your health information could be revealed to your employers or insurance company. How can you evaluate the advantages and the disadvantages of the IoT to ensure you achieve the positives of the technology without experiencing any of the negatives?

In this chapter,
you will

- learn vocabulary related to the Internet of Things;

- use passive voice accurately to emphasize action;

- summarize and reference to avoid plagiarism;

- edit and improve your own writing;

- recognize the differences between academic and popular texts;

- weigh advantages and disadvantages to develop a unique opinion;

- write two summaries and integrate them into a persuasive essay.

GEARING UP

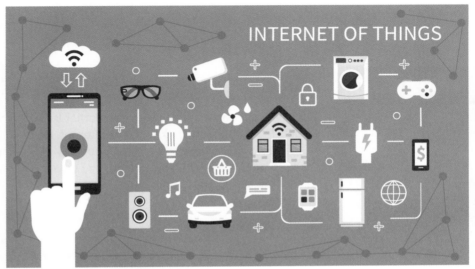

INTERNET OF THINGS

A. In a group of four students, think about how you use the Internet to find information or a service. Make a list of all the websites you visit for these purposes. These are examples of human interaction with the Internet.

Purchase from Amazon,
_____

_____

B. In your group, list the ways you use the Internet for human-to-human communication. These are examples of how the Internet facilitates human-to-human communication.

Skype,
_____

_____

C. With your group, list examples of machine-to-machine (M2M) communication that assist human activity.

Traffic data on Google maps,
_____

_____

D. Discuss the following questions in your group: Do you believe the interactions and activities you listed in tasks A, B, and C are advantageous? Do M2M interactions have any disadvantages? What are they?

Below are the key words you will practise in this chapter. Check the words you understand then underline the words you use. Highlight the words you need to learn.

nouns
app
Big Brother
breach
gadget
hacker
household appliance
query
vehicle*
vulnerabilities

verbs
configured
embedded
exploiting*
expose*
invade
invoke*
resolved*
reveal*

IoT

adjectives
conventional* hybrid
domestic* integrated*
embedded

adverbs
autonomously
conversely*
presumably*
remotely

other
dubious utility (expression)

* Appears on the Academic Word List

READING ❶ Introduction to the Internet of Things

Machines can communicate with each other through computer chips that are embedded in them and linked to the Internet. Have you ever left home and worried that you left the stove on? If your stove contained a computer chip that could communicate with your phone, you would be able to use your phone to turn off the stove. That's efficient!

A. The following sentences are based on Reading 1. Choose the best word(s) from the box to complete each sentence, and write the definition of the word on the line below.

> autonomously ~~configured~~ conventional conversely
> embedded household appliance integrated invokes query

❶ For example, a dishwasher could be _____ *configured* _____ to delay the wash cycle until off-peak hours, when the cost of electricity drops.

Definition: *arranged to work with other equipment, in a particular way*

❷ The appliance can send a _____ query _____ to find the cost of electricity at various times, and adjust its schedule of actions accordingly.

Definition: ask question about something

❸ Communication between a Household applia (for example, a dishwasher) and the energy company does not need a human at either end to send data.

Definition: usually electrical that are in our home such as

4 Unlike traditional computers, the IoT has applications that are built into a device and connected to other, similar devices. The resulting network forms a(n) ___embedded~~Conventional~~___ system.

Definition: _____

_____

5 Through the IoT, each individual household appliance acts ___autonously___ to turn on or off by itself, based on data it has collected from the energy company.

Definition: _____

_____

6 The device might be configured to contact the energy company before it turns on to determine the price of energy at that time. ___Conversely___, the energy company could send information to each household appliance whenever the energy rates change so the appliance always has current price information.

Definition: _____opposite_____

_____

7 ~~integrated~~ The IoT is a series of household appliances with embedded computer chips that are constantly in contact with each other. The computer chips are ___~~Conventiembedded~~___ so the appliances can act together and get work done.

Definition: _____combined / working_____

_____

8 When a shopper walks up to the display, the system uses a camera to capture an image, and ___invokes___ software that can analyze the image.

Definition: _____start to used_____

9 ___integrated___ computers allowed people to interact with the Internet; the IoT allows computers to interact with other computers or appliances.

Definition: _____

_____

Before You Read

A. Discuss these questions with your classmates.

① What do you already know about M2M communication? In what ways is your life already influenced by M2M communication (or the IoT)? Do you think that you benefit from M2M communication? Why?

② In some places in the world, energy companies try to balance the demand for electricity (usually high during the day and low at night) by charging more for energy during high-demand (peak) hours and charging less during low-demand (off-peak) hours. Does this happen in the country you are from or where you live? Are you familiar with other ways of balancing, or reducing, the demand for energy? Do you think these approaches are effective?

③ In what ways could M2M communication be used in your home or in places where you shop (in retail)?

④ Do you think there might be any disadvantages to M2M communication?

While You Read

B. While you read, think about the writer's purpose. What kind of text is this? How do you know? What audience is the writer addressing? Consider the text organization, vocabulary, and content. When you finish reading, discuss your answers with the class.

_____

_____

_____

_____

The Internet of Things

1. Introduction

For over thirty years, the Internet was focused on providing communications that involve humans. Applications like electronic mail (email), chat, and voice over Internet **protocol** (VoIP telephony) require two human participants who interact. Applications 5 like web surfing, search, and file transfer arrange for a human to access a service.

protocol (n.): accepted or established system of rules

This chapter explores a new use of the Internet: communications among machines. Researchers and networking professionals are using the terms _machine to machine (M2M)_ and the _Internet of Things[1] (IoT)_ to describe the concept. This chapter explains the motivation for [developing] machines that communicate with each other.

10 2. Embedded Systems

Unlike earlier applications that use **conventional** computers, IoT applications focus on _embedded systems_. That is, computing and communications [capabilities] are **integrated** into a device, such as a light switch, **household appliance**, a heating or

---

1. Although in many ways it fails to capture the idea, the term _Internet of Things_ seems to have gained acceptance.

air conditioning system. According to Farnam Jahanian of the National Science Foundation, "Today, the number of networked devices equals the number of people on Earth. In three years, Internet devices will outnumber people by a factor of three."

Why would a household appliance need to communicate over the Internet? One reason involves home automation—if all electrical devices in a home had connectivity, an owner could contact the devices to determine their status and control them. Without returning home, an owner could answer a question such as, did I leave the iron on? More importantly, the owner could turn the iron or the lights off, or could start an oven preheating while he or she was on the way home.

2.1 Embedded Systems in the Smart Grid

The examples above involve humans controlling devices. Does machine-to-machine communication also make sense? Yes. One instance where machine-to-machine communication will be important arises from the concept of a *smart grid*. In a smart grid, an appliance has an **embedded** controller and network connectivity. The appliance can send a **query** to find the cost of electricity at various times, and adjust its schedule of actions accordingly. For example, a dishwasher could be **configured** to delay the wash cycle until off-peak hours when the cost of electricity drops. Similarly, an air conditioning system could raise the temperature slightly during peak hours, and then cool the house during off-peak hours.

Communication between an appliance and the energy company does not need a human at either end—the embedded system in the appliance acts **autonomously** to contact a server at the energy company and obtain information about schedules and pricing. **Conversely**, systems at an energy company could be configured to download rates and schedules to systems at each residence whenever a change occurs.

2.2 Embedded Online Security Systems

Home automation systems allow an owner to monitor or control electrical devices. Intelligent security systems take one step beyond home automation by being proactive. That is, the system acts on its own to inform the owner when an unexpected event occurs. For example, if a motion sensor is **tripped** by a robber, the system can contact the owner's smartphone, turn on the lights, and supply a video stream from a camera. The system can then accept commands to ignore the event, reset the sensor, or take further action.

The significant advantage of an intelligent security system lies in its ability to have a list of contingencies. That is, the system can take action depending on the event that occurs, the time of day, and the actions of the owner. For example, the system might be **configured** to inform two or more smartphones for a given event. Furthermore, if an owner does not respond within a specified time, the system could choose to inform the local police.

2.3 Embedded Systems in Retail

The Internet of Things includes much more than household appliances. One interesting use of embedded systems involves retail locations. For example, some shopping malls have electronic displays with sophisticated embedded systems. When a shopper walks up to the display, the system uses a camera to capture an image, and **invokes** software that can analyze the image. The software identifies human faces, analyzes each, and estimates traits, such as the individual's age and sex. The display then selects ads that are targeted for the individual's demographic profile.

tripped (v.): switched on or activated (e.g., a mechanism)

Electronic displays in malls do much more than merely show ads; they send data in
60 both directions. In terms of gathering information, the systems track each viewer,
calculate how long the person continues to look at the display, and report statistics
back to a server in the cloud. The **cloud server** takes information from the displays
as well as information from other sources, and … combines the information. Once
new decisions are made, the cloud server downloads the information to the displays.
65 For example, a cloud server might sample weather at each site, and decide to advertise
umbrellas during a rainstorm or air conditioners during a heat wave.

A similar technology is used in grocery stores. Cameras mounted over shelves and
refrigerated cases gather images of shoppers. The images are analyzed to determine
the amount of time each shopper stands at a particular spot and the approximate
70 location of the items the shopper considers. The data is then fed back to a cloud
server that combines information from many stores and recommends product
placement for each individual store.

(871 words)

Comer, D. (2015). *Computer networks and Internets* (6th ed., pp. 567–569). Boston: Pearson.

cloud server (n.): main
network computer that
controls other computers
and allows for online
processing and storage

After You Read

C. Answer the following questions to check your comprehension.

1 What is an IoT device (or smart appliance)?

_____

_____

2 In column 2 of the table, list the IoT applications mentioned in each section
of the reading. In column 3, write the advantages associated with these IoT
devices. Some of the information has been provided for you in the table.
The complete list will be useful when you write your final assignment.

SECTION OF READING	EXAMPLES OF IOT APPLICATIONS	ADVANTAGES OF IOT APPLICATIONS
2. Embedded Systems	• *light switch*	• *energy savings* • *peace of mind (you don't have to worry that you left your lights on)*
2.1 Embedded Systems in the Smart Grid	• *dishwasher*	
2.2 Embedded Online Security Systems	• *intelligent home security systems*	

SECTION OF READING	EXAMPLES OF IOT APPLICATIONS	ADVANTAGES OF IOT APPLICATIONS
2.3 Embedded Systems in Retail	• *electronic displays in stores and malls*	

3 How many of these applications have you experienced?

_____

4 The writer introduced definitions of three terms in this reading in an interesting way. Use the line numbers below to find the three terms and their definitions. Complete the sentence to explain how the writer introduced the definitions of these terms. Then, to help you remember the meaning of the terms, write out their definitions.

The writer introduces the definitions by _____

_____

a) (line 12) embedded systems _____

_____

b) (line 40) proactive

_____

_____

c) (line 47) contingencies _____

_____

5 Does the author mention any disadvantages of the IoT? Do you think there may be disadvantages to the IoT?

_____

_____

_____

My Bookshelf > My eLab >
Exercises > Chapter 7 >
The Internet of Things

FOCUS ON ACCURACY

Using the Passive Voice

In Reading 1, you may have noticed that the writer sometimes wants to refer to an action that happened without emphasizing who performed the action. When you want to de-emphasize the person who did the action, you use the passive voice verb form. You can use the passive voice in the following situations:

1. When it doesn't matter, or you don't know, who did the action

   Example: A computer chip **is embedded** in a household appliance to connect it to the Internet.

   Note: You don't know who put the computer chip in the household appliance, and the doer's name is not relevant to your point.

2. When you want to emphasize the action more than the person/people who did the action

Example: The car's security system **was hacked** before the police were aware of the problem.

Note: The reader does not know who hacked the car's security system. What is most important is that it happened, not who did it.

3. When you want to emphasize the action more than the person/people who did the action even when the doer is mentioned (usually in a "by phrase" after the verb)

Examples: The weaknesses in the Internet connection **were discovered** *by researchers from Pen Test Partners*.

It's surprising that these weaknesses **were not detected** *by Mitsubishi* beforehand.

Note: Even though the "by phrases" include the people (or company) that acted (discovered or detected), they appear after the verb and therefore seem less important than the action.

4. When you want to be objective, for example in scientific and technical writing

Example: 2.5D multi-chip modules **are installed** in thousands of devices every day.

5. When you want to be polite and not mention who made a mistake

Example: The disadvantages of IoT enabled devices **should have been discovered** sooner.

The table shows how to form the passive voice in the present, past, and future tenses.

	PASSIVE VOICE FORMATION			
	SUBJECT receives the action	BE shows the tense	MAIN VERB past participle form	BY PHRASE AND/OR REST OF SENTENCE
PRESENT TENSE	A computer chip	is	embedded	in the device.
PAST TENSE	A computer chip	was	embedded	in the device.
FUTURE TENSE	A computer chip	will be	embedded	in the device.

To make a passive voice sentence negative, add *not* after the first auxiliary verb (see #3 above).

A. Underline the passive voice verb form with one line, and the "by phrase" (if there is one) with two lines.

1. That is, computing and communications facilities <u>are integrated</u> into a device, such as a light switch, household appliance, a heating or air conditioning system. (Reading 1)

2. For example, if a motion sensor is tripped by a robber, the system can contact the owner's smartphone, turn on the lights, and supply a video stream from a camera. (Reading 1)

3. The on-board diagnostics (OBD) port is accessed after the door is locked. (Reading 3)

4. A similar technology is used in grocery stores. (Reading 1)

The passive voice is used with modals to show degrees of possibility and obligation.

PASSIVE VOICE WITH MODALS				
SUBJECT receives the action	**MODAL**	**BE**	**PAST PARTICIPLE**	**BY PHRASE AND/OR REST OF SENTENCE**
Traffic lights	can	be	configured	to reduce congestion.
Traffic lights	could	be	configured	to reduce congestion.
Traffic lights	should	be	configured	to reduce congestion.
Traffic lights	might	be	configured	to reduce congestion.

_____
To make a passive voice sentence negative, add *not* after the modal.

B. Underline the passive voice modal plus the main verb form with one line, and the "by phrase" (if there is one) with two lines.

1. For example, a dishwasher could be configured to delay the wash cycle until off-peak hours when the cost of electricity drops. (Reading 1)

2. The weaknesses in the car's IoT security system could not be detected by Mitsubishi because the company's technology was simply not advanced enough (Reading 3).

3. All this data also can be sold by data brokers around the world. (Reading 2)

4. Any object that can connect to the Internet can make you an invasion-of-privacy victim, because it can be hacked. (Reading 2)

C. Fill in the blanks with the passive voice of the verbs in parentheses to complete the sentences. Use a modal if it is appropriate. After, underline the "by phrases" with two lines.

1. A light switch (connect) *can be connected* to a computer chip so the owner can turn the house lights on and off from a cellphone.

2. To create a machine-to-Internet connection, a computer chip (embed) _____ in a household appliance.

3. An air conditioning system (control) _____ by an IoT connection to turn on when the cost of electricity is low.

4. With an IoT connection, you never have to worry about leaving your oven on again. The oven (turn off) _____ even when you are out of the house.

5. Before the IoT, homes (monitor, not) _____ remotely by owners when the owners were out of the house.

6. Your privacy (invaded) _____ by hackers hoping to steal your personal information.

The passive voice is used frequently in technical or scientific communication that describes a process. It is useful when you want to emphasize the process rather than the person completing the process. However, in general, avoid using the passive voice too often as it distances the reader from the action.

My Bookshelf > My eLab > Exercises > Chapter 7 > Focus on Accuracy

Avoiding Plagiarism by Summarizing

In Chapter 5, you learned how to avoid plagiarism by providing a reference when quoting. In Chapter 6, you learned to provide a reference when paraphrasing. It is also important to cite a reference when summarizing.

Learning how to summarize is an essential skill for students. You can use this technique to help you

1. write a formal summary for your professors;
2. support a point in your own writing;
3. refute a writer's ideas in your own writing;
4. study efficiently.

Like a paraphrase, a summary translates another person's ideas into your own words. However, a summary is only approximately one-third of the original text length. In a summary, give the main points of the writing and eliminate all the details and examples.

Here is an approach to try:

1. Before beginning, read the original source carefully, and underline only the main points.
2. Begin by referring to the author, title, and source of the article.
3. Paraphrase the underlined sections of the original source.
4. Eliminate details, examples, and repetitious points.
5. Write a reference to acknowledge the ideas contained in your summary.

A. With one or two partners, on a separate page, practise summarizing the text in the box. Follow the steps above. Refer to the Models Chapter (page 253) to see an example and to learn more about writing a summary. Include the reference for this text.

Handwritten notes:
① Title
② Author
③ Type of source
④ Reporting Verb
⑤ Main Idea

The Article by Comer d Computer network and internet is part of IOT

> Unlike earlier applications that use conventional computers, IoT applications focus on *embedded systems*. That is, computing and communications facilities are integrated into a device, such as a light switch, household appliance, a heating or air conditioning system. According to Farnam Jahanian of the National Science Foundation, "Today, the number of networked devices equals the number of people on Earth. In three years, Internet devices will outnumber people by a factor of three."
>
> Why would a household appliance need to communicate over the Internet? One reason involves home automation—if all electrical devices in a home had connectivity, an owner could contact the devices to determine their status and control them. Without returning home, an owner could answer a question such as, did I leave the iron on? More importantly, the owner could turn the iron or the lights off, or could start an oven preheating while he or she was on the way home.
>
> ———
> Comer, D. (2015). *Computer networks and Internets* (6th ed., pp. 567–568) Boston: Pearson.

My Bookshelf > My eLab > Exercises > Chapter 7 > Focus on Writing

B. When the class has finished, write your summaries on the board. Look for successful summarizing techniques in each. As a class, read each summary and identify its best features.

Handwritten: Assignment *Sheet*

WARM-UP ASSIGNMENT
Write a Short Summary

A. Summarize the following text from Reading 1. Write your summary on a separate page. Use the academic perspective (third-person present tense). Pay careful attention to subject-verb and pronoun-antecedent agreement (see Chapter 6, page 169). Use the passive voice when you want to de-emphasize the person who did the action. Don't forget to include the reference for the text at the end of your summary.

The Internet of Things includes much more than household appliances. One interesting use of embedded systems involves retail locations. For example, some shopping malls have electronic displays with sophisticated embedded systems. When a shopper walks up to the display, the system uses a camera to capture an image, and invokes software that can analyze the image. The software identifies human faces, analyzes each, and estimates traits, such as the individual's age and sex. The display then selects ads that are targeted for the individual's demographic profile.

Electronic displays in malls do much more than merely show ads; they send data in both directions. In terms of gathering information, the systems track each viewer, calculate how long the person continues to look at the display, and report statistics back to a server in the cloud. The cloud server takes information from the displays as well as information from other sources, and ... combines the information. Once new decisions are made, the cloud server downloads the information to the displays. For example, a cloud server might sample weather at each site, and decide to advertise umbrellas during a rainstorm or air conditioners during a heat wave.

A similar technology is being used in grocery stores. Cameras mounted over shelves and refrigerated cases gather images of shoppers. The images are analyzed to determine the amount of time each shopper stands at a particular spot and the approximate location of the items the shopper considers. The data is then fed back to a cloud server that combines information from many stores and recommends product placement for each individual store.

(265 words)

_____
Comer, D. (2015). *Computer networks and Internets* (6th ed., pp. 568–569). Boston: Pearson.

> ❶ When you receive feedback from your teacher or your classmates on this Warm-Up Assignment, you will have information that you can use to improve your writing on the Final Assignment.

Academic
Survival Skill

Editing Your Own Writing

What do you do with feedback on your writing? It can be discouraging to receive instructor or peer feedback when there are many corrections or several different kinds of corrections. However, you can use the feedback to improve your writing if you think about it in a systematic way.

First, stop for a moment to appreciate the positive feedback that you almost certainly received. If you are using this book, you are already a skilled writer of English. You may still want to improve your English writing, but take some time to think about what you have done well.

Next, identify and write down your three most significant—top three—challenges or areas needing improvement. These could relate to how you

- organize your ideas;
- develop (or elaborate on) your ideas;
- choose words to express your ideas;
- choose grammatical structures to express your ideas.

Next, decide how you can improve in those three areas. If you have made several similar grammatical errors, make sure you know how to eliminate them in future writing. If your goal is to develop your writing more, find out how you can do that (e.g., give more examples, provide more details, or write about an opposing idea).

You can ask your instructor or classmates for help, or you can search grammar books, dictionaries, and websites for examples of how to improve or make corrections.

Take notes on techniques you could use, or write a few example sentences to illustrate the grammar point you would like to master. This will help you easily review what you want to improve.

Do your best to understand why you have these challenges. For example, if you do not elaborate enough on your ideas, you may not be allowing yourself enough time, or you may be trying to write as little as possible to minimize the number of mistakes you make. In these cases, you probably need to allow yourself more time or to try to make your writing as complex as your thinking. Understanding your challenges is an important part of editing and improving your writing.

Here is an example of a student's top three challenges.

MY WRITING CHALLENGES	WAYS TO IMPROVE MY WRITING
❶ Elaborate on information in body paragraphs.	• Add details by giving examples, being more descriptive, or introducing an opposing idea and showing how it is incorrect.
❷ Use more formal words.	• More formal/academic verbs I **get** feedback on my writing. (informal) Students **receive** feedback on their writing. (more formal/academic) • Write differently than I talk IoT stuff is really a hot topic these days. (informal) IoT-enabled devices are popular and their uses are increasing. (more formal/academic)
❸ Check use of the passive voice.	• Don't forget that the main verb in the passive is in the past participle form. The computer chip was embed**ded** in the thermostat to control the temperature.

A. Return to the last writing assignment for which you received feedback. Identify and write down your top three challenges.

B. Consider how you might approach these challenges: ask your instructor or classmates, look at useful grammar books, or do research online. Write a few example sentences that illustrate your challenges. Do your best to understand why you have these challenges. Keep your list close by for your next writing assignment.

C. For your next assignment or assignment draft, proofread your writing specifically for your top three challenge areas. When you get feedback again, add the next top three challenges to your list. As your writing improves, you will be able to delete some of your top challenges.

(handwritten: 10 words from Chapter)

READING ② Too Clever for Comfort

In this reading, you will learn about many different applications of M2M communication. Some of the applications are funny and entertaining, others offer significant advantages, and still others are associated with potential negative outcomes. In addition, the writer expresses a clear opinion. As a student of English who is often asked to express opinions in academic work, you may find it interesting to see how this writer expresses his views.

VOCABULARY BUILD

(handwritten: 10 words)

In the following exercises, explore key words from Reading 2.

A. Match each word or expression to its definition. When you have finished, check your answers with the class.

WORDS		DEFINITION
❶ Big Brother	*d*	a) doubtful usefulness
❷ breach	*e*	b) small, cleverly designed tool
❸ domestic	*h*	c) show something that is usually covered or hidden
❹ dubious utility	*a*	d) character in George Orwell's novel *1984* who was never seen, but was represented in posters with the slogan, "Big Brother is watching you"; used to refer to a government that watches everyone and has complete power over people's lives
❺ expose	*c*	e) action that breaks a law, rule, or agreement
❻ gadget	*b*	f) used to say that something is probably true
❼ hackers	*i*	g) make something known that was previously secret
❽ invade	*j*	h) related to life at home
❾ presumably	*f*	i) people who secretly use and change information on other people's computers (informal)
❿ reveal	*g*	j) get involved in something in an unwanted or annoying way

B. Fill in the blanks with the key words (first column) to complete the short story. Don't forget to capitalize or make a word plural if required.

An Imagined Future World

In the future, governments will watch their citizens more closely than ever before. This ___Big Brother___ approach to observing people will become common. Citizens, especially smart ___hackers___, will invent ___gadget___ that attempt to avoid governmental observation. These gadgets will be installed in ___domestic___ locations

▶

where the governments are unlikely to find them. Governments will make laws that prevent the invention of these gadgets. However, hackers will _breach_ the laws and continue to develop avoidance devices. _Presumably_ everyone will want such a device, not only criminals; the potential market for these gadgets will be enormous. Governments will _invade_ retail stores and _reveal_ large quantities of the devices. The citizens will _expose_ the government observation plans, and they will insist that such close observation serves a _dubious utility_ since most citizens are good.

Before You Read

A. Carefully consider the words and expressions in the table above. Which ones seem to have negative meanings?

_____

B. Based on how these words are used, can you predict the author's opinion about the IoT? Is this different from the author's opinion in Reading 1? Discuss this with your class. Write your prediction here:

_____

While You Read

C. Read this text to determine if your prediction of the author's opinion of the IoT is correct. When you have finished, discuss with the class whether your predictions were correct.

Too Clever for Comfort

As the smart devices of the Internet of Things invade your home, hackers and Big Brother are close behind.

1. I've always been a fan of useless **gadgets**. High on my list were pizza scissors, the smartphone case that doubles as a hairbrush, and a battery-powered, swirling
5   spaghetti fork. Lately, thanks to the Internet of Things (IoT)—loosely defined as everyday devices linked to the Internet, thereby making them smart—I've got lots of choice.

2. As far as I can tell, the IoT involves sticking a computer chip into something you can buy at Home Depot or Walmart, from fridges to baby monitors, and linking it
10   to an app. You can buy smart toothbrushes, thermostats, and [even a personal health monitor] … Starting at $1200 (all currency in US dollars), **faucet** maker Moen has a smart shower **contraption** that allows you to control the heat of your water from your smartphone. No more waiting naked for ten or twenty [painful] seconds while the water warms up.

15 3. My favourite is a $199 automated cup …, made by a San Francisco company, that is advertised … as a hydration and nutrition tracker. Pour in a liquid, make sure the cup is charged up, and it will identify your drink. Pour in beer, and the word

faucet (n.): tap; device that controls the flow of water from a pipe

contraption (n.): piece of equipment that looks strange or funny, and is unlikely to work well

beer will light up on the outside. Confirmation is always appreciated, I guess, and
imagine the fun you could have trying to confuse your smart cup by filling it with
20   a mix of Coke and red wine.

4. The IoT wasn't invented merely to entertain us, of course; some of it is genuinely
useful. Smart cities have the potential to solve public problems like traffic congestion;
Internet-connected self-driving cars promise a transportation revolution. The IoT
market is potentially massive, assuming that consumers keep buying into the
25   dream of a connected **domestic** heaven … Gartner, an information technology
research firm, estimates that more than twenty billion **gadgets** and appliances will
be connected to the Internet by 2020.

5. But the IoT also has a dark side. Any object that can connect to the Internet can
make you an invasion-of-privacy victim, because it can be hacked. Reports of
30   hacking are piling up, and you have to wonder whether the IoT will lose popularity
in the same way that the early IT companies lost popularity in the early 2000s. A
house-renovator friend in Toronto told me that enthusiasm for home automation
is already [decreasing], partly because so many of the devices, like Bluetooth-
enabled door locks, are of dubious utility. But many homeowners also don't [like
35   the thought of] turning living rooms and kitchens into potential listening devices
for hackers and advertisers.

6. Many of the security **breaches** so far seem **malicious**. In March, documents
published by **WikiLeaks** … **reveal** that the **CIA** had launched a program called
Weeping Angel, which found ways to turn Samsung Internet-connected TVs into
40   devices that could record conversations even when sets were turned off. The CIA
declined to comment … WikiLeaks also said the CIA was looking into hacking
car-control systems, **presumably** making the cars vulnerable to crashes, which
"would permit the CIA to engage in nearly undetectable assassinations."

7. Last year, hackers attacked the electronic key-card system of a hotel in Austria,
45   preventing guests from getting back into their rooms. The hotel's manager sent a
ransom of $1800 worth of bitcoin—typically the currency of choice of blackmailers—
to unlock the doors. Early this year, hackers **exposed** more than two million
messages [of] parents and children playing with Internet-enabled teddy bears.
What these various [breaches] proved is that many makers of consumer products
50   can't be bothered, or can't afford, to invest in **sophisticated encryption software**.

8. Another annoyance with IoT gadgets is perfectly legal monitoring by collectors of
massive amounts of consumer data, among them Amazon, Facebook, Google and
Twitter. "Smart devices are all about surveillance—tracking your habits," says Jacob
Silverman, author of *Terms of Service: Social Media and the Price of Constant
55   Connection*. "The question is whether they use your data responsibly."

9. As artificial intelligence makes the IoT more sophisticated, the gadgets' ability to
monitor your behavioural habits rises. The [use] of intelligent, voice-activated
personal assistants like Siri (used by Apple) and Alexa (Amazon) has the potential
to expose every aspect of your domestic life to Big Data capitalism. Ask Alexa a
60   health question and you might get bombarded with ads for Fitbit exercise trackers.
All this data also can be sold around the world by **data brokers**.

malicious (adj.): unkind and cruel

WikiLeaks (n.): multinational online media organization that publishes controversial government documents

CIA (n.): Central Intelligence Agency; the US government agency that collects information about people

ransom (n.): amount of money that is used to free someone who is being held prisoner, or get something back that was stolen

sophisticated encryption software (collocation): computer program that creates a complicated code that prevents illegal use of the software or computer

data brokers (n.): people who collect and sell personal information for profit

10. The best way to fight all these invasions of privacy is to [stay away from] Internet-enabled gadgets. The IoT and all its cleverness are better suited for big fixes, like making cities safer, cleaner and less congested. Besides, do you really need a Bluetooth-enabled frying pan or smart garbage can?

65

(792 words)

Reguly, E. (2017). Too clever for comfort. *Report on Business: The Globe and Mail, 33*(9), 21.

After You Read

D. Answer the following questions to check your comprehension.

1 Based on the first paragraph of the reading, how does the author feel about "useless gadgets"?

_____

_____

2 After reviewing paragraphs 2 and 3, explain the author's feelings about the smart Moen faucet and the $199 automated cup. What is the author's tone in these paragraphs? How do you know?

_____

_____

_____

_____

_____

3 In paragraph 4, what does the author suggest is a good use for the IoT?

_____

_____

4 The last sentence of paragraph 4 (line 25) is similar to a sentence in Reading 1 (page 183, line 15). In both readings, the writers include a statistic about the IoT. Why do you think these two very different readings contain similar sentences? You may want to use a statistic for the same purpose in your own writing.

_____

_____

_____

_____

5 What words signal to the reader that the author is going to present a different opinion about the IoT in the next paragraphs?

_____

6 In paragraphs 5 to 10, the writer refers to many IoT devices (listed in the second column of the next table). For each application, write the potential disadvantage. This information will clarify the negative aspects of the IoT.

PARAGRAPH NUMBERS	IoT APPLICATIONS	POTENTIAL DISADVANTAGES
5	Bluetooth-enabled door lock	*Dubious utility (Do you really need it?)*
5	other "smart" appliances in living rooms and kitchens	
6	Samsung Internet-connected TV	
6	car-control systems	
7	electronic key-card system in hotel	
7	Internet-enabled teddy bears (toys)	
7	IoT consumer products	
8	Amazon, Facebook, Google, Twitter	*Extensive (though legal) personal data collection may not be used responsibly.*
9	"smart" voice-activated personal assistants	
10	Bluetooth-enabled fry pan or "smart" garbage can	

7 When you look at the table above, which (if any) of these negative aspects of the IoT worry you?

_____

E. To help you summarize the content in the final five paragraphs of the text, write the paragraph number next to its purpose.

PURPOSE OF THE PARAGRAPH	PARAGRAPH NUMBER (5–10)
1 IoT devices can invade your privacy, and many are not that useful.	5
2 In addition, hackers seem to be gathering personal information from IoT devices.	
3 These problems won't just disappear. Increasing use of IoT devices means our personal information will be more available than ever before.	
4 It seems that even legal organizations are using IoT devices in illegal ways.	
5 IoT applications are better used for large (city-wide) projects than for personal devices.	
6 Large companies collect personal data all the time, and they may not use that information wisely.	

F. Which paragraph best expresses the author's opinion about the IoT? Do you agree with the author? Why or why not?

_____

_____

My Bookshelf > My eLab >
Exercises > Chapter 7 >
Too Clever for Comfort

FOCUS ON READING

Recognizing the Differences Between Academic and Popular Texts

You probably noticed some differences in the writing between Readings 1 and 2. One is academic, and the other is a popular text. Even though both readings are about the IoT, their genres are very different.

A. In the first row of the table, identify which reading is academic and which is popular. Write the number in the appropriate column.

B. Using the questions in the first column, write notes on the differences between the two readings.

DIFFERENCES IN THE TEXTS	ACADEMIC TEXTBOOK: READING _____	POPULAR MAGAZINE: READING _____
❶ Who is the audience for the reading?		
❷ What is the writer's purpose for writing?		
❸ What perspective does the author choose (first person or third person)?		
❹ Does the writing seem more formal, or more like the author is speaking to the reader?		
❺ Can the reader see a clear organizational pattern in the text?		
❻ In general, how do the lengths of paragraphs compare?		
❼ Is the choice of words more formal or informal?		
❽ Does the author express opinions directly?		
❾ Does the author demonstrate a sense of humour?		
❿ How do the references differ?		
⓫ Do you have other points of comparison? If so, write them here.		

C. Academic textbooks and popular magazines are kinds of texts, referred to as *genres*. Write some other genres of communication that you are familiar with.

_____

_____

D. How do authors decide which genre they will write?

_____

_____

Genres are associated with conventions (or reader expectations). For example, if a writer decides to write an academic essay (a kind of text / genre), one of the things the reader will expect to see toward the end of the introduction is a thesis. Once authors decide on their audience and the genre they will use, they have a good idea of the conventions their writing should follow to meet readers' expectations.

E. Which genre of reading do you prefer? Which is easier to read?

_____

READING ③ **Researchers Hack the Mitsubishi Outlander SUV**

In this reading, you will learn about a group of researchers who successfully hacked into a car's control systems through an insecure Internet-enabled application. In their hacking experiments, the researchers looked for weaknesses in the IoT application that allowed car owners to unlock, heat, and/or cool their cars, and turn on or off the infotainment systems via an app installed on their cellphones. The researchers discovered that it was possible.

VOCABULARY BUILD

A. Read each sentence and circle the letter of the word or phrase that best matches the meaning of the word in bold. When you have finished, check your answers with a partner and confirm them with the class.

❶ The car's systems can be controlled from an **app** installed on a cellphone.
   a) application form that you complete when you apply to college
   b) piece of software that provides easy access to information or a service
   c) appliance with an embedded computer chip

❷ Hackers who are **exploiting** the car's weaknesses know how to use the technology.
   a) using the car's weaknesses to do something unlawful
   b) taking the car parts to build a better car
   c) using the car's weaknesses to help the owner

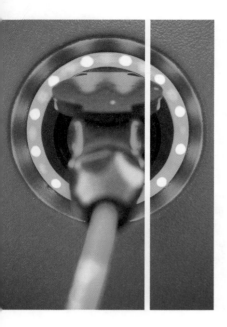

3. **Hybrid** cars are becoming more popular as the price of oil and gas increases.

   a) cars that have characteristics of bigger cars

   b) cars that are manufactured by two companies

   c) cars that use both gas and electricity

4. IoT devices can be controlled **remotely** through an app, usually installed on the owner's cellphone.

   a) by only one person

   b) completely

   c) from a distance

5. Until the weaknesses of the security system are **resolved**, many car owners will worry about parking their cars in public places.

   a) fixed in a satisfactory way

   b) shown to be incorrect

   c) applied to a new rule

6. Mitsubishi Outlander is a popular **vehicle** sold around the world.

   a) motorized form of transportation

   b) way to get exercise

   c) dating service

7. Similar **vulnerabilities** were discovered in the Jeep Cherokee last year.

   a) exceptional cases

   b) weaknesses

   c) understandings

My Bookshelf >
Exercises > Chapter 7 >
Vocabulary Review

Before You Read

A. There are many car- and security-related expressions in this reading. The author assumes that the audience is familiar with these expressions and often simply uses acronyms to refer to them. Here is a list of the acronyms and their full meanings in this reading. Match the acronym (and term) to the best definition. When you have finished, compare your answers with a partner.

CAR- AND SECURITY-RELATED EXPRESSIONS		DEFINITIONS
❶ SUV (sport utility vehicle)	_____	a) car's self-diagnostic reporting function
❷ SSID (service set identifier)	_____	b) expensive class of large vehicles with a lot of power, designed for city driving
❸ OBD (on-board diagnostics)	_____	c) password used by a mobile device when it connects to the wireless local area network (WLAN)

B. Who is the author's intended audience?

_____

_____

C. Based on the title of Reading 3, do you think this author will have a positive or a negative opinion about the IoT?

_____

_____

While You Read

D. Consider this question: If you were the owner of a Mitsubishi Outlander SUV, how secure would you feel after reading this text? Why?

Researchers Hack the Mitsubishi Outlander SUV, Shut Off Alarm Remotely

Mitsubishi Outlander, a popular **hybrid** SUV sold around the world, can be easily broken into by attackers **exploiting** security weaknesses … that allow the car to be **remotely** controlled via an **app**.

The weaknesses were discovered by Pen Test Partners, and include:

5 • The mobile app connects to the car through a Wi-Fi access point, making the app impossible to use if the owner is not in range of the car's wireless network.

• This wireless network's Wi-Fi pre-shared key is written on a piece of paper included in the owners' manual, but its format is too simple and too short, allowing attackers to [break in] easily and relatively quickly.

10 • The car's Wi-Fi access point has a unique SSID, but in a predictable format. This allowed the researchers to geolocate the various Outlanders throughout the United Kingdom.

After discovering the SSID and the pre-shared key, the Pen Test Partners researchers connected to an … IP address within a network's subnet, and this allowed them to 15 find the Wi-Fi connection and send messages to the car. Through these messages they were able to turn the car's lights, air conditioning and heating on and off, change the charging program and, most importantly, to disable the car's anti-theft alarm. "Once unlocked, there is potential for many more attacks. The on-board diagnostics (OBD) port is accessible once the door is unlocked. While we haven't looked in detail 20 at this, you may recall that the hack of some BMW **vehicles** suggested that the OBD port could be used to code new keys for the car," they noted. "We also haven't looked at connections between the Wi-Fi module and the Controller Area Network (CAN). There is certainly access to the infotainment system from the Wi-Fi module. Whether this extends to the CAN is something we need more time to investigate."

25 The researchers have tried to get in touch with Mitsubishi and share these discoveries responsibly but didn't have much luck initially. Only after the investigators made these concerns public did the company contact them. Mitsubishi is currently working on new firmware for the Wi-Fi module that should fix these problems. Until [it's ready, company engineers] advised owners to deactivate the Wi-Fi using the "Cancel Vehicle 30 Identification Number (VIN) Registration" option on the app, or by using the remote app cancellation procedure. "While obviously disturbing, this hacking only affects the

car's app, therefore with limited effect to the vehicle (alarm, charging, heating). It should be noted that without the remote control device, the car cannot be started and driven away," the company pointed out, and added that they are willing to work
35 with the researchers in order to understand and solve the problem.

For a long-term fix, Mitsubishi needs to re-engineer the … Wi-Fi app-client connection method completely, the researchers advised. "The problem is that any time you connect physical devices, objects or machines to the Internet, you are taking the risk that these could one day be **compromised** due to **vulnerabilities**," Justin Harvey,
40 chief security officer at Fidelis Cybersecurity, told Help Net Security. "There is no doubt that owners of Mitsubishi Outlander hybrid cars will be reluctant [to drive their cars] after this latest hack—at least until it is **resolved**. Indeed, it's not the first time we've seen hackers gain access to a car system; it's reminiscent of the security vulnerabilities found by researchers in the Jeep Cherokee last year."

45 "While it's surprising that these vulnerabilities were not detected by Mitsubishi beforehand, both consumers and enterprises must evaluate the risks of Internet of Things (IOT) devices before using them. The physical nature of these "things" represents a kinetic danger to the real world and, in reality, they could cause an accident or a serious injury. While no damage
50 was done on this occasion, there is no doubt that similar vulnerabilities will be detected in the years to come," he concluded.

"The Mitsubishi Outlander vulnerability
55 is another example of why a [protected] identity … approach to connected device management is essential in reducing risk and enhancing user experience," noted Simon Moffatt, Director of Advanced
60 Customer Engineering at ForgeRock. "As more and more objects join the Internet of Things, high-end items such as connected cars will become increasingly attractive targets for hackers. While manufacturers focus on end-user experience
65 and device connectivity, there needs to be a more joined-up approach to security, including a strong focus on device, service and user identity management."

"It is important that devices, such as a car or a mobile phone application, have individual identity profiles, with validated, authenticated, and authorized services, that can restrict the operations or data made available," he added. Doing so allows
70 Internet-connected devices to confirm that the digital identity of the user and device is in fact fully [protected], and the right people are accessing the right services at the right time—making **malicious** activities more difficult."

(807 words)

Zorz, Z. (2016, June 6). *Researchers hack the Mitsubishi Outlander SUV, shut off alarm remotely*.
Retrieved from https://www.helpnetsecurity.com/2016/06/06/researchers-hack-mitsubishi-outlander/

compromised (adj.): unable to work properly

After You Read

E. In your final assignment, you will be asked to summarize the content in Reading 3. To prepare, answer these questions which highlight the main points of the reading. Answering the questions in your own words will provide you the beginning of a good summary.

1 Who wrote this article, what is the title, and when was it published?

Author: _____

Title: _____

Date of publication: _____

2 What genre is this reading? Is it more like Reading 1 or 2 of this chapter?

_____

3 What is the author writing about? What is this an example of?

_____

_____

_____

4 What is Pen Test Partners and what do the researchers do (you will have to search online to find this information)?

_____

_____

5 What disadvantages did the Pen Test Partners researchers discover in the Mitsubishi Outlander's IoT setup?

_____

_____

_____

_____

6 How did Mitsubishi respond to the researchers' discoveries?

_____

_____

7 In general, what should consumers be aware of before they purchase an IoT-enabled product?

_____

_____

_____

F. Look carefully at lines 1, 4, 18, 21, 42, 45, 49, and 50 (eight lines total). What do they have in common?

_____

G. Look carefully at lines 10, 14 and 69 (three lines total). What useful expression do these lines have in common? This expression means that something (the subject of the sentence) creates the conditions for something else to happen.

1 Write the sentences according to the grammar pattern. Note that you don't have to complete the sentence.

	SUBJECT	VERB	DIRECT OBJECT	INFINITIVE OF MAIN VERB + REST OF SENTENCE
LINE 10	*This*			*to geolocate the ...*
LINE 14				
LINE 69				

2 Complete the following sentences with the verb *allow* following the grammar pattern above.

a) The weaknesses in the IoT application _____

_____

b) The vulnerabilities in the Outlander's security system _____

_____

c) The collection of personal data _____

_____

My Bookshelf > Exercises >
Chapter 7 > Researchers Hack
the Mitsubishi Outlander SUV

FOCUS ON
CRITICAL
THINKING

Weighing Advantages and Disadvantages to Develop Your Unique Opinion

You may already be aware that when you write following Western academic conventions, your readers often expect you to express your opinion. Most writers who face this challenge wonder how they will develop a unique perspective that their readers will value. How can their opinions differ from those of many other people who write about the same issues? The following task may help you develop a unique opinion.

A. You have now read texts in which writers are very positive or less supportive of IoT-connected devices. With a small group of students, discuss how you feel about these devices. Would you purchase IoT devices? Do you see their benefits, or are you concerned about their weaknesses? Or can you understand both sides of the IoT issue?

B. Often when people want to think carefully about an issue, they list the advantages and disadvantages in a chart. Complete the table to help you summarize all the advantages and disadvantages of IoT devices. Refer to your answers from the readings.

- Summarize the advantages of IoT devices that you listed in Reading 1, task C, question 2, page 184.
- Summarize the advantages and disadvantages of IoT devices that you listed in Reading 2, task D, question 6, page 195.
- Summarize the disadvantages of IoT car control systems that you listed in Reading 3, task E, question 5, page 201.

ADVANTAGES	DISADVANTAGES

The information in this kind of chart may not help you decide whether you think positively or negatively about an issue because the advantages and disadvantages may not be equally important to you. Sometimes a single advantage may be significant enough to outweigh several disadvantages, or vice versa.

C. Using a chart that lists advantages and disadvantages as significant, somewhat significant, and less significant might be helpful. Working on your own, rewrite the advantages and disadvantages from the first chart in the second chart, categorizing each as significant, somewhat significant, or less significant.

	ADVANTAGES	DISADVANTAGES
Significant		
Somewhat Significant		
Less Significant		

The distribution of the points in this chart should demonstrate your unique opinion about the issue of IoT-enabled devices because you have ranked the points according to how you value them. Your table will show a "unique profile" because the way you value each point will be different from how other people value them. You will have an opportunity to express your unique opinion in your final written assignment.

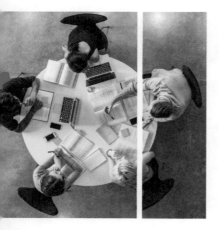

FINAL ASSIGNMENT
Integrate a Summary into a Persuasive Essay

You will write a persuasive essay in which you integrate the summary from the Warm-Up Assignment and a summary of Reading 3. Follow these steps to complete this assignment.

A. Summarize Reading 3 on a separate page. Use the techniques you learned in this chapter. Refer to the Models Chapter (page 253) for more information on how to write a summary and to see a model summary.

- You should now have two summaries: one from the Warm-Up Assignment and another of Reading 3.

B. Define your audience (your instructor, classmates, parents, school newspaper, friends, or another group). You might write differently depending on your audience.

C. Establish your unique opinion about whether the advantages outweigh the disadvantages (or the opposite) of the IoT. You will present this opinion to your audience.

D. As you write your persuasive essay, use what you have learned in this chapter.

- Use vocabulary about IoT-enabled devices.
- Use the passive voice to de-emphasize the doer of the action (refer to Focus on Accuracy, page 185).
- Integrate your two summaries into your writing. Include both in-text citations and final references.
- Refer to the Models Chapter (page 247) for more information on how to write a persuasive essay and to see an example.

E. Edit your writing, then proofread it for your top three challenges (refer to Academic Survival Skill, page 189).

Critical Connections

Use this approach to develop a unique opinion by applying the framework from Focus on Critical Thinking to another issue. The framework involves using two tables. In the first table, list the advantages and disadvantages of the issue. In the second, categorize the advantages and disadvantages as significant, somewhat significant, or less significant. Your categorization will likely be unique because it is based on your values.

A. Consider one of the issues from the previous chapters in this book or suggest another issue. For example, outline the advantages and disadvantages of one of the following issues:

- The internationalization of education
- The promotion of products using advertising
- Trying fad diets
- Using a digital currency

B. Once you have decided on the issue you will discuss, write it at the top of the table. Work with a small group of students to brainstorm advantages and disadvantages, and list them on a separate page using the table below as a model.

Issue: _____

ADVANTAGES	DISADVANTAGES

C. When you have finished, work on your own to weigh the advantages and disadvantages and categorize them. Use the format below.

	ADVANTAGES	DISADVANTAGES
Significant		
Somewhat Significant		
Less Significant		

D. Compare your table with that of a classmate. You will most likely have listed the information in a unique way; this demonstrates that your opinion is different from your classmate's. Use this approach when you want to develop a unique opinion for a writing assignment.

CHAPTER 8

The Slow Food Movement

How often do you make your own meals and eat them with friends and family? How often do you shop at a market for fresh, locally grown food? Participants in the Slow Food movement try to do these things daily. They also believe that buying locally grown food is the best way to enjoy tasty food, ensure sustainable production, and support local farmers. The Slow Food movement encourages gastronomic pleasure, sustainable agriculture, and cultural revitalization. However, not everyone agrees that it will achieve these goals. Is the Slow Food movement the best way to address today's rapid pace of life, destruction of farmland, and loss of cultural traditions?

In this chapter,
you will

- learn vocabulary related to the Slow Food movement;

- choose effective vocabulary to express your opinion;

- clarify the subject of a sentence when writing;

- apply tips to help you read multi-clause, multi-phrase sentences;

- learn how to express opposing ideas;

- find academic sources;

- write persuasive essays.

GEARING UP

A. Are you a gastronome? If you are not sure what a gastronome is, read the following characteristics, as defined by Carlo Petrini, the founder of the Slow Food movement. Check the ones that apply to you.

CHARACTERISTICS OF GASTRONOMES	YES	NO	SOMETIMES
1 insist on and take pleasure in eating good-quality food	☐	☐	☐
2 appreciate food diversity and seek out new culinary experiences	☐	☐	☐
3 avoid fast food (e.g., McDonald's) and object to it on principle	☐	☐	☐
4 search for like-minded friends with whom you can share *good, clean,* and *fair* food	☐	☐	☐
5 have an interest in learning about and understanding the complexity of the systems that bring food to our tables	☐	☐	☐
6 believe that food should be produced in a sustainable way that does not damage the Earth	☐	☐	☐
7 believe farmers should be paid a reasonable wage for the food they produce, to bring a new dignity to food production	☐	☐	☐
8 believe that many of the world's problems are a result of our methods of food production	☐	☐	☐

B. Discuss your answers with the class. Which characteristics are the most important for you and your classmates?

C. Go to the Slow Food International website. There are Slow Food groups, *convivia* (n. pl.), all over the world. Where is the *convivium* (n. sing.) nearest to you?

Below are the key words you will practise in this chapter. Check the words you understand, then underline the words you use. Highlight the words you need to learn.

nouns

barbarians
distinction*
element*
erosion*
folly
homogenization
ideology*
inputs*

intervention*
luxury
notion*
pesticides
propaganda
sphere*
standardization

verbs

abandoned*
advocated* (for)
conferring*

cultivated
procuring

slow food movement

adjectives

abundant
affluent
charismatic
crucial* (factor)
empirical evidence*

indigenous
intensive*
rigorous
stratified

adverbs

previously*

other words

despite* (prep.)
in pursuit* of (exp.)

* Appears on the Academic Word List

READING ❶ In Praise of Slowness: Turning the Tables on Speed

You might think the Slow Food movement is about taking more time to prepare and enjoy the food that you eat at your table—and you would be right. In fact, the expression *turning the tables* means reversing the situation to gain an advantage. However, Slow Food advocates are also concerned about the chain of actions that brings food to your table: the production, harvesting, and transporting of food, as well as the preparation and eating of it. This broader view of the food chain encourages concern for food-related issues, including the preservation of the environment, biodiversity, and local culture.

VOCABULARY BUILD

In the following exercises, explore key words from Chapter 8.

A. Read the following sentence that features the word *pesticides*.

Pesticides are believed to kill thousands of birds each year.

❶ Write the definition of pesticides.

_____

_____

❷ What is the root word in pesticides? What does it mean?

_____

_____

❸ What is the suffix? What does it mean? What other words do you know that finish with this suffix?

_____

_____

B. Read each sentence and write one synonym and one antonym (where indicated) for each key word in bold.

SENTENCE	SYNONYM	ANTONYM
1 The need for an **abundant** supply of cheap food has led to standardized production of plants and animals.	*ample*	*scarce*
2 Carlo Petrini, a **charismatic** culinary writer, launched the Slow Food movement.		
3 The Slow Food movement is strongest in Europe, which has a rich tradition of **indigenous** cuisine and where fast food culture is less strongly established.		
4 Members of the Slow Food movement believe that the use of chemical fertilizers and pesticides, and **intensive** feeding of animals, makes crops and livestock grow unnaturally quickly.		
5 According to Slow Food proponents, the **rigorous** breeding of pigs and cows to achieve maximum weight is also unnatural.		
6 In France, the Slow Food movement has **advocated for** the Pardigone plum and a delicate goat's cheese called Brousse du Rove.		
7 A defence of quiet material pleasure is the only way to oppose the universal **folly** of Fast Life.		
8 In the food industry, efficiency leads to **homogenization.**		
9 Manufacturers can process **inputs**—be they turkeys, tomatoes, or turnips—more quickly if they are all the same.		
10 Slow Food members also idealize "eco-gastronomy"—the **notion** that eating well can, and should, go hand in hand with protecting the environment.		

Before You Read

A. Working with a small group of classmates, discuss the following questions. When you have finished, share your answers with the rest of the class.

1 How much time do you spend preparing meals each week? How much time do you spend eating meals each week?

2 What methods do farmers (producers) use to speed up the natural growth processes of plants and animals? Here are some key words and phrases that you can use to discuss this question:

- pesticides
- antibiotics
- genetic modification
- speeding up animals' day/night cycle
- standardizing farming production

3 Consider the following quote from this reading: "A firm defence of quiet material pleasure is the only way to oppose the universal folly of Fast Life ... Our defence should begin at the table with Slow Food." Do you agree or disagree? Why?

While You Read

B. While you read, think about where you could place the following headings in the reading. The spaces between the paragraphs have been assigned letters. Determine the best position for these headings, and write the corresponding letters next to the headings listed in the table. The first one has been done for you.

SUGGESTED HEADINGS	LOCATION
1 Fast Food Equals Fast Life	*A*
2 Fast Farming Methods	_____
3 History of Slow Foods to the Current Day	_____
4 What Slow Food Activists Do	_____
5 Slow Food in Europe and America	_____
6 Slow Food Supports Organic Farming and Biodiversity	_____

C. Compare your answers to a classmate's. Fill in the headings in the text to help see the organization of the reading.

In Praise of Slowness: Turning the Tables on Speed

A:

Today, most meals are little more than refuelling **pit stops**. Instead of sitting down with family or friends, we often eat solo, on the move or while doing something else—working, driving, reading the newspaper, surfing the Net. Nearly half of Britons
5 now eat their evening meal in front of the TV, and the average British family spends more time together in the car than they do around the table. When families do eat together, it is often at fast food [restaurants] like McDonald's, where the average meal lasts eleven minutes ...

B:

10 The acceleration at the table is mirrored on the farm. Chemical fertilizers and pesticides, **intensive** feeding, antibiotic digestive enhancers, growth hormones, **rigorous** breeding, genetic modification—every scientific trick known to man has been deployed to cut costs, boost yields, and make livestock and crops grow more quickly. Two centuries ago, the average pig took five years to reach 286 kilograms;
15 today, it hits 484 kilograms after just six months and is slaughtered before it loses its baby teeth. North American salmon are genetically modified to grow four to six times faster than the average. The small landowner gives way to the factory farm, which **churns** out food that is fast, cheap, **abundant**, and standardized.

pit stops (n.): quick stops a driver makes to refuel or for service repairs (e.g., in a car race)

churns (v.) out: produces large quantities of something without concern about the quality

C:

20 As our ancestors moved into the cities and lost touch with the land, they fell in love with the idea of fast food for a fast age. The more processed, the more convenient, the better … Many of us have swallowed the idea that when it comes to food, faster is better. We are in a hurry, and we want meals to match. But many people are waking up to the drawbacks of the "gobble, gulp, and go" philosophy. On the farm, in the
25 kitchen, and at the table, they are slowing down. Leading the change is an international movement with a name that says it all: Slow Food …

D:

It all started in 1986, when McDonald's opened a branch beside the famous Spanish Steps in Rome. To many locals, this was one restaurant too far … To roll back the fast
30 food **tsunami** sweeping across the planet, Carlo Petrini, a **charismatic** culinary writer, launched Slow Food. As the name suggests, the movement stands for everything that McDonald's does not: fresh, local, seasonal produce; recipes handed down through the generations; sustainable farming; **artisanal** production; leisurely dining with family and friends. Slow Food also idealizes "eco-gastronomy"—the **notion** that eating well
35 can, and should, go hand in hand with protecting the environment …

E:

Petrini thinks this is a good starting point for **tackling** our obsession with speed in all aspects of life. The group states: "A firm defence of quiet material pleasure is the only way to oppose the universal **folly** of Fast Life … Our defence should begin at the
40 table with Slow Food."

F:

With its very modern message—eat well and still save the planet—Slow Food has attracted seventy-eight thousand members in more than fifty countries. In 2001, *The New York Times* named it one of the "eighty ideas that shook the world …" Aptly
45 enough, Slow Food takes the snail as its symbol, but that does not mean the members are lazy or [slow] …

G:

All over the world, Slow Food activists organize dinners, workshops, school visits, and other events to promote the benefits of taking our time over what we eat. Education is
50 key. In 2004, Slow Food opened its own University of Gastronomic Sciences at Pollenzo, near Bra, Italy, where students study not only the science of food but also its history and sensual character. The movement has already persuaded the Italian state to build "food studies" into the school curriculum. In 2003, Petrini himself helped the German government lay the groundwork for a nationwide "taste education" program.

55 **H:**

On the economic side, Slow Food seeks out artisanal foods that are on the way to extinction and helps them find a place in the global market. It puts small producers in touch with one another, shows them how to … promote their products to chefs, shops, and gourmets around the world. In Italy, over 130 dying delicacies have been
60 saved, including lentils from Abruzzi, Ligurian potatoes, the black celery of Trevi, the

tsunami (n.): large wave caused by extreme conditions (like an earthquake) that causes damage when it reaches land

artisanal (adj.): relating to artists

tackling (v.): dealing with a difficult problem

Vesuvian apricot, and purple asparagus from Albenga … Similar rescue operations are underway in other countries. Slow Food is working to save the Firiki apple and traditional olive oil-soaked ladotiri cheese in Greece. In France, it
65 has **advocated for** the Pardigone plum and a delicate goat's cheese called Brousse du Rove.

I:

As you might expect, Slow Food is strongest in Europe, which has a rich tradition of **indigenous** cuisine and
70 where fast food culture is less strongly established. But the movement is also growing across the Atlantic. Its American membership is eight thousand and rising. In the United States, Slow Food helped persuade *Time* magazine to run a feature on the Sun Crest peach of
75 Northern California, a fruit that tastes sublime but travels badly. After the article appeared, the small producer was overwhelmed with buyers wanting to sample his crop.

Slow Food is also leading a successful campaign to bring back the tasty rare-breed turkeys—Narragansett, Jersey Buff, Standard Bronze, Bourbon Red—that were the
80 centrepiece of every American family's Thanksgiving supper until bland factory-farmed birds took over …

J:

As part of its ecological beliefs, Slow Food opposes the genetic modification of foodstuffs and promotes organic farming. Nobody has conclusively proven that organic
85 food is more nutritious or better tasting than non-organic, but it is clear that the methods used by many conventional farmers **take a toll on** the environment, polluting the water table, killing off other plants and exhausting the soil. According to the Smithsonian Migratory Bird Center in the United States, pesticides, directly or indirectly, kill at least sixty-seven million American birds every year. By contrast, a
90 well-run organic farm can use crop rotation to enrich the soil and manage pests—and still be very productive.

take a toll on (exp.): have a bad effect over a long period of time

K:

Slow Food fights for biodiversity. In the food industry, efficiency leads to **homogenization**: manufacturers can process **inputs**—be they turkeys, tomatoes, or turnips—more
95 quickly if they are all the same. So the farmers are required to concentrate on single strains or breeds. Over the last century, for instance, the number of artichoke varieties grown in Italy has tumbled from two hundred to about a dozen. Besides narrowing our choice of flavours, the loss of animal variety upsets delicate ecosystems … In addition, when all you have is one breed of turkey, a single virus can wipe out the
100 whole species.

(1088 words)

Honoré, C. (2004). *In praise of slowness: How a worldwide movement is challenging the cult of speed* (pp. 54–63). San Francisco, CA: Harper San Francisco.

After You Read

D. Answer the questions to check your comprehension.

1 To increase efficiency, what "scientific tricks" must farmers use, and what benefits do they provide?

_____

_____

_____

_____

2 How did the Slow Food movement start?

_____

_____

_____

_____

3 Globally, what do Slow Food activists do?

_____

_____

_____

_____

4 Why does the Slow Food movement support organic farming and oppose genetic modification?

_____

_____

_____

_____

5 Why does the Slow Food movement support biodiversity?

_____

_____

_____

6 The author of this reading is Carl Honoré; his book *In Praise of Slowness* is famous for exploring how to apply the Slow Food philosophy to many fields of human experience. Honoré has made a career of talking and writing about the Slow movement. Search online to learn about some of the activities he has been involved with. List some of them here.

_____

_____

_____

7 Look online to discover some of the fields that Honoré suggests the Slow philosophy can be applied to. List them here.

_____

_____

_____

My Bookshelf > My eLab > Exercises > Chapter 8 > In Praise of Slowness

FOCUS ON WRITING

Choosing Vocabulary to Express Opinions

As you know, writers write about facts, but they also express their opinions about facts. When writers use expressions such as _in my opinion_ or _I believe that_, it is easy to identify their opinions. But these first-person expressions are not always appropriate in academic writing. So how do academic writers manage to express their opinions?

Read the following sentence from Reading 1, in which the writer expresses his disgust with modern methods of food production. How do you, the reader, recognize the writer's opinion?

> "Chemical fertilizers and pesticides, intensive feeding, antibiotic digestive enhancers, growth hormones, rigorous breeding, genetic modification—every scientific trick known to man has been deployed to cut costs, boost yields, and make livestock and crops grow more quickly."

The writer uses the word _trick_ to refer to methods employed in commercial farming. In this context, _trick_ has a pejorative connotation—a negative meaning that goes beyond the actual definition. By using this word, the author conveys his opinion that modern food production is an unnatural or unfair game used to increase efficiency. If the writer used the word _method_ instead, the reader would not get the same impression of the writer's opinion.

In the following sentence, also from Reading 1, the writer again expresses his dissatisfaction with modern methods of food production. What words does he use to express his opinion?

> "Two centuries ago, the average pig took five years to reach 286 kilograms; today, it hits 484 kilograms after just six months and is slaughtered before it loses its baby teeth."

The words _hits_ and _slaughtered_ convey the writer's disapproval; _before it loses its baby teeth_ also suggests that the animal is being killed at too young an age. Consider how different your understanding would be if the writer wrote the sentence this way.

> Two centuries ago, the average pig took five years to reach 286 kilograms; today, it _weighs_ 484 kilograms after just six months and is _butchered while the meat is still tender_.

You might expect to find this sentence in a text about the benefits of modern methods of food production. You would think that the writer approves of these methods.

You can see that careful choice of vocabulary can be effective to express opinion without the use of the first person.

A. Now, read one more sentence from Reading 1 and underline the words that express the writer's opinion.

"The small landowner gives way to the factory farm, which churns out food that is fast, cheap, abundant, and standardized."

B. Working with a partner, read the following sentences. The sentences are neutral; they do not express opinions. Keeping the facts the same, replace some of the words with synonyms that have negative connotations, to express unhappiness with modern methods of food production. When you have finished, compare your answers with the class.

1 Today, North American salmon are genetically modified to grow four to six times faster than they would in the wild.

_____

_____

_____

2 With new strains of rice, farmers can grow two or more harvests of grain within a single year.

_____

_____

_____

3 There are varieties of peaches that can be picked when they are hard and shipped over long distances.

_____

_____

_____

_____

My Bookshelf > My eLab >
Exercises > Chapter 8 >
Focus on Writing

FOCUS ON ACCURACY

Clarifying the Subject of a Sentence

You may have noticed that the writer of Reading 1 discusses the Slow Food organization as if it were a person. Look at the following sentences from the reading that clearly show this practice.

> Slow Food idealizes eco-gastronomy.
> Slow Food opened its own university ...
> Slow Food seeks out artisanal foods ...
> Slow Food opposes genetic modification.
> Slow Food fights for biodiversity.

To be strictly accurate, it is the *people* in the Slow Food movement who idealize, open, seek out, oppose, and fight on behalf of the movement.

▶

To clarify the subject of these sentences and accurately refer to the people who perform these actions, the writer could have revised these sentences in the following ways.

> Slow Food *members* idealize eco-gastronomy.
> *People in the Slow Food movement* opened *their* own university.
> Slow Food *supporters* seek out artisanal foods.
> Slow Food *advocates* oppose genetic modification.
> Slow Food *activists* fight for biodiversity.
>
> Note that the word *activist* implies aggressiveness, so it matches well with the verb *fight*.

A. Why do you think the author wrote about the Slow Food organization as if it were a person? What does this achieve? Read the following reasons and check the ones that you believe are true.

The author wrote about the Slow Food organization as if it were a person to

☐ suggest that all the people in the movement are united;

☐ make the Slow Food movement seem more alive;

☐ use fewer words;

☐ emphasize the movement more than the people in the movement.

B. Rewrite the following sentences to emphasize the people involved in the movement rather than the movement itself.

❶ Slow Food is working to save the Firiki apple and traditional olive oil-soaked ladotiri cheese in Greece.

_____

_____

_____

_____

❷ In France, Slow Food has advocated for the Pardigone plum and a delicate goat's cheese called Brousse du Rove.

_____

_____

_____

_____

❸ In the United States, Slow Food helped persuade *Time* magazine to run a feature on the Sun Crest peach of Northern California, a fruit that tastes sublime but travels badly.

_____

_____

_____

_____

④ Slow Food is also leading a successful campaign to bring back the tasty rare-breed turkeys—Narragansett, Jersey Buff, Standard Bronze, Bourbon Red—that were the centrepiece of every American family's Thanksgiving supper until bland factory-farmed birds took over.

_____

_____

_____

_____

My Bookshelf > My eLab >
Exercises > Chapter 8 >
Focus on Accuracy

When you write about the Slow Food movement, as you will in the Warm-Up and Final Assignments, you should follow academic writing conventions, and be clear about the subject of your sentences.

FOCUS ON READING

Reading Multi-Clause, Multi-Phrase Sentences

The writer of Reading 2 uses many long sentences containing multiple clauses and phrases that can make the sentences challenging to read and understand. Identifying the start and end points of the clauses and phrases in these sentences can help you make sense of them.

Each clause and phrase packages, or groups, content to help you, the reader, understand.

A. Here is the first sentence of the reading. Underline each clause. Circle the coordinate conjunctions. Highlight the relative pronoun.

> "Food production is rising, the amount of cultivated land is increasing, and 22 percent of the world population (almost half of the total workforce) is engaged in agriculture, but the food produced for twelve billion people is in fact not enough to feed the six billion who actually live in the world."

As you can see, the sentence begins with three independent clauses that are linked by commas and the coordinate conjunction *and*.

The writer uses commas to show that he is combining the independent clauses as items in a series. The coordinate conjunction *but* (preceded by a comma) begins another independent clause that presents contrasting information. Finally, the relative pronoun *who* introduces an adjective clause that describes the preceding noun phrase, *six billion (people)*.

The punctuation and conjunctions help the reader understand the content and construction of the sentence.

If you find you need to reread long sentences several times to understand them, highlight the punctuation and conjunctions to help you divide up the content.

B. Here is another long sentence from Reading 2. To understand how the content is packaged in this sentence, underline the clauses and prepositional phrases, and highlight the adjective clause.

> "Biodiversity is rapidly diminishing, especially agro-biodiversity, with a continual reduction in the number of animal breeds and vegetable varieties that have for centuries contributed to the sustenance of entire regions in a perfectly sustainable alliance between man and nature."

In this sentence, the independent clause is extended with a prepositional phrase ("with a continual ..."), an adjective clause beginning with *that* (to describe the animal breeds and vegetable varieties), and another prepositional phrase ("in a perfectly ..."). Recognizing the divisions between the clauses and phrases can help you understand the meaning more easily.

C. Working with a partner, underline the clauses and phrases in the following sentences. Highlight the conjunctions, relative pronouns, and prepositions that signal the divisions between clauses and phrases. When you have finished, discuss the meaning of the sentences with the class.

1 Executioner, because the unsustainable methods of agro-industry have led to the disappearance of many sustainable production methods that were once part of the identity of the communities that practised them and were one of the highest pleasures for the gastronome in search of valuable knowledge and flavours.

2 Victim, because the same unsustainable methods—originally necessary in order to feed a larger number of people—have since turned the sphere of food and agriculture into a neglected sector, completely detached from the lives of billions of people, as if procuring food required no effort at all.

3 Politicians show little interest in it, except when pressured to do so by the most powerful international corporations of agro-industry, while the average consumer either does not reflect on what he or she is eating or has to make a titanic effort to obtain the information that will explain it.

4 As Debal Deb stated in a 2004 publication, modern agricultural and forestry sciences have created a simplification and homogenization of nature in order to minimize uncertainty and ensure an efficient production of commercial goods; agriculture today consists of an intensification of a few crops, to the detriment of a magnificent genetic diversity created through millennia of experimentation.

READING ❷   Restoring Food to Its Central Place

In this reading, Carlo Petrini, the Italian man who founded the Slow Food movement, invites you to think about what has been lost in the push to produce enough food for the world's growing population.

A. Choose the best word or phrase from the box to complete each sentence, and write a definition underneath. The first one has been done for you.

> ~~abandoned~~   crucial factor   cultivated
> despite   element   procuring
> empirical evidence   previously   sphere

❶ In some places, agriculture has been _____abandoned_____ because it was not profitable.

Definition: _left behind, stopped_____

❷ Food production is rising, the amount of _____ land is increasing, and 22 percent of the world population (almost half of the total workforce) is engaged in agriculture.

Definition: _____

❸ During the past twenty years, we have used more than twice as many chemical fertilizers as we had ever _____ produced!

Definition: _____

❹ _____ the evidence of the adverse consequences of large-scale industrial agriculture, it has become the dominant model.

Definition: _____

❺ Unsustainable methods of food production … have since turned the _____ of food and agriculture into a neglected sector …

Definition: _____

❻ People should still regard food as a central _____ in their lives.

Definition: _____

7. There is _____ that agro-industry is not fulfilling its promise of eradicating world hunger.

Definition: _____

8. Agriculture has become completely detached from the lives of billions of people, as if _____ food required no effort at all.

Definition: _____

9. The formulas of chemical fertilizers ... have been the _____ in the escalation of modern industrial agriculture and its unnaturalness.

Definition: _____

Before You Read

A. How much do you know about where your food comes from?

1. When you purchase these foods, do you know where they come from? Check the ones you know.

☐ apples   ☐ dates

☐ oranges   ☐ rice

☐ olives   ☐ fish

☐ beans

2. When you consume these foods, do you know how they were produced? Check the ones you know.

☐ pasta   ☐ cheese

☐ meat   ☐ coffee

☐ cookies

If you're not sure, you're probably like most people in the world: you are not thinking about where your food comes from. Petrini suggests that we join the Slow Food movement and become aware of the processes that bring food to our tables.

While You Read

B. In the previous reading, Carl Honoré called Petrini "a charismatic culinary writer" (page 211). You probably remember that people who are charismatic are persuasive and attract others with their arguments. As you read, ask yourself if you are convinced by Petrini's arguments.

1. Do you believe that people have lost touch with where their food comes from?

2. Do you believe that the agricultural industry (agro-industry) has damaged Earth?

3. Do you believe that a new sustainable agriculture can restore cultural food traditions that have been lost?

C. When you finish reading, discuss these questions with your class, and decide how persuasive Petrini has been.

Restoring Food to Its Central Place

Food production is rising, the amount of **cultivated** land is increasing, and 22 percent of the world population (almost half of the total workforce) is engaged in agriculture, but the food produced for twelve billion people is in fact not enough to feed the six billion who actually live in the world. Moreover, this effort of production has not achieved
5 its aims. It has subjected the Earth to such stress that the land either turns to desert or dies because of the excessive use of chemical products. Water resources are running out. Biodiversity is rapidly diminishing, especially agro-biodiversity, with a continual reduction in the number of animal breeds and vegetable varieties that have for centuries contributed to the sustenance of entire regions in a perfectly sustainable
10 partnership between man and nature.

Something must have gone wrong, because if we consider the problem of satisfying the primal need for food and analyze it over the long term, the hunger for production has done more harm than good.

The contradiction in agro-industrial terms is clearly emerging: agro-industry has
15 given us the illusion that it could solve the problem of feeding the human race. I would go even further: over the last fifty years, it has turned food production into both executioner and victim. Executioner, because the unsustainable methods of agro-industry have led to the disappearance of many sustainable production methods that were once part of the identity of the communities that practised them and were one
20 of the highest pleasures for the gastronome in search of valuable knowledge and flavours. Victim, because the same unsustainable methods—originally necessary in order to feed a larger number of people—have since turned the **sphere** of food and agriculture into a neglected sector, completely detached from the lives of billions of people, as if **procuring** food … required no effort at all. Politicians show little interest
25 in it, except when pressured to do so by the most powerful international corporations of agro-industry, while the average consumer either does not reflect on what he or she is eating or has to make a **titanic** effort to obtain the information that will explain it.

titanic (adj.): big, strong, and impressive

Food and its production must regain the central place that they deserve among human activities, and we must re-examine the criteria that guide our actions. The crucial
30 point now is no longer, as it has been for all too long, the quality of food that is produced, but its complex quality, a concept that ranges from the question of taste to that of variety, from respect for the environment, ecosystems, and the rhythms of nature to respect for human dignity. The aim is to make a significant improvement to everybody's quality of life without having to submit, as we have done until now,
35 to a model of development that is incompatible with the needs of the planet.

Agro-Industry?

It should be stated at the beginning that if food is to regain its central place, we will have to concern ourselves with agriculture. It is impossible to discuss food without discussing agriculture. Every gastronome should be aware of this because the present
40 situation in the world is the result of the history of Western agriculture (and the damage it has done to nature), an agriculture that has lost sight of some of the aims that are most important to anyone who cares about the quality of food …

The formulas of chemical fertilizers were first developed in the 1840s, and they have been the **crucial factor** in the escalation of modern industrial agriculture and its
45 unnaturalness (Bevilacqua, 2002). The trend toward chemistry did not just carry on

the tradition of introducing **elements** alien to existing ecosystems but introduced inorganic elements that have been overused. During the past twenty years, we have used more than twice as many chemical fertilizers as we had ever **previously** produced! Can the Earth sustain such a change in its balance?

50 As Debal Deb stated in a 2004 publication, modern agricultural and forestry sciences have created a simplification and homogenization of nature in order to minimize uncertainty and ensure an efficient production of commercial goods; agriculture today consists of an intensification of a few crops, **to the detriment of** a magnificent genetic diversity created through millennia of experimentation. The **monocultures** of those
55 varieties that are valid from the commercial point of view have shaped modern agriculture, which rapidly eliminates life forms, impoverishes the soil, and destroys the systems that support life on Earth. The worst thing, Deb goes on to say, is that, **despite** the **empirical evidence** of the adverse consequences of large-scale industrial agriculture, this has become the model to follow for agricultural development in all
60 the countries that try to imitate the Western model of growth (2004, p. 4).

The **absurd** idea (it is a contradiction in terms!) of industrial agriculture—agriculture carried out according to the principles of industry—is thus dominant. Under industrial agriculture, the fruits of nature are considered raw materials to be consumed and processed on a mass scale. The subversion of the natural order has affected the entire
65 food production system. The agro-industry of food production has become the model of development in a world in which technology reigns. And if it has done enormous damage in the Western world that invented it, the imposition of a single method of development … has created even worse problems elsewhere. It has done untold harm to the environments and people of the countries that are poorest in material wealth
70 (though certainly not in biodiversity), and to traditions and cultures that have existed for centuries in perfect harmony with their ecosystems …

The final balance sheet is beginning to show the effects of these changes: enormous damage caused to the ecosystem; an increase in food production that has not solved the problems of hunger and malnutrition; and an incalculable loss from cultural and
75 social points of view. From this latter viewpoint, ancient traditions and knowledge have been thrown away; the rural population has **abandoned** the countryside to fill up the cities (a phenomenon that is reaching catastrophic proportions in developing countries, creating megalopolises like New Delhi or Mexico City); and there has been a loss of culinary knowledge that was once the basis of a correct—as well as enjoyable—
80 use of agricultural resources. We are witnessing a form of cultural destruction that has affected the countryside of every part of the world, on a scale that has never before been seen in human history.

There is therefore an urgent need for new kinds of farming, a truly *new agriculture*. Sustainable methods can take their starting point from the small (or large, depending
85 on where in the world you are) amount of knowledge that has not been eliminated by agro-industrial methods. This will not be a return to the past, but rather a new beginning that grows out of the past, with an awareness of the mistakes that have been made in recent years. It will involve making productive again those areas where agriculture has been abandoned because it was not profitable according to industrial criteria; preserving,
90 improving, and spreading knowledge of the traditional practices that are demonstrating that other ways of production are possible; and giving new dignity and new opportunities to the people who have been **marginalized** by the globalization of agriculture.

to the detriment (n.) **of**: causing harm or damage to

monocultures (n.): large, single cultures that have no diversity

absurd (adj.): completely unreasonable

marginalized (v.): made to feel powerless in an unfair way (pushed to the margins of society)

Only through a new sustainable agriculture that respects both old traditions and modern
95 technologies (for the new technologies are not bad in themselves—it all depends on how one uses them) can we begin to have hopes of a better future. And only through its global acceptance will gastronomes be able to move
100 from their present state of protesters against the prevailing trends to that of fulfilled people who still regard food as a central element in our lives.

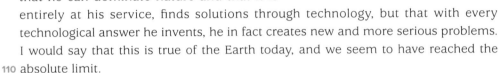

The Gastronome

105 There is a theory that man, since he [believes] that he can dominate nature and that it is entirely at his service, finds solutions through technology, but that with every technological answer he invents, he in fact creates new and more serious problems. I would say that this is true of the Earth today, and we seem to have reached the
110 absolute limit.

This situation demands much more than a simple change, of course: it demands a radical change in mentality, more complexity of thought, more humility, and a greater sense of responsibility toward nature.

(1389 words)

References

Bevilacqua, P. (2002). *La mucca è savia.* Rome, Italy: Donzelli.

Deb, D. (2004). *Industrial vs. ecological agriculture.* New Delhi, India: Navdanya/RFSTE.

Petrini, C. (2005). *Slow food nation: Why our food should be good, clean, and fair* (pp. 22–28). New York, NY: Rizzoli Ex Libris.

After You Read

D. Answer the following questions to check your comprehension.

1 What characteristics of Petrini's writing show him to be charismatic?

_____

_____

_____

2 Why does Petrini think that something has gone wrong with modern agriculture?

_____

_____

_____

_____

3 Petrini writes that modern methods of agro-industry have made food production both "executioner" and "victim." What does he mean?

_____

_____

_____

_____

4 Why does Petrini argue that food must regain its central place in our lives?

_____

_____

_____

5 What does Petrini blame Western agriculture for?

_____

_____

_____

6 What are the dangers of creating an agricultural monoculture?

_____

_____

_____

7 Why is the term _agro-industry_ a contradiction?

_____

_____

_____

8 What damage does the "final balance sheet" display?

_____

_____

_____

9 What characteristics should the new agriculture include?

_____

_____

_____

_____

10 What does Petrini believe the situation demands now?

_____

_____

_____

My Bookshelf > My eLab >
Exercises > Chapter 8 >
Restoring Food to Its Central Place

WARM-UP ASSIGNMENT
Write a Short Persuasive Essay

A. To prepare for your Final Assignment, write a short persuasive essay either agreeing or disagreeing with the following statement.

The Slow Food movement will improve the condition of the environment.

A persuasive essay, like other essay types, has an introduction with a thesis statement (that expresses your opinion), a body, and a conclusion. Remember that the essay should aim to convince your readers to accept your viewpoint.

B. Choose vocabulary that expresses your opinion without using the first-person perspective.

C. Write accurately to emphasize the people in the movement rather than writing about the movement as if it were a person.

Refer to the Models Chapter (page 247) to see an example of a persuasive essay and to learn more about how to write one.

> **❶** When you receive feedback from your teacher or your classmates on this Warm-Up Assignment, you will have information that you can use to improve your writing on the Final Assignment.

Academic
Survival Skill

Expressing Opposing Ideas

Readings 1 and 2 presented a positive view of the Slow Food movement and its benefits. Suppose your instructor now asks you and your classmates to consider some of its possible negative consequences. If, for example, everyone adopted Slow Food as a philosophy of life and of economic and environmental balance, what might some of the negative consequences be?

In response, you might list the following concerns:

1 Slow Food farming means not using fertilizers or pesticides to grow food. This will reduce farmers' production, leading to lower incomes.

2 Slow Food farming means not shipping produce over long distances. This will conserve fuel, but it also means some foods will not be available in some countries. For example, it may be difficult to get fruit and vegetables during winter in countries with cold climates.

3 Slow Food farming means diversifying animal and plant varieties rather than standardizing strains. This could lead to higher food prices.

④ Slow Food cooking means shopping for fresh food and spending time preparing meals in the old-fashioned way. These activities are time-consuming, and might be difficult for some people who are busy with family and work.

Your instructor then asks you to write about these concerns. You may feel uncomfortable writing negatively about a movement that seems to have so many advantages. You may think that your concerns are not significant or may not want to criticize such a popular movement. And you may consider that academic writing should just deal with the facts, not the writer's opinion. However, in many academic communities, it is appropriate and necessary to express divergent opinions to show you are capable of independent thought on various topics. Your challenge is to find appropriate ways to express views that oppose those of other writers.

Here are some "sentence frames" to help you express opposing thoughts.

Use the active voice to oppose a specific writer.

- Although / even though Petrini believes that ..., he has not considered ...
- Petrini states that ...; however, he must also think about ...
- Scholars/researchers continue to disagree about Petrini's statement that ...
- Scholars/researchers dispute/take issue with Petrini's suggestion that ...
- Critics of the Slow Food movement differ sharply with Petrini's conclusion that ...
- Petrini is mistaken when he states that ...

Use the active voice to oppose an idea.

- Women are divided on the issue of ...
- There is disagreement/dispute about how ...
- There is controversy about ...
- This ... is a contentious issue in the Slow Food movement.
- This ... is a divisive issue in the Slow Food movement.

Use the passive voice to avoid criticizing the writer(s) directly.

- Not enough thought/consideration/attention has been given to ...
- More thought/consideration/attention should be given to ...
- Despite ..., not enough importance has been attached to ...
- Despite ..., more importance should be given to ...

A. Can you think of other ways to express disagreement with a writer or an idea? If so, share them with the class.

B. On a separate page, use the sentence frames to express opposition to the Slow Food movement. You can use the opposing ideas previously mentioned, or you may be able to think of other points. When you have finished, write your sentences on the board and discuss their effectiveness with the class.

The Ideology of Slow Food

This reading is an academic article in which the writer criticizes the Slow Food movement for a variety of reasons. As Slow Food movement supporters appear to have good intentions, you may be surprised by the number of objections mentioned here.

VOCABULARY BUILD

A. Choose the best word to complete each sentence. Use a dictionary if required.

B. Confirm your answers with a classmate. Continue working together to write another sentence using the same word. Write your best sentences on the board to share with the rest of your class.

① Members of the Slow Food movement must be _____ because they need to have the money to buy expensive food, and the time to prepare it.

  a) affluent   b) stratified   c) standard

  Your sentence: _____

② Our cooking traditions form part of our culture. Petrini believes that if we ignore our cooking traditions, we are no better than _____.

  a) ideologies   b) distinctions   c) barbarians

  Your sentence: _____

③ Quality food is associated with the good life. For this reason, quality food is responsible for _____ high status on the people who consume it.

  a) intervening   b) conferring   c) eroding

  Your sentence: _____

④ Quality food confers high status and _____ to people who can afford it.

  a) intervention   b) distinction   c) standardization

  Your sentence: _____

⑤ People like fast food because it can be eaten quickly and cheaply; its popularity does not demonstrate the _____ of a culture.

  a) erosion   b) ideology   c) luxury

  Your sentence: _____

⑥ The _____ of the Slow Food movement includes several related beliefs about the speed of living and eating, the destruction of farmland, and the return to traditional cooking and farming methods.

  a) distinction   b) intervention   c) ideology

  Your sentence: _____

7 Simonetti, in his 2012 article "The Ideology of Slow Food," suggests that members of the Slow Food movement believe that agriculture is a human

_____ that contradicts the natural processes of the Earth.

a) distinction   b) intervention   c) propaganda

Your sentence: _____

8 Spending time eating and preparing quality food are _____ activities that only the affluent can afford.

a) luxury   b) affluent   c) stratified

Your sentence: _____

9 Supporters of the Slow Food movement believe that the popularity of fast

food must be due to _____ and the mass media that try to create false needs; otherwise, people would never buy fast food.

a) propaganda   b) ideology   c) barbarians

Your sentence: _____

10 In the industrial age, time spent _____ pleasure was not valued because it reduced the amount of time people had to produce goods.

a) in pursuit of   b) in order to   c) because of

Your sentence: _____

11 Petrini believes that fast food and agro-industry have led to the

_____ of food.

a) standardization   b) intervention   c) distinction

Your sentence: _____

12 Simonetti believes that a return to an idealized past would be an unfortunate

return to a _____ society where people had little ability to move from one social class to another.

a) affluent   b) stratified   c) distinct

Your sentence: _____

My Bookshelf > My eLab >
Exercises > Chapter 8 >
Vocabulary Review

Before You Read

A. Some of the reasons the writer cites to criticize the Slow Food movement are mentioned in the abstract of the article. Read the abstract (page 230), and list the reasons why the writer disagrees with the Slow Food movement. Compare your answers with a classmate's to confirm your understanding.

_____

_____

_____

_____

_____

_____

While You Read

B. For each of the first seven paragraphs, you will find a one-sentence summary in the box below. Read the first seven paragraphs, and write the one-sentence summary in the table that follows, next to the corresponding paragraph number. (The first one has been done for you.) Then read the next seven paragraphs, and fill in the table with your own one-sentence summary statements.

Summary Statements for the First Seven Paragraphs

- This paragraph gives a short history of the Slow Food movement.
- Slow food advocates believe that fast food destroys food customs and traditions.
- ~~The abstract provides an overview of what the article will be about.~~
- Time and access to good food are luxuries.
- The Slow Food movement's main goals emphasize the rights of people to enjoy good-quality, local, culturally appropriate food produced by traditional, sustainable methods of agriculture that promote biodiversity.
- The existence of fast food is justified because people may want quick, inexpensive food.
- Slow food believers think that fast food is a modern phenomenon, but it's not.

PARAGRAPH NUMBER	ONE-SENTENCE SUMMARY STATEMENT
1	*The abstract provides an overview of what the article will be about.*
2	
3	
4	
5	
6	
7	

PARAGRAPH NUMBER	ONE-SENTENCE SUMMARY STATEMENT
⑧	
⑨	
⑩	
⑪	
⑫	
⑬	
⑭	

C. When you have finished, work with a small group of students to compare your paragraph summaries. Confirm your understanding of the content with your class.

The Ideology of Slow Food

Abstract

This article addresses the **ideology** of Slow Food (SF), an influential movement founded in Italy in 1986. Through an analysis of a wide range of texts, ranging from SF's opposition to fast food to its ambition to establish a new "gastronomic science" and
5 a new "development model" based on the three criteria of *buono* (good), *pulito* (clean), and *guisto* (tasty), the article … claims that SF's understanding of the capitalist system is limited, that its idea of a new agriculture and a new economy is simply that of returning to a primitive, pre-industrial economy (without explaining how that economy could feed the present world population), that its ideal of a new world is that of a
10 **stratified** and [unchangeable] society, and that its main goal is to combine the commercial promotion of high-price **luxury** food products with political engagement.

…

SF's main goals are the following:

- placing the right emphasis on the pleasure of food, and learning how to appreciate
15 different recipes and tastes, in order to recognize the various places and skills of production, and to respect the rhythms of the seasons and of the *convivium*;

- sustaining the education of taste as a defence against poor quality, food fraud, and the **standardization** of our meals;
20 - safeguarding local cuisines, traditional production systems, and vegetable and animal species at risk of extinction;
- sustaining a new model of agriculture that is less intensive and cleaner;
- defending biodiversity and the right of the people to food sovereignty.[1]

SF was created in the late 1980s by people feeling a "snobbish distaste for that consumerist and TV-addicted Italy" and a desire to "contain this barbaric invasion"
25 (Petrini & Padovani, 2005, p. 92). Its origins date back to a reaction to the first Italian fast food outlets (the first McDonald's restaurant in Italy opened in 1985), but from the very beginning it was opposed not just to a food model but to an entire culture: "Fast food was backed by a new culture and a new civilization having one value only: profit. Pleasure is totally incompatible with productivity, since the time spent in its
30 **pursuit** is subtracted from production" (Petrini & Padovani, 2005, pp. 90–91). Thus, in the SF Manifesto, we read that modern civilization started under "the signs of … acceleration," taking the machine as a model for man himself and velocity as the "dominant ideal." SF proposes to "defeat the virus of fast." … This is SF's "modest proposal for a gradual as well as progressive recovery of man, both as an individual
35 and as a species, in the long-delayed process of environmental recovery, in order to make life livable again, starting from basic desires."

It is striking that SF ignores the fact that fast food (i.e., food rapidly bought and eaten outside the home) has always existed, from ancient Rome to medieval China, from seventeenth-century France to pre-Columbian America. On the other hand, what is
40 very recent and typical of modern bourgeois civilization … is precisely the meal slowly consumed at the family table. It is therefore wrong to consider fast food as a modern phenomenon.

By its own admission, SF's hostility to fast food is due to cultural reasons: namely, fast food would upset the … "customs," the complex of habits and behaviours followed
45 by a people … Fast food with its planetary standardization has totally erased these traditions, these "customs" as regards to eating, and is consequently, … immoral … Even conceding that consumers of fast food get the same pleasure from it that others get from a glass of wine or from a dinner in good company, SF would [state that if we abandon the habits, rhythms, and cultural layers which form our history, and our
50 identity, we turn ourselves into **barbarians**] (Petrini, 2001).

The major weakness of this kind of criticism is that it is based on the untested conviction that consumption of certain products (i.e., fast food) cannot be **aesthetically** enjoyed[2] and cannot have another rational justification; the success of that product, therefore, must be due to **propaganda** such as mass media or advertising, to mass
55 conformism, or to the **debasement** of culture. But the basis of this argument is not only **elitist**[3] but unproven. These prejudices prevent SF from recognizing that fast food, like other mass products, attracts consumers not because of their lack of culture

aesthetically (adv.): in a way that gives pleasure through the senses

debasement (n.): lowering of value or respect of someone or something

elitist (adj.): describes a system in which a small group of people have power and privilege

---

1. See the SF website at https://www.slowfood.com/about-us/

2. "Critics have a tendency to dismiss popular taste, to imagine that people couldn't really like McDonald's food or really enjoy listening to Celine Dion" (Heath and Potter, 2005, p. 239). The problem is studied with unparalleled finesse by Williams (1989 [1961]: 305ff).

3. "Whenever you look at the list of consumer goods which (according to the critic) people don't really need, what you invariably see is a list of consumer goods that middle-aged intellectuals don't need" (Heath and Potter, 2005: 108).

or the hypnotic influence of media and advertising, but because it can be consumed quickly and at a low price by people without much time and/or money. These are quite reasonable motives, and are wholly capable of explaining the success of fast food (Jones, Shears, Hillier, Comfort, & Lowell, 2003, p. 302ff), with no need to assume [the **erosion** of culture.] …

Having personal relations with producers and suppliers [as SF recommends], as well as spending time at the table in good company, are costly and time-consuming activities: in other words, they are *luxury goods* … [SF adherents] are **affluent** because the products promoted by SF are *luxury* goods, and as such they are necessarily intended for a minority … On the one hand, the emphasis the movement puts on hand-crafted and local produce implies a limited production, with obvious consequences for prices. On the other hand, it is the nature of quality goods that makes them products that only have "quality" as opposed to "mass" or standardized production; it is precisely for this reason that quality goods are capable of **conferring** status and **distinction**.

…

In SF's system, a crucial role is played by the critique of industrial agriculture and by praise of "traditional" farming. The history of Western agriculture is seen by SF as a gradual but unstoppable passage from "naturalness" to "unnaturalness" (Petrini, 2005, p. 22). However, the concept of natural agriculture is problematic. In fact, since none of the plants grown by man exist in nature … one must conclude that agriculture—like most human activities—is an artificial **intervention** in nature, and alteration of it and even a violence toward it … In fact, the artificiality of agriculture is common knowledge in Western culture.[4] [What this means is] that "naturalness" cannot be the [division] between what can and cannot be done in agriculture because "naturalness" does not exist.

Conversely, for SF, agriculture became "unnatural" only recently, after the triumph of chemistry (i.e., fertilizers and pesticides). SF proponents prefer the growing of only "native varieties and races," which, being "inserted into the ecosystem which saw their birth and evolution, guarantee the conservation of that ecosystem" (Petrini, 2005, p. 22). In the first place, do such things as "millennial ecosystems" and "native varieties and races" actually exist? … The truth is that there are no agricultural products "well suited to their original ecosystems" because there are no original agricultural ecosystems. The products of agriculture and breeding are the most globalized on earth.

…

SF's critique of modern industrial agriculture is also based on other premises. The main one is that, notwithstanding the increase in the extent of cultivated land, the use of fertilizers, water consumption and pollution, output is still not sufficient to feed everyone (Petrini, 2005, pp. 24–25). On the contrary, agro-industry "in some way gave us the illusion that the food problems of mankind could be solved" (Petrini, 2005, p. 20). So we would conclude that these problems could be solved and that all other efforts must stop in order to return to the old ways. But SF explains neither how we could get back to the previous situation nor how we could feed the present world population … Therefore, [SF] is a movement that objects to industrial and intensive farming because it is unable to solve the hunger problem, only to put in its place an agriculture that would produce even less.

…

---

4. Thus Leopardi (1976 [1827], p. 181) wrote: "most of what we call natural, is not, but is instead artificial."

We can gather that the great novelty proposed
105 by SF is nothing less than a return to primitive
society ... It was, as we now know after decades
of interdisciplinary studies,[5] the kind of society
which not only suffered from a systematic
scarcity, but which, like all pre-industrial
110 societies,[6] far from being more "human" and
"generous" than modern ones, was actually
based on robbery, violence and the systematic
exploitation of nature and other people.[7] But
SF ignores this debate.

115 ...

We are dealing with ... idealizations of an
imaginary past, of which SF selects only the
appealing features, systematically forgetting
all others. Thus, the idea of a return to ...
120 "a government ruled by the values of a nation
of farmers" (Petrini & Padovani, 2005, pp. 208–
209) is greeted with enthusiasm by SF without

taking into consideration that one of those values was slavery. Similarly, when SF
praises the "traditional role of women in the food chain" (Petrini, 2006, p. 6), we
125 should also remember that for centuries the role of women was an extremely
subordinate one, and that their emancipation in developed countries was achieved
precisely by overthrowing this traditional role (Allen & Sachs, 2007, p. 15ff; Walter,
2009, pp. 9–10).

...

130 The portrait of the "slow man" is that of a person rich in money and leisure time.
The fact that the means that enable the "slow man" to exert his taste and his senses
originate precisely from the **diabolical** activities of speed, industrialization, and
standardization—in short, capitalism—is something that SF does not even notice.
And SF does not realize that such a way of life cannot be affordable below a given
135 level of income, and so cannot be the basis for a "new model of development." ...
Moreover, attributing to pre-industrial, backward, or even primitive societies the leisure
to think, to cultivate human relations, etc., is pure myth. Developed societies are in
fact only those that can afford to "lose time," since increases in productivity allow
them to produce more in less time. Rather, traditional pre-industrial, underdeveloped
140 societies are those that devote most of their time to production for their own **subsistence**,
that are most obsessed with production, and that exploit natural resources most
mercilessly and endanger the environment.[8]

...

diabolical (adj.): evil
(relating to the devil)

subsistence (n.): the
condition of having just
enough money or food
to survive

---

5. A debate among anthropologists, historians, archaeologists, classicists, economists, philosophers, etc.,
   starting from the rediscovery of Marx's Forms which precede capitalist production, and stimulated by
   the work of Polanyi. An interesting survey can be found in Carandini (1979, p. 208ff).

6. As explained, among others, by Cipolla (2002 [1974], p. 31ff). See, in particular, p. 35: "in those centuries
   gift and robbery as an alternative to exchange were economically more relevant than exchange itself."

7. In particular, slavery was a typical characteristic of all Mediterranean societies: see Braudel (2002 [1949],
   pp. 797–798); Horden and Purcell (2006 [2000], p. 388).

8. There would be thousands of references. Here it will suffice to quote Cipolla (2002, p. 87 and *passim*).

If SF were to present itself as a movement of gourmets, no harm could be done.
145 But when it claims to know the secret formula for protecting biodiversity, feeding the starving, and even creating new sustainable growth, then there is a danger that "the best for the few is the enemy of the good of the many" (Laudan, 2004, p. 143). As long as there are starving people in the world, the way to help them is not to maintain culinary and agricultural traditions, but to change them … The fact is that SF is anti-
150 scientific, worshipping traditional societies, fond of little … communities [that are] eternally fixed, uninterested in and ignorant of history and the realities of production, and thus incapable of seeing complex contradictions and historical fictions [the movement embraces].

(1775 words)

References

Allen, P., & Sachs, C. (2007). Women and food chains: the gendered politics of food. *International Journal of Sociology of Food and Agriculture, 15*(1), 1–23.

Jones, P., Shears, P., Hillier, D., Comfort, D., & Lowell, J. (2003). Return to traditional values? A case study of Slow Food. *British Food Journal, 105*(4/5), 297–304.

Laudan, R. (2004). Slow food, the French terroir strategy, and culinary modernism. *Food, Culture and Society, 7*(2), 133–149.

Petrini, C. (2001). *Slow Food: Le ragioni del gusto*. Rome, Italy: Laterza.

Petrini, C. (2005). *Buono, pulito e giusto*. Turin, Italy: Einaudi.

Petrini, C. (2006). Sovranità alimentare. *Slow, 54*, 6–7.

Petrini, C., & Padovani, G. (2005). *Slow Food revolution*. Milan, Italy: Rizzoli.

Walter, L. (2009). Slow food and home cooking: Toward a relational aesthetic of food and relational ethic of home. *Provisions: The Journal of the Center for Food in Community and Culture, 1*, 1–23.

———————

Simonetti, L. (2012). The ideology of Slow Food. *Journal of European Studies, 42*(2), 168–189.

After You Read

D. Answer the following questions.

1. Why does Simonetti start by listing the main goals of the Slow Food movement?

_____

_____

2. Does the writer refer to Slow Food as if the movement were a person? Give an example to support your answer.

_____

_____

3. What do you think of the Slow Food movement now? Do you agree that it is an admirable movement that will help improve the world? Why?

_____

_____

4. Did you find the writer's arguments against the Slow Food movement persuasive? Which criticisms (if any) do you find most persuasive?

_____

_____

My Bookshelf > My eLab >
Exercises > Chapter 8 >
The Ideology of Slow Food

Finding an Academic Source

As you prepare for the Final Assignment, you may wish to find more information to quote, summarize, and/or paraphrase in your persuasive essay.

A. First, you can think about the information you already have about the Slow Food movement based on the readings in this chapter. Complete this table with the titles of the readings to help you categorize this information.

IN SUPPORT OF THE SLOW FOOD MOVEMENT	CRITIQUE(S) OF THE SLOW FOOD MOVEMENT

B. Next, consider the online searches you completed while going through this chapter. In Gearing Up (page 207), you found the Slow Food International website. In Reading 1, After You Read (p. 213), you read more about the author, Carl Honoré. Add these sources of information to the table above in the appropriate column.

You can see that you have more sources in support of than against the Slow Food movement. It would be a good idea to find at least one more source that critiques the Slow Food movement before you write your final essay.

As you will be writing an academic essay, the sources should be academic. Although it's possible to find academic sources online, you can also use this opportunity to become familiar with your school library. Try to find either a book or an academic journal to make sure your source is academic.

Your instructor may take you to the library, or may arrange for a librarian to come and speak to your class. You may also go on your own and consult with a librarian. Be sure to learn how to find books in the library, and how to search the library databases to find an academic journal.

Find one academic source (either a book or an academic journal) that is critical of the Slow Food movement. Be sure to get all the information required to cite the source in your References section. Read and think about how this new information fits with what you already know about the Slow Food movement. Use this information in the Final Assignment.

FINAL ASSIGNMENT
Write an Extended Persuasive Essay

A. Write a persuasive essay of approximately three to four pages. Whichever position you take, present the opposing view as well, using the sentence frames from Academic Survival Skill (page 225).

B. Agree or disagree with one of the following statements, and explain your reasons.

  1 If more people adhere to the Slow Food movement, it will be beneficial to women.

  2 If more people adhere to the Slow Food movement, it will reduce the cost of food.

  3 If more people adhere to the Slow Food movement, it will be beneficial for the environment.

  4 If more people adhere to the Slow Food movement, it will ensure farmers are paid more for the food they produce.

C. Be sure to
- use vocabulary from the readings to write about the Slow Food movement;
- clarify the subjects of your sentences so you accurately write about the people in the movement;
- choose vocabulary carefully to express your opinion without using a first-person perspective;
- express opposing ideas by using the sentence frames you learned in Academic Survival Skill;
- quote, paraphrase, and/or summarize from the readings in this chapter and others you have found through your own research. Don't forget to list the readings in a Reference section at the end of your essay.

Refer to the Models Chapter (page 254) to see an example of an extended persuasive essay and to learn more about how to write one.

Critical Connections

Use your abilities to find academic sources of information and to express opposing perspectives to think about the topics in the other chapters of this book.

A. Read the sentences below (one for each of the first seven chapters of this book) which summarize the main ideas in each chapter. Select one or two of the summary sentences, and find an academic source (either a library book or a journal article) that presents an opposing view.

SUMMARY SENTENCES	OPPOSING PERSPECTIVES
❶ Robots will solve many of the world's problems.	
❷ The benefits of pursuing education internationally are obvious; therefore, all students should study internationally.	
❸ Companies must constantly innovate to keep existing customers and win new ones. As a result, constant innovation is a requirement for success.	
❹ Marketing provides consumers with information about the products they want.	
❺ A healthy diet will lead to a healthy life.	
❻ Investing in bitcoin shows confidence in the future of digital currency.	
❼ The Internet of Things will make our lives more convenient than ever before.	

B. In the second column of the table, choose one of the sentence frames you used in Academic Survival Skill (page 225) to state the opposing perspective from the new source of information. Develop this into a full paragraph on a separate page.

MODELS CHAPTER

This chapter provides models of the writing assignments that you may be required to write as you progress through this textbook. All of the assignments are about water, allowing you to see how the same information can be arranged to meet the demands of different writing assignments.

Before each model assignment,

you will find

- instructions that highlight the key characteristics of the writing assignment;
- the outline that the writer used to prepare for the writing assignment.

MODEL 1 **How to Write Short Answers**

In the first sentence,

- repeat the important words from the question;
- respond to the first word in the question (for example, *what, when, why, how, explain, define*).

In the rest of the short answer,

- provide correct and detailed information to answer the question;
- organize the information (for example, first to last, simple to complex).

Question 1: What is the water cycle?

WRITER'S PLAN
• sky to Earth to sky (vapour to liquid to vapour) • rain and snow falls • falls on ground, rivers, and oceans • evaporates from land and returns to atmosphere

Answer

The **water cycle** is the process of water movement from the sky to the Earth and back to the sky again. Water is a vapour in the atmosphere, but it changes to liquid rain or solid snow as it falls to Earth. Once on land, the water flows into the earth, rivers, and oceans. The heat from the sun will cause the water to evaporate and become a vapour again as it returns to the atmosphere.

Question 2: What are the differences between a watershed and an aquifer?

WRITER'S PLAN	
WATERSHED	AQUIFER
• all land from which water drains into a common body of water • is natural—not based on political borders • example	• water in the ground • water travels downwards until it hits rock • aquifer is the layer of water above the layer of rock • can be large or small • example

Answer

A **watershed** is all the land from which water drains into a common body of water, while an **aquifer** is an underground layer of water found just above a layer of rock.

A **watershed** is a natural dividing line that does not reflect political borders. As a result, countries may share watersheds. Canada and the United States share a number of watersheds, such as the Pacific Ocean watershed west of the Rocky Mountains that drains into the Pacific Ocean, and the Great Lakes-St. Lawrence watershed that drains into the Atlantic Ocean.

An **aquifer**, or layer of water stored underground, is created as water from rain or melting snow sinks into the ground. Aquifers are important because people drill wells down to the aquifer to find water. Canada and the United States also share a number of large aquifers, such as the Abbotsford-Sumas transboundary aquifer shared between the province of British Columbia in Canada and Washington State in the United States.

Question 3: How can we conserve water around our homes?

WRITER'S PLAN
TWO WAYS TO CONSERVE WATER • use less water—repair, collect rain, be water-efficient • avoid contamination—use non-toxic cleaners, reduce pesticide and salt use

Answer

People can conserve water around their homes in two ways. First, they can use less water. By repairing leaky taps and toilets, collecting and using rainwater, reducing water use for the lawn, and using water-efficient shower heads and taps, people can save a significant amount of water. Second, people must avoid contaminating their water supply with toxic cleaners, fertilizers, pesticides, and salt.

MODEL 2   How to Design a Survey

A survey is designed to collect information from people (respondents/participants). To create a survey, you should

- decide what information you want to gather (limit yourself to finding one or two pieces of information);
- select two different groups of respondents you want to find information about (for example, men and women, older and younger, Chinese and Canadian);
- write a *hypothesis* (a sentence that explains what you expect to discover);
- ask five or six questions that will give you the information you want, including yes/no questions, multiple-choice questions, or Likert scale questions (to which participants can answer a) always, b) often, c) sometimes, d) rarely, or e) never);
- write the questions so that you can easily record the respondents' answers;
- conduct the survey (ask the survey questions);
- ask the same number of respondents from each of the groups;
- summarize the information in a table;
- consider whether your hypothesis was correct, and try to explain the outcome(s) based on the information you have gathered.

Example Survey

Hypothesis: *Older people use more water than younger people.*

1 How old are you?
☐ thirteen to thirty ☐ thirty-one or over

2 How many showers or baths do you take per day?
☐ one or less ☐ two ☐ more than two

3 On average, how many times do you flush the toilet per day?
☐ one to three times ☐ four or five times ☐ six times or more

4 How many times per week do you use the clothes washer?
☐ once or less ☐ twice ☐ more than twice

5 How many times per week do you use the dishwasher?
☐ once or less ☐ twice ☐ more than twice

6 Do you water your lawn?
☐ yes ☐ no

Summary of Survey Results

QUESTIONS	TOTAL NUMBER AGED THIRTEEN TO THIRTY (TEN)			TOTAL NUMBER AGED THIRTY-ONE OR OVER (TEN)		
1 How old are you?	**% TOTAL** 50%			**% TOTAL** 50%		
2 How many showers or baths do you take per day?	**<1 or 1** 7	**2** 3	**>2** 0	**<1 or 1** 10	**2** 0	**>2** 0
3 On average, how many times do you flush the toilet per day?	**1–3** 0	**4–5** 8	**>6** 2	**1–3** 0	**4–5** 4	**6 or >6** 6
4 How many times per week do you use the clothes washer?	**<1 or 1** 5	**2** 5	**>2** 0	**<1 or 1** 0	**2** 0	**>2** 10
5 How many times per week do you use the dishwasher?	**<1 or 1** 2	**2** 7	**>2** 1	**<1 or 1** 0	**2** 0	**>2** 10
6 Do you water your lawn?	**YES** 0		**NO** 10	**YES** 4		**NO** 6

MODEL 3 How to Write a Report

A report is designed to explain data or information. The following guidelines will help you write an effective report.

• Divide the report into sections. Many reports are divided into *introduction, methods, results*, and *discussion* sections. However, your sections will depend on the information that you need to explain.

• Select logical section headings.

• In your introduction section, explain why the information was collected.

• In your methods section, explain how the information was collected.

• In your results section, explain what you discovered. You may include tables or charts in this section.

• In your discussion section, highlight the value of the report's results, mention any limitations of the report, and provide your ideas for further research.

Example Report on the Model Survey

WRITER'S PLAN	
INTRODUCTION	• general information about fresh water • importance of conservation • importance of public education campaigns to encourage water conservation • segment of the population that would be best to target with these campaigns • hypothesis
METHODS	• explain survey design • explain participant selection (by age)

RESULTS	• hypothesis correct
	• summarize major results:
	  - younger people have showers more frequently
	  - older people use toilets, dishwashers, clothes washers, and lawn sprinklers more frequently
	  - overall, older people use more water than younger people

DISCUSSION	• limitations: is water use related to age or size of household? • more research needs to be done to target water reduction campaigns effectively

Water Conservation Efforts Best Targeted to Older People

Introduction

Water conservation is becoming an important issue as world population increases. Although the world is covered with water, approximately 97 percent of that water is salt water, and much of the remaining 3 percent is held in glaciers in the North and South Poles (United States Geological Society, 2016). Only a small percentage of the Earth's water is available to support human life. Water conservation is essential if people want to preserve their quality of life. The expression, "Think globally, act locally," encourages individuals to reduce their water consumption.

Scientists and governments are trying to educate people to reduce their water consumption and protect the quality of existing water. In order to do this, individuals should use less water by repairing leaky taps, collecting and using rainwater, buying water-efficient bathroom fixtures, eliminating grass watering, and reducing the use of toxic cleaners, fertilizers, pesticides, and salts. Although most people are aware they should be conserving water, many people do not actually make an effort to reduce their water consumption where it counts most: in the home. The public needs to be educated about how to reduce and protect water.

To develop effective public education campaigns, it is important to know who uses the most water. Do older people use more water than younger people? If this is true, then the government can target older people with its water use reduction campaigns. If younger people use more water, then the government can target younger people in these campaigns. This survey was based on the hypothesis that older people (aged thirty-one and over) used more water than younger people (aged thirteen to thirty).

Method

The survey was designed to cover all the areas where water is often wasted in the home: showers (baths), toilets, clothes washers, dishwashers, and lawns. There was one question for each of these areas. Here is a list of the questions.

1. How old are you?
   (This question divided the respondents into "younger" or "older" age groups.)

2. How many showers or baths do you take per day?

3. On average, how many times do you flush the toilet per day?

4. How many times per week do you use the clothes washer?

5. How many times per week do you use the dishwasher?

6. Do you water your lawn?

Showers (which use up to 42 litres per person per day), toilets (which use up to 54 litres per person per day), clothes washers (which use up to 36 litres per person per day), and faucets (which use up to 42 litres per person per day) consume a large amount of water every day (Alliance for Water Efficiency, 2016). These questions were designed to find out if the individuals were using less or more water.

Twenty people completed the survey. These people were selected, based on their age, so that half the survey population was between thirteen and thirty, and half was older than thirty. Children younger than thirteen were not surveyed because these individuals probably do not have the responsibility for cleaning their homes and clothes, and therefore, probably use less water than adults, who have greater responsibility in these areas.

Results

The results prove the hypothesis correct. Older people (aged thirty-one and over) use more water than younger people (aged thirteen to thirty). For only one question (Question 2), the results show that older people use less water than younger people; more senior people have fewer showers per day, consuming less water in this area only. The answers to the third question demonstrate that older individuals consume slightly more water than younger individuals by flushing the toilet more times per day. One hundred percent of both older and younger people said they flushed the toilet more than four times per day, yet 60 percent of older people flushed more than six times per day compared to only 20 percent of younger people. This suggests that more senior individuals are flushing slightly more often than younger individuals.

Responses to Questions 4 and 5 clearly show that older people use significantly more water per day than younger people. In response to the questions, "How many times per week do you use the clothes washer, and the dishwasher?," 100 percent of older people said they use these appliances more than twice a week. For these same questions, 100 percent of younger people said they used the clothes washer two times or less per week, and 90 percent said they used the dishwasher two times or less per week. These differences result in significantly reduced water consumption for younger people.

Similarly, when asked if they water their lawns, 100 percent of younger individuals responded "no" while only 60 percent of older individuals answered "no." As a result, younger people were again using less water than older people.

Discussion

The results support the hypothesis that older people use more water than younger people. Older participants used the toilet, clothes washer, dishwasher, and sprinkler more frequently than younger respondents. Older individuals only used less water in the shower as they had fewer showers than younger people.

It is possible that age is not the reason why more senior people use more water than more junior people. All the older respondents had children, and therefore larger households than the younger respondents. It is likely that having children results in more clothes and dishes to wash, and possibly more toilets to flush during the day. Of the younger people in the survey, only one of them had children. It is suggested that any follow-up survey should divide the respondents according to whether they have children or not.

More research should also be done to determine whether water reduction campaigns should be aimed at younger or older people, or if some other segment of the population should be the focus of encouragement to reduce water use.

References

Alliance for Water Efficiency. (2016). Residential end uses of water study (2016, 1999). Retrieved from http://www.allianceforwaterefficiency.org/residential-end-uses-of-water-study-1999.aspx

United States Geological Society. (2016, December 2). The world's water. Retrieved from https://water.usgs.gov/edu/earthwherewater.html

---

MODEL 4 How to Write a Process Essay

Process essays are written to explain *how* something is done. Therefore, often a process essay explains the steps in a process. The following guidelines will help you write an effective process essay.

- Like all essays, a process essay must have three general sections: an introduction, a body, and a conclusion. Unlike in a report, you may not use these section titles as headings in the essay.
- The introduction announces the topic of the essay. Although there are many good ways to start an essay, the introduction usually begins with a general statement about why the topic is important.
- The introduction finishes with a *thesis statement*. A thesis statement is a sentence that includes the topic of the essay and the opinion that the essay will present. It may or may not include the main steps of the process that you are writing about.
- The body of the essay will contain a number of paragraphs. For a short process essay, usually each paragraph describes one step in the process.
- Each body paragraph should start with a topic sentence that clearly indicates the topic of the paragraph. If your thesis listed the main steps of the process, you can repeat key words (or a synonym of the key words) from the thesis.
- Each body paragraph should finish with a sentence that clarifies the point of the paragraph.
- The conclusion summarizes the main steps in the process. It often finishes with a sentence that restates (but does not repeat) the thesis.

Example Process Essay

How is dirty water cleaned for drinking?

WRITER'S PLAN	
INTRODUCTION	NOT MUCH WATER AVAILABLE FOR USE • dirty water must be cleaned and reused • this is the water treatment process • three steps: sedimentation, filtration, and disinfection
BODY	• sedimentation removes tiny particles from the water: alum is added; water thickens; particles stick together and sink to the bottom • filtration: water is passed through a sand filter to remove any remaining waste • disinfection: chlorine is added to remove bacteria; fluoride may be added
CONCLUSION	• three steps in the water treatment process provide clean drinking water

Cleaning our Water

Although the world is covered with water, 97 percent of that water is salt water, and much of the remaining 3 percent is held in glaciers in the North and South Poles (United States Geological Society, 2016). Only a small percentage of the Earth's water is available to support human life. This means it is important to use less water and avoid polluting water. It also means that people must clean dirty water if they want to have enough. The process of cleaning dirty water so that it is safe to drink is called *the water treatment process*. Dirty water is often treated by sedimentation, filtration, and disinfection before it is clean.

Sedimentation of dirty water is the first step in the water treatment process. To start, a chemical called *alum* is mixed into the water to make small particles stick to each other. With gentle mixing, more and more small particles stick together. As a result, the heavy particles that are produced sink to the bottom of the tank, leaving the water cleaner, but not clean enough to drink.

After sedimentation, the water is filtered to remove the remaining particles. The water is passed through layers of stones, called *gravel*, and sand. These layers form a filter that further cleans the water. Once the water is through the filter, it is free of particles, but it is still not clean enough to drink.

To complete the water treatment process, disinfection destroys any bacteria or viruses that are present in the water. Chlorine, a chemical used to kill bacteria, is added to the water. *Chlorine* not only kills bacteria during the treatment process, but it also maintains the quality of the water as it is carried through the water distribution system. Another chemical, *fluoride*, may be added to the water to help reduce tooth decay. The overall treatment results in water that is clean and ready to drink.

If dirty water is not treated properly, people and animals may become sick from the dirt and bacteria in the water. The water treatment process is constantly monitored to make sure this does not happen. An effective water treatment process that includes sedimentation, filtration, and disinfection is essential if people want enough safe water to drink.

Reference

United States Geological Society. (2016, December 2). The world's water. Retrieved from https://water.usgs.gov/edu/earthwherewater.html

How to Write a Cause and Effect Essay

Cause and effect essays are written to demonstrate that something is the cause of something else (the effect). The following guidelines will help you write an effective cause and effect essay.

- Like all essays, a cause and effect essay must have three general sections: an introduction, a body, and a conclusion. Unlike in a report, you may not use these section titles as headings in the essay.
- The introduction announces the topic of the essay. Although there are many good ways to start an essay, the introduction usually begins with a general statement about the cause and the significance of the effects.
- The introduction finishes with a *thesis statement*. A thesis statement is a sentence that presents the cause and effect relationship you will write about as well as an opinion about the relationship. It may or may not list the specific effects that you will write about.
- The body of the essay will contain a number of paragraphs. For a short cause and effect essay, usually each paragraph explains one effect.
- It may be helpful to use expressions that you learned in Chapter 4 (Focus on Accuracy, page 94) that demonstrate cause and effect relationships.
- Each body paragraph should start with a topic sentence that clearly indicates the topic of the paragraph. If your thesis listed specific effects, you can repeat key words (or synonyms of the key words) from the thesis.
- Each body paragraph should finish with a sentence that clarifies the point of the paragraph.
- The conclusion summarizes the main effects and why the essay opinion is correct. It often finishes with a sentence that restates (but does not repeat) the thesis.

Example Cause and Effect Essay

What was the effect on the Aral Sea of building dams on the Syr Darya and Amu Darya rivers?

WRITER'S PLAN	
INTRODUCTION	GENERAL INFORMATION • location of Aral Sea and Syr Darya and Amu Darya rivers • building of dams in 1960s • significance of effects on water supply, agriculture, and people in the area
BODY	• impact of dams on water supply to the sea • impact of dams on agriculture and soil quality in the area • impact of dams on human health
CONCLUSION	• current changes now improving water, agricultural, and health outcomes in the Aral Sea area • demonstrates there is hope that seemingly irreparable damage may be addressed • Aral Sea an example of how uninformed decisions can destroy an ecosystem

Destruction of an Ecosystem: Lessons from The Aral Sea

In the 1950s, the Syr Darya and Amu Darya rivers flowed into the Aral Sea, which was the world's fourth largest lake, situated in Central Asia between south Kazakhstan and north Uzbekistan. The water supply from the two rivers and the annual rainfall combined to create a productive ecosystem that was home to a wide variety of fish, plants, and animals, and supported a growing population base that relied on fishing as its economic base. In the early 1960s, the Soviet government decided to dam the two rivers, the Syr Darya in the north and the Amu Darya in the south, and divert the river water to create cotton farms in the deserts that lay upstream of the Aral Sea. This ill-advised water diversion plan had a momentous impact on the Aral Sea ecosystem, diminishing the water supply, destroying the soil quality, and devastating human health outcomes in the area.

The building of the Syr Darya and Amu Darya river dams resulted in the reduction of the water supply to the Aral Sea. By 1970, the small fishing village of Muynak, originally located on an island in the Aral Sea, was 10 kilometres away from the water; by 1980, the water was 40 kilometres away; by 2000, the water was 75 kilometres away (de Villiers, 2015, p. 277). Not only was the water supply reduced, but also the water quality was diminished. The Aral Sea was naturally a saltwater lake, but the reduced water supply caused the salt content in the lake to increase so that the fish in the sea died. Fishing was no longer a sustainable way to earn a living, and the economic base of the region disappeared.

The increased salt content of the Aral Sea led to increased salt content of the earth and soil, both in the dry area around the shrinking sea and in the cotton growing farmland upstream of the Sea. As the Aral Sea became smaller and its salt content higher, salt entered the groundwater, spreading salt throughout the watershed and the soil. Upstream, water from the naturally salty rivers concentrated in the soil and groundwater of the cotton farms, causing the soil to lose its productivity. In response, the farmers used increased amounts of chemical fertilizer, which increased chemical pollution both in the soil, and in the Aral Sea downstream of the farms ("The Aral Sea crisis," n.d.). The increase in dry soil and salt generated dust and salt storms that devastated the productivity of the land and the water.

As the effects of the river dams became more extreme, the diminished fishing economy resulted in increasing poverty for the people in the area. Birth and death rates rose significantly, and life expectancy fell ("The Aral Sea crisis," n.d.). In addition, increased concentrations of chemical fertilizers in the air and reduced water quality gave rise to high disease rates. People in the area suffered from high rates of tuberculosis, infections, typhus, and hepatitis ("The Aral Sea crisis," n.d.). Increased poverty and reduced health outcomes for the people living in the Aral Sea region were the results of the water diversion from the river dams.

In effect, the Syr Darya and Amu Darya river dams destroyed the ecosystem of the Aral Sea region. This destruction contributed to a reduced amount of water in the Sea, an increased amount of salt in the soil, and an increased number of human deaths from disease. Fortunately, in 2000, the World Bank financed a rebuilding of the river dams and surrounding canals, which has diverted more water to the small North Aral Sea. These changes are responsible for increased water supply and quality, and a slow return of some fish and animals to the region (Conant, 2006). Although these are welcome changes, the lessons from the Aral Sea region have been devastating and should not be forgotten.

References

The Aral Sea crisis. (n.d.). Retrieved from http://www.columbia.edu/~tmt2120/introduction.htm

Conant, E. (2006, September 1). Return of the Aral Sea. *Discover, 27*(9), 54–58.

de Villiers, M. (2015). *Back to the well: Rethinking the future of water.* Fredericton, NB: Goose Lane Editions.

How to Write a Persuasive Essay

Persuasive essays are written to persuade, or convince, people that a particular opinion about a topic is correct. The following guidelines will help you write an effective short persuasive essay.

- Like all essays, a persuasive essay must have three general sections: an introduction, a body, and a conclusion. Unlike in a report, you may not use these section titles as headings in the essay.

- The introduction announces the topic of the essay. Although there are many good ways to start an essay, the introduction usually begins with a general statement about why the topic is important.

- The introduction finishes with a *thesis statement*. A thesis statement is a sentence that includes the topic of the essay and the opinion that the essay will present. It may or may not include the main reasons why the opinion of the essay is correct.

- The body of the essay will contain a number of paragraphs. For a short persuasive essay, usually each paragraph explains one reason why the essay opinion is correct.

- Each body paragraph should start with a topic sentence that clearly indicates the topic of the paragraph. You can repeat key words (or synonyms of the key words) from the thesis.

- Each body paragraph should finish with a sentence that clarifies the point of the paragraph.

- The conclusion summarizes the main reasons why the essay opinion is correct. It often finishes with a sentence that restates (but does not repeat) the thesis.

Example Persuasive Essay

Water is becoming contaminated with a new form of pollution. Medicines (drugs or pharmaceuticals) used by humans and animals are entering the water system. Governments should make every effort to eliminate water pollution from pharmaceuticals. Agree or disagree and explain why.

WRITER'S PLAN	
INTRODUCTION	GENERAL INFORMATION • where: groundwater, surface water, and drinking water • what: types of medicines (pharmaceuticals) • source: humans and animals GOVERNMENTS SHOULD NOT ELIMINATE THIS FORM OF POLLUTION BECAUSE • pollution levels are low • money could be spent better elsewhere
BODY	POLLUTION LEVELS VERY LOW • parts per billion, and parts per trillion • so much less than prescribed doses • only sensitive equipment allows us to find this kind of pollution VERY EXPENSIVE TO REMOVE MEDICINE POLLUTION FROM THE WATER • levels very low: hard to find, test, and monitor • money could be spent better in researching the long-term effects of this pollution

CONCLUSION	• water pollution from pharmaceuticals is worrying
	• deserves further study, *but* remember
	  - pollution levels are low
	  - money could be spent better elsewhere

Water Pollution from Pharmaceuticals Requires More Study

It is well recognized that water is essential for life, and consequently, water should be protected from pollution. In order to protect the water supply, water treatment processes are designed to eliminate many forms of harmful pollution. Recently, scientists have begun to find a new type of pollution in ground, surface, and drinking water. They have discovered that human and animal medicines, such as antibiotics, are polluting the water. People expect governments to eliminate pollution from medicines or pharmaceuticals in their water. However, at the moment, governments should not attempt to remove medicines from the water supply because the levels of this kind of pollution are very low, and the removal of the pollution would cost money that could be spent on research.

The levels of pharmaceutical pollution in the water supply are extremely low. It is true that research in Europe and the United States has found some form of pharmaceutical pollution in almost all ground, surface, and drinking water. However, measurements at levels this low have only become possible because of sensitive measurement equipment that was not available to scientists in the past. Scientists measure the amounts of pharmaceutical pollutants in nanograms per litre. These amounts of pollution from medicines are so low that they are unlikely to cause a human health risk (Crowe, 2014).

In order to remove these low levels of pharmaceutical pollution from water, governments would have to spend a lot of money. The current water treatment processes remove many harmful particles and bacteria from the water, but they are not as effective at removing low levels of pharmaceutical pollution. Only advanced water treatment technologies would remove medicines from the water supply, and even then, some pharmaceuticals might not be eliminated. At this point, the money needed to remove all medicines from water would be better spent on research related to the long-term effects of pharmaceutical pollution on humans and animals.

Although the thought of medicines in the water supply is worrying, it would not be useful for governments to spend large amounts of money to change current water treatment processes to try to eliminate all pharmaceutical pollution. This kind of pollution is so minimal that it is difficult to measure. Furthermore, low levels of medicines are not likely to cause health problems in the short term. Instead of spending large amounts of money to modify water treatment processes, governments should spend money on research to identify the long-term effects of exposure to low levels of pharmaceuticals.

Reference

Crowe, K. (2014, September 22). *Drinking water contaminated by excreted drugs a growing concern.* [Radio broadcast]. CBC News. Retrieved from http://www.cbc.ca/news/health/drinking-water-contaminated-by-excreted-drugs-a-growing-concern-1.2772289

MODEL 7 How to Write a Compare and Contrast Essay

Compare and contrast essays are written to show the similarities and differences between two items. When you compare items, you show the similarities; when you contrast items, you show the differences. The following guidelines will help you write effective compare and contrast essays.

• Decide what points of comparison or contrast you wish to explain to your reader.

- Decide which pattern of organization fits your information best. There are two standard ways to organize a compare and contrast essay: block style organization and point-by-point style organization. Generally, block style organization is best for less technical information while point-by-point style organization is best for more technical information. Both styles of organization are demonstrated here.

- Like other kinds of essays, a compare and contrast essay has three general sections: an introduction, a body, and a conclusion. Unlike in a report, you may not use these section titles as headings in the essay.

- The introduction announces the topic of the essay. Although there are many good ways to start an essay, the introduction usually begins with a general statement about why the topic is important.

- The introduction finishes with a *thesis statement*. A thesis statement is a sentence that includes the topic of the essay and the opinion that the essay will present. It may or may not include the main points of comparison or contrast.

- The body of the essay will contain a number of paragraphs. For a short compare and contrast essay, usually each paragraph explains one point of comparison or contrast.

- Each body paragraph should start with a topic sentence that clearly indicates the topic of the paragraph. You can repeat key words (or synonyms of the key words) from the thesis.

- Each body paragraph should finish with a sentence that clarifies the point of the paragraph.

- The conclusion summarizes the points of comparison and/or contrast. It often finishes with a sentence that restates (but does not repeat) the thesis.

Example Compare and Contrast Essay

Compare and contrast two different technologies that could be used to solve water shortages.

Block Style Essay

WRITER'S PLAN FOR A BLOCK STYLE COMPARE AND CONTRAST ESSAY

• compare and contrast desalination with atmospheric water vapour processing
  - both are ways of producing pure drinking water
  - some differences in source, waste products, and final product

DESALINATION	ATMOSPHERIC WATER VAPOUR PROCESSING

• explain the process; give an example
  - source: ocean water
  - waste products: salty brine
  - final product: salty (transport inland)
	• explain the process; give an example
	  - source: water vapour in the air
	  - waste products: none
	  - final product: very pure

• desalination and water vapour processing are useful because
  - sources are accessible
  - few waste products
  - final product = drinking water

Desalination and Atmospheric Water Vapour Processing

Desalination, or the process of removing salt from ocean water, and atmospheric water vapour processing, the process of turning water vapour into water, are both ways of producing drinking water for human consumption. Although desalination and atmospheric water vapour processing are distinct because they extract water from unique sources and produce different waste and final products, both are useful to increase the amount of water available for human use.

Producing drinking water from salty ocean water is the process of desalination. This process is used in the Middle East, where Saudi Arabia operates the largest desalination plant in the world. The source of water for desalination plants is ocean water. As ocean water is 97 percent of the world's water (United States Geological Society, 2016), there is a large supply of water that could be processed with desalination technology. The process does result in some unwanted waste products. Desalination plants produce salty brine, as well as some chemical wastes that must be properly disposed of. If the waste products are simply returned to the environment, they will pollute rivers and groundwater, but they can be properly managed so the environment is not damaged. Finally, the desalination process works by removing the salt from ocean water; however, it is impossible to remove all the salt. Therefore, the final product of desalination is drinking water with a salty taste.

Atmospheric water vapour processing pulls water vapour from the air, cools it, and condenses it into drinking water. This technology is often used in disaster relief situations when water from regular sources is scarce. The main source of water for this kind of treatment is humid air, which is free in large quantities. As for waste products, it is true that in order to cool the water vapour, a refrigerant is used. However, refrigerants, also found in refrigerators and dehumidifiers, can be used for long periods of time before they become waste. The final product of atmospheric water vapour processing is appealing, too. It is one of the cleanest forms of water. Pollutants in the air that adhere to rain drops do not stick to water vapour; consequently, the final product of this process is very pure.

Both desalination and water vapour processing technologies are useful methods for producing clean drinking water in countries where there is a lack of natural water supply. The sources of water for these processes are easily available, their waste products can be properly managed so they don't harm the environment, and the end products are clean drinking water for human consumption.

Reference

United States Geological Society. (2016, December 2). The world's water. Retrieved from https://water.usgs.gov/edu/earthwherewater.html

Point-By-Point Style Essay

WRITER'S PLAN FOR A POINT-BY-POINT STYLE COMPARE AND CONTRAST ESSAY	

• compare and contrast desalination with atmospheric water vapour processing
  - both ways of producing pure drinking water
  - some differences in source, waste products and final product	

SOURCE OF WATER	• desalination: ocean water • water vapour processing: air
WASTE PRODUCTS	• desalination: salty brine • water vapour processing: none
FINAL PRODUCT	• desalination: tastes salty • water vapour processing: pure

• water vapour processing and desalination are useful because
  - sources are accessible
  - few waste products
  - final products = drinking water	

Desalination and Atmospheric Water Vapour Processing

Desalination, or the process of removing salt from ocean water, and atmospheric water vapour processing, the process of turning water vapour into water, are both ways of producing drinking water for human consumption. Although desalination and atmospheric water vapour processing are distinct because they extract water from unique sources and produce different waste and final products, both are useful to increase the amount of water available for human use.

Each of these water creation technologies has a unique source of water. Producing drinking water from salty ocean water is the process of desalination. This process is used in the Middle East, where Saudi Arabia operates the largest desalination plant in the world. The main source of water for desalination plants is ocean water. As ocean water is 97 percent of the world's water (United States Geological Society, 2016), there is a large supply of water that could be processed with desalination technology. Alternatively, atmospheric water vapour processing pulls water vapour from the air, cools it, and condenses it into drinking water. This technology is often used in disaster relief situations when water from regular sources is scarce. The main source of water for this kind of treatment is humid air, which is free in large quantities. Each process is based on an abundant natural resource.

Every technology must be evaluated to determine if it produces waste products that will be dangerous to the environment. Desalination technology does result in some unwanted waste products: salty brine, as well as some chemicals. If the waste products are simply returned to the environment, they will pollute rivers and groundwater, but they can be properly managed so the environment is not damaged. Similarly, water vapour processing uses a refrigerant to cool the water vapour. However, refrigerants, also found in refrigerators and dehumidifiers, can be used for long periods of time before they become waste. Both processes produce waste products that need to be disposed of properly.

The taste of the final product is also a significant consideration when evaluating water technologies. The desalination process works by removing the salt from ocean water; nevertheless, it is almost impossible to remove all the salt. Therefore, the final product of desalination is drinking water that tastes salty. In contrast, the final product of water vapour processing is one of the cleanest forms of water. Pollutants in the air that adhere to rain drops do not stick to water vapour; consequently, the final product of this process is very pure. However, both processes produce drinking water for human consumption.

Desalination and water vapour processing technologies are useful methods for producing clean drinking water in countries where there is a lack of natural water supply. The sources of water for these processes are easily available, their waste products can be properly managed so they don't harm the environment, and the end products are clean drinking water for human consumption.

Reference

United States Geological Society. (2016, December 2). The world's water. Retrieved from https://water.usgs.gov/edu/earthwherewater.html

How to Write a Paraphrase

The goal of a paraphrase is to restate the ideas of another author without copying the author's words. Paraphrasing is an effective way to avoid plagiarism. Use the following guidelines to write a paraphrase.

- All paraphrases start with a reference to the original author. Common ways to start paraphrases are the following:

    In her 2018 article, (author's name) states that …

    In his book of 2017, (author's name) suggests that …

    According to (author's name) in her article of 2018, …

    (Author's name) website maintains that …

- A paraphrase is approximately the same length as the original writing.

- To restate the main ideas of an author without repeating the same words, you can use writing techniques such as finding synonyms for key words, changing the structure of sentences, changing word forms, and changing the voice from active to passive (or passive to active). See pages 165–167 for examples of these writing techniques.

- You may need to use more than one of these techniques to complete a successful paraphrase.

- Be sure to include a full reference to the original text at the end of your writing.

Example Paraphrase

Paraphrase the following text:

> We tend to think of water in terms of a particular purpose: is the quality of the water good enough for the use we want to make of it? Water fit for one use may be unfit for another. We may, for instance, trust the quality of lake water enough to swim in it, but not enough to drink it. Along the same lines, drinking water can be used for irrigation, but water used for irrigation may not meet drinking water standards. It is the quality of the water that determines its uses.
>
> ### Reference
> Government of Canada. (2015). *Introduction to water quality.* Retrieved from http://www.ec.gc.ca/eau-water/default.asp?lang=En&n=2C3144F5-1

Example paraphrase:

When we consider the uses to which water can be put, we must first determine its purity, states Environment Canada on its website (2015). A single source of water may not be suitable for all uses. For example, we may be sufficiently confident of a lake's water quality to swim in it; however, we would likely think twice before drinking it. Similarly, water pure enough to drink can be used for crops although not vice versa. Water use is dependent on its purity.

Reference

Government of Canada. (2015). *Introduction to water quality.* Retrieved from http://www.ec.gc.ca/eau-water/default.asp?lang=En&n=2C3144F5-1

MODEL 9   How to Write a Summary

The goal of a summary is to restate the ideas of another author without copying the author's words. Summarizing, like paraphrasing, is an effective way to avoid plagiarism. Follow these guidelines to write a summary.

- All summaries, like paraphrases, start with a reference to the original author. Common ways to start summaries are the following:

  In her 2018 article, (author's name) states that ...

  In his book of 2017, (author's name) suggests that ...

  According to (author's name) in her article of 2018, ...

  (Author's name) website maintains that ...

- A summary, unlike a paraphrase, is approximately one-quarter to one-third the length of the original writing.

- To summarize an original text, you should:

  - read the original text carefully;

  - underline the main points of the original text, leaving out supporting details, repetitions and examples;

  - paraphrase the underlined sentences.

- To paraphrase the underlined sentences, you can use writing techniques such as finding synonyms for key words, changing the structure of sentences, changing word forms, and changing the voice from active to passive (or passive to active). See pages 165–167 for examples of these writing techniques.

- You may need to use more than one of these techniques to complete a successful summary.

- Be sure to include a full reference to the original text at the end of your writing.

Example Summary

Summarize the following text:

> Like many industrialized countries, Canada has used its water resources to promote economic development, without questioning the impact on the natural world. In the post-war era, progress was seen as ... good, and millions were lifted out of poverty. Water, land, forests, and minerals were so abundant it was hard to imagine any serious threat to them. Canada built its economic and development policies on the myth of abundance, assuming that nature would always provide. It is only in hindsight that we begin to see the impact of industrial development on our water heritage.
>
> As a consequence, generations have dumped whatever waste we wanted into water, overextracted it for ... commercial food production, and diverted it from where it was needed to sustain a healthy ecosystem to where it was convenient for industry and urban populations. We [drained] wetlands and canals, built mighty dams, hardened shorelines, moderated watershed levels, and modified waterways, once in the name of survival, later in the name of economic prosperity.

> Our understanding of the implications of such wholesale intervention in freshwater sources is slowly catching up to the damage we have caused, both planned and [unintended], but the time for complacency is over. While it is true that compared to many parts of the world, Canada is blessed with plentiful clean water, there are serious limits and threats to it, and too little is known for us to be complacent. Centuries of abuse and neglect are catching up.
>
> ### Reference
>
> Barlow, M. (2016). *Boiling point: Government neglect, corporate abuse, and Canada's water crisis* (pp. 2–3). Toronto, ON: ECW Press.

Example summary:

Barlow (2016) states that Canada, like other developed nations, has sacrificed water quality for economic progress. After the Second World War, many Canadians benefited from the improved quality of life that resulted from this progress, and they assumed that the plentiful natural resources for which Canada is famous would exist forever. As a result, Canadians have not taken particularly good care of their water resources, using their substantial water supply to drive economic development. However, Canadians are beginning to understand the damage they have caused to their water supply. While much of Canada still has access to high-quality water, that water is now in danger due to centuries of neglect.

Reference

Barlow, M. (2016). *Boiling point: Government neglect, corporate abuse, and Canada's water crisis* (pp. 2–3). Toronto, ON: ECW Press.

MODEL 10   How to Write an Extended Persuasive Essay

Persuasive essays are written to persuade, or convince, people that a particular opinion about a topic is correct. The following guidelines will help you write an effective persuasive essay.

- Like all essays, a persuasive essay must have three general sections: an introduction, a body, and a conclusion. In a short persuasive essay, the introduction and conclusion are each usually one paragraph long, and the body of the essay has as many paragraphs as you have main points to make. However, in an extended persuasive essay, the introduction and conclusion may each be more than one paragraph long, and the body of an extended essay has as many sections as you have main points to make. Each section may contain one or more paragraphs.

- The introduction announces the topic of the essay. Although there are many good ways to start an essay, the introduction usually begins with a general statement about why the topic is important.

- The introduction finishes with a *thesis statement*. A thesis statement is a sentence that includes the topic of the essay and the opinion that the essay will present. It may or may not include the main reasons why the opinion of the essay is correct.

- The body of the essay will contain a number of sections. For an extended persuasive essay, usually each section explains one reason why the essay opinion is correct. Each section may contain one or more paragraphs. The number of paragraphs per section depends on the content.
- Each section should start with a topic sentence that clearly indicates the topic of the section. You can repeat key words (or a synonym of the key words) from the thesis.
- Within each section, each paragraph should start with a topic sentence that clearly indicates the topic of the paragraph and how it relates to the main point of the section.
- Each body paragraph should finish with a sentence that clarifies the point of the paragraph.
- The conclusion summarizes the main reasons why the essay opinion is correct. It often finishes with a sentence that restates (but does not repeat) the thesis.

Example of an Extended Persuasive Essay

Water redistribution is the key to solving global water shortages. Agree or disagree and explain why.

WRITER'S PLAN			
INTRODUCTION	Water redistribution is no longer the key to solving global water shortages. There are other methods that will do a better job of eliminating water shortages.		
REDISTRIBUTION	• historically: redistribution by dams and pipes • now: too many dams (give numbers) • no new rivers to dam • now what?		
NOT USEFUL METHODS OF REDISTRIBUTION	• glaciers • water bags • old oil tanker		
Are there really water shortages? Some people don't agree with this statement. They say • aquifers may be only temporarily low: in the process of establishing a steady state, we can adapt to sinking ground levels; • scientists will develop new technologies to eliminate the threat of water shortages. However, this is a minority viewpoint.			

What can be done about water shortages?	OTHER METHODS		
	• desalination • atmospheric water vapour processing • elimination of poverty • education and conservation		

DESALINATION	WATER VAPOUR	POVERTY	EDUCATION
• ocean water • energy consumption • waste product	• humid air • energy consumption • pure water	• complex • essential to address	• long-term • essential

CONCLUSION	• water redistribution is no longer the best method to solve water shortages • other methods, although they have drawbacks, are much more effective • desalination, water vapour processing, the elimination of poverty, education, and conservation will be more efficient in solving the world's water shortages

Meeting the Challenge of Water Shortages

Water shortages are fast becoming a fact of life, not only in undeveloped countries, but also in developed countries. Even those countries with the money to spend on wells, pumps, pipes, and distribution systems are running out of water. The solution to this problem seems simple. If there is a shortage of water in one place and an abundance of water in another place, all that is required is the transportation of the water to the area without water. However, water shortages are complex problems; as a result, simple redistribution of water is no longer the most effective method of solving global water shortages.

Historically, redistribution of water has been very successful at eliminating water shortages. This redistribution was achieved by building dams on rivers, blocking the natural flow of water, and creating a reservoir, or extra water storage, above the dam. And while the dams have created environmental disruptions, they have been successful in sharing water among regions. However, today, 60 percent of the world's major rivers have been dammed (Black & King, 2009, p. 36). Any river left to be dammed is too small, or too distant. The cost of building dams on the remaining rivers is too high. As a result, the traditional method of redistributing water through a dam is no longer economically possible.

Other methods of redistribution have been proposed. A Saudi prince, Mohammed Al-Faisal, thought it might be possible to tow glaciers from the poles to warmer countries where water shortages exist; however, scientific studies indicated the glaciers would melt too quickly (de Villiers, 2015, p. 193). A number of people have tried to float fresh water, contained in huge bags, through the ocean to thirsty countries. But the water bags remain theoretical (de Villiers, 2015, p. 195). Others have suggested water be carried in tanker ships that are too old to carry oil. But the costs of cleaning the tanker ships are too high (de Villiers, 2015, p. 194). There have always been theories about how water could be redistributed, but for reasons of cost and politics, these theories have not been achieved. With the limited number of rivers left to dam, and the high cost of other redistribution methods, this is no longer the most efficient way of preventing water shortages.

It is important to consider if there really are water shortages. There are some scientists who believe that although there may be water shortages, there is no crisis. These people point out that shrinking aquifers may simply be moving to a new steady state, and that we do not know enough about replenishment cycles of aquifers to know if they are really disappearing. These scientists suggest humans need only to adapt to sinking ground levels due to groundwater withdrawal; and they recommend people put their faith in emerging technologies to solve any water crisis in the future. However, this is a minority view. Most scientists point to prolonged water shortages in developing countries, the shrinking of the Aral Sea in former Soviet Asia, and the depleting of the aquifer under Mexico City as examples that a water crisis is not looming in the future, but here now, in the present.

As the majority of scientists believe there really is a water crisis, other ways of addressing the problem of global water shortages must be considered. Desalination, or the process of removing salt from ocean water, is a reality in the Middle East. This solution has the advantage of a water source that is easily available, provided a piece of coastline is accessible. Desalinated water from the ocean can then be pumped inland. This process consumes a lot of energy and produces some waste products, but these wastes can be properly managed so as not to damage the environment. Desalination is more than just a theory. It works in reality to fight water shortages.

Furthermore, atmospheric water vapour processing is providing hope for many areas experiencing water shortages. Water vapour processing pulls water vapour from warm, humid air, and cools and condenses it into pure water. Processors have been used in countries where there have been natural disasters in order to provide clean drinking water. The main source of water for this kind of treatment is humid air, which is free in large quantities. This technology is already fighting water shortages.

The World Bank, in a 2017 report on reducing inequity in the supply of water in developing countries, ties water supply to poverty. Poor countries are less able to build or maintain a water supply for their populations, and this negatively impacts human health, nutrition, and educational outcomes for their citizens. This report notes that a lack of water significantly disadvantages rural, small city, and poor people in eighteen countries included in the study. Although this is not an easy solution to achieve, the report indicates that eliminating water shortages and fighting poverty are connected.

Education about water conservation is also essential in the struggle against water shortages. In order to preserve water quantity and quality, people must learn how to conserve water around their homes and industries. Information about waste disposal and pollutants must become common knowledge, so water quality is protected. Again, this is a long-term solution, but still essential in order to eliminate water shortages.

It is clear now that water shortages are becoming a fact of life in all countries of the world. Traditional methods of water redistribution, such as building dams, are no longer possible, and other redistribution theories are too costly. Other methods, although they have drawbacks, are much more effective at addressing water shortages today. Desalination, water vapour processing, the elimination of poverty, education, and conservation will be methods scientists use to solve the global water shortages of tomorrow.

References

Black, M., & King, J. (2009). *The atlas of water: Mapping the world's most critical resource* (2nd ed.). Los Angeles, CA: University of California Press.

de Villiers, M. (2015). *Back to the well: Rethinking the future of water.* Fredericton, NB: Goose Lane Editions.

World Bank Group. (2017). *Reducing inequalities in water supply, sanitation, and hygiene in the era of the sustainable development goals: Synthesis report of the WASH Poverty Diagnostic Initiative.* Washington, DC: World Bank. Retrieved from https://openknowledge.worldbank.org/bitstream/handle/10986/27831/W17075.pdf?sequence=5&isAllowed=y

PHOTO CREDITS

SHUTTERSTOCK

p. viii, 2: © Lauren Elisabeth; pp. 3, 17: © Phonlamai Photo; p. 5: © asharkyu; p. 6: © Power best; p. 8: © Willyam Bradbury; p.10: © Bas Nastassia; p.11: © Robin Atzeni; pp.13, 14: © M.M. art; p. 16: © GaudiLab; pp.18, 40, 64, 69, 91, 98, 101, 107, 125, 235: © Rawpixel.com; p.20: © iurii; p.23: © Nestor Rizhniak; p. 24: © Gorodenkoff; p. 25: © Lightfield Studios; p. 27: © Photodiem, p. viii, 28: © Ekaterina Pokrovsky; p. 29: © VLADGRIN; p. 30: © Roman Samborskyi; p.32: © Electric Egg; p. 34, 67, 116, 204: © Jacob Lund; p. 37: © PORTRAIT IMAGES ASIA BY NONWARIT; p. 38: © DavidPinoPhotography; p. 43: © Markgraf; p. 43: © oneinchpunch; p. 44: © fivetrees; p. 48: © sdecoret; p. 50: © 4 PM production; p. 53: © Rusly95; p. 54: © 9dream studio; p.57: © AnemStyle; p. 58: © DW labs Incorporated; p. 59: © chuckstock; p. viii, 60: © dotshovk; p. 61: © Sammby; p. 62: © patat; p.71: © Blend Images; p. 72: © Ed Aldridge; p. 75: © Unconventional; p. 77: © zimmytws; p. 78: © Pedro Monteiro; p. 81: © MAStock; pp. 82, 229: © hxdbzxy; p. 84: © Have a nice day Photo; p. 85: © balein; p. 86: © astephan; p. 97: © javi_indy; p. 89: © elenansl; p.93: © Bloomicon; p.94: © Twin Design; p. 96: © phloxii; p. 97: © Gutesa; p. 102: © Zolnierek; p. 105: © ChameleonsEye; p. 108: © Jim Barber; p. 110: © Eric Crama; p.113: © totojang1977; p. 114: © Luciano Mortula – LGM; p. 119: © gst; p. 121: © Yuriy Maksymiv; p. 122: © Kerdkanno; p. 126: © Elena Elisseeva; p. 128: © Yulia Furman; p. 129: © Monkey Business Images; p. 131: © Hanna_photo; p. 135: © ch_ch; p. 136: © CandyBox Images; p. 139: © LStockStudio; p. 140: © Africa Studio; p. 141: © mdurson; p. 144: © BestPhotoStudio; p. 145: © Alex Berger; p. 147: © tgavrano; p. ix, 150: © Michal Steflovic; p. 151: © Natalia Dar; p. 153: © PixieMe; p. 155: © Omer N Raja's; p.156: © Hadrian; p. 158: © Ryzhi; p. 159: © khoamartin; p. 161: © dnaveh; p. 164: © Thunderstock; p. 165: © michaeljung; p. 167: © MaxxiGo; p. 169: © wavebreakmedia; pp. 172, 189: © Zapp2Photo; p. 175: © YAKOBCHUK VIACHESLAV; p. ix, 178: © Busakorn Pongparnit; p. 179: © Irina Strelnikova; p.181: © REDPIXEL.PL; pp. 182, 225: © ESB Professional; p. 185: © vierra; p. 188: © BoonritP; p. 190: © ByEmo; p. 191: © Sergey Nivens; p. 194: © Serebryakova Ekaterina; p. 196: © George Rudy; p. 197: © bondvit; p. 198: © nikkytok; p. 200: © Lucky business; p. 202: © MJgraphics; p. ix, 206: © Alicja Neumiler; p. 207: © medejaja; p. 208: © KHARCHENKO VLADIMIR; p. 211: © Syda Productions; p. 214: © Gajus; p. 212: © Sea Wave; p. 216: © Jack Frog; p. 217: © Max Maier; p. 219: © Peter Gudella; p. 220: © simona pavan; p. 223: © Mert Toker; p. 226: © nito; p. 230: © ranimiro; p. 233: © Chris Bence; p. 236 : © SasinTipchai

UNSPLASH

p. viii, 88: © Jenna Day; p. viii, 118: © Mical Grosicki

TEXT CREDITS

CHAPTER 1

pp. 6–8 "Robot Futures" by I. R. Nourbakhsh. Excerpts from Nourbakhsh, Illah Reza, *Robot Futures*, pp. xiv-xviii, © 2013 Massachusetts Institute of Technology, by permission of The MIT Press. p. 15 "Aeryon Deploys SkyRangers to Support Hurricane Irma Response" reprinted by permission of Aeryon.com. pp. 21–23 "Here Come the Robots" by A. Ross. Excerpts from *Industries of the Future* by Alec Ross, pp. 15–19, © 2016 by Alec Ross. Reprinted with the permission of Simon & Schuster, Inc. All rights reserved.

CHAPTER 2

pp. 45–48 "The Contemporary Landscape of University Internationalization" AUCC. © 2014. Canada's Universities in the World: AUCC Internationalization survey. Retrieved from: https://www.univcan.ca/wp-content/uploads/2015/07/internationalization-survey-2014.pdf. pp. 52–55 "The Internationalization of Higher Education" by E. Egron-Polak & R. Hudson. Extract from the Executive Summary of the 4th IAU Global Survey on Internationalization of HE.

CHAPTER 3

pp. 65–66 "Introduction to Innovation" by J. Blythe; pp. 80–82 "Adoption of Innovation" by J. Blythe. Excerpts from Blythe, J. © 2013 *Consumer Behaviour* (2nd ed.) London: Sage Publications Ltd. pp. 71–74 "The Buyer Decision Process for New Products" by G. Armstrong et al. Excerpts from Armstrong, G., Kotler, P., Trifts, V., Buchwitz, L. & Gaudet, D. © 2017 "Understanding Consumer and Business Buyer Behaviour" in *Marketing: An Introduction 6e*, reprinted with permission by Pearson Canada Inc.

CHAPTER 4

pp. 92–93 "What Is Marketing?" by G. Armstrong et al. Excerpt from Armstrong, G., Kotler, P., Trifts, V., Buchwitz, L. & Gaudet, D. © 2017 "Brand Strategy and Management" in *Marketing: An Introduction 6e;* Reprinted with permission by Pearson Canada Inc. pp. 100–105 "Social Criticisms of Marketing" by G. Armstrong et al. Excerpts from Armstrong, G., Kotler, P., Trifts, V., Buchwitz, L. & Gaudet, D. © 2017 "Sustainable marketing, social responsibility and ethics" in *Marketing: An Introduction 6e;* Reprinted with permission by Pearson Canada Inc. pp. 113–114 "Culture Jam" by K. Lasn. Excerpt from pp. 18–21 from *Culture Jam: The Cooling of America* by Kalle Lasn. Reprinted by permission of Harper Collins Publishers.

CHAPTER 5

pp. 122–127 "Understanding Healthy Bodyweight" by J. Thompson & M. Manore. Excerpts from Thompson, Janice J.; Manore, Melinda, *Nutrition for Life,* 4th Ed., © 2016 Reprinted and electronically reproduced by permission of Pearson Education, Inc. New York, NY. pp. 133–137 "Of Bananas and Cavemen" by A. Maxfield and A. Rissing. Excerpts from Maxfield, A. & Rissing, A. © 2017 "Of bananas and cavemen: Unlikely similarities between two online food communities" in K. Cargill (Ed.), *Food cults: How fads, dogma, and doctrine influence diet* (pp. 141–155). London, U.K.: Rowman & Littlefield. pp. 146–147 "Losing Weight, Gaining Life" by A. Agatston. Adapted from *The South Beach Diet: The Delicious, Doctor-Designed, Foolproof Plan for Fast and Healthy Weight Loss* by Arthur Agatston, M.D. Copyright © 2003. All rights reserved. Used by permission of Rodale Inc., Emmaus, PA.

CHAPTER 6

pp. 154–156 "Digital Cash for a Digital Age" by P. Vigna & M. Casey. Excerpts from *The age of cryptocurrenty; how bitcoin and digital money are challenging the global economic order* © 2015 Paul Vigna © 2015 Michael J. Casey. Reprinted by permission of St Martin's Press. All Rights Reserved. pp. 160–163 "Frequently Asked Questions from the Bitcoin Website." Excerpts from Bitcoin.org website FAQ, Creative Commons Bitcoin Project 2009–2017. Released under the MIT license. pp. 174–176 "The Rise of Bitcoin" by D. L. K. Chuen. Excerpts from Chuen, D.L.K © 2015, *Handbook of digital currency: Bitcoin, innovation, financial instruments, and big data* (pp. xxi-xxiii). Amsterdam: Academic Press, Elsevier.

CHAPTER 7

pp. 182–184 "The Internet of Things" by D. Comer. Excerpts from Comer, Douglas E., *Computer Networks and Internets,* 6th ed., © 2015. Reprinted and electronically reproduced by permission of Pearson Education, Inc., New York, NY. pp. 192–194 "Too Clever for Comfort" by E. Reguly. Excerpts from "Too clever for comfort," Eric Reguly, *Report on Business: The Globe and Mail*. pp. 199–200 "Researchers Hack the Mitsubishi Outlander SUV, Shut Off Alarm Remotely" by Z. Zorz. (June 6, 2016). "Researchers hack the Mitsubishi Outlander SUV, shut off alarm remotely." Help Net Security. https://www.helpnetsecurity.com/2016/06/06/researchers-hack-mitsubishi-outlander/

CHAPTER 8

pp. 210–212 "In Praise of Slowness: Turning the Tables on Speed" by C. Honoré. Excerpt from Honoré, C. © 2004 *In Praise of Slowness: How a worldwide movement is challenging the cult of speed* (pp. 54–63). Harper Collins, Penguin Random House, Orion Publishing Group London. pp. 221–223 "Restoring Food to Its Central Place" by C. Petrini. Excerpt from *Slow Food Nation*, by Carlo Petrini published in English in 2007. Reprinted by permission of Rizzoli Ex Libris, New York. Copyright (c) 2005 by Slow Food Editore s.r.l. Bra, Italy. pp. 230–231 "The Ideology of Slow Food" by L. Simonetti © 2012 "The ideology of slow food." *Journal of European Studies* 42(s), pp. 168–189, Sage Publications Ltd.

NOTES

NOTES

NOTES

~~Improved Cost Management increased in communic at~~
~~Cyber security~~

10 points popular and academic source

purpose inform
3rd person
objective
formal
in a rllogical
in text citation
references
I ~~is~~ possible that
shorter
Academic
Chapter 6 Paraphrasing
Materials of Pharaphrasing & Summarising

25 - 30 % Summary
Each paragraph get the main Idea

165 use appropriate Synonymy